Children's Book Corner

# Children's Book Corner

## A READ-ALOUD Resource

with Tips, Techniques, and Plans
for Teachers, Librarians, and Parents

Level Grades 3 and 4

## Judy Bradbury

*Photographs by Gene Bradbury*

**LIBRARIES**
U N L I M I T E D
A Member of the Greenwood Publishing Group

Westport, Connecticut • London

**Library of Congress Cataloging-in-Publication Data**

Bradbury, Judy.
  Children's book corner : a read-aloud resource with tips, techniques, and plans for teachers, librarians, and parents : grades 3 and 4 / Judy Bradbury ; photographs by Gene Bradbury.
     p. cm.
  Includes bibliographical references and index.
  ISBN 1–59158–046–3 (pbk. : alk. paper)
  1. Oral reading. 2. Reading (Elementary) 3. Children—Books and reading. 4. Book selection.  I. Title.
LB1573.5.B73  2005
372.45'2—dc22     2005011401


British Library Cataloguing in Publication Data is available.

Library of Congress Catalog Card Number: 2005011401
ISBN: 1-59158-046-3

First published in 2005

Libraries Unlimited, 88 Post Road West, Westport, CT 06881
A Member of the Greenwood Publishing Group, Inc.
www.lu.com

Printed in the United States of America

The paper used in this book complies with the Permanent Paper Standard issued by the National Information Standards Organization  (Z39.48–1984).

10   9   8   7   6   5   4   3   2   1

# Dedication

For educators everywhere who strive to find ways to connect children with books and nurture a lifelong love of the written word through their daily practices, their literate-rich rooms, and their deep respect for the wonders found between the covers of a book.

# Contents

# Acknowledgments

Third and fourth graders! Such gleeful abandon and unabashed hopefulness earmarks this age. The best of the books for youngsters celebrate their endearing approach to life while gently suggesting paths to explore. These books reach, teach, and touch middle graders, helping them to navigate prickly, often complex issues as they grow and mature. Friends, enemies, school issues, standardized tests, playground pranks, triumphs on the sports field, insecurities, curiosity about body parts, and giggling fests about bodily noises and everything gross, as well as aging grandparents, sibling rivalry, navigating divorce, and an awareness of the world and the environment, are all themes near and dear to the hearts of middle graders. Lighthearted, moving, warm and wacky, gently spooky, and those with a fresh perspective are the books middle graders clutch in their muddy, sturdy, growing hands.

And the people who impact middle graders' lives, the best of them, honor and celebrate this tender time. They encourage, support, guide, and share in the daily activities that will make these the happy days middle graders look back on when they become middle-agers. It was my pleasure to immerse myself in the world of the middle grader through the hundreds of books I read in preparing this resource. A nod of thanks goes to those at the publishing houses who kindly and enthusiastically participated in this project by assisting in my selection of books: Kimberly Lauber, Marketing Assistant, Educational and Library Assistant, and Michelle Fadlalla, Associate Marketing Director, Education & Library, Simon & Schuster Children's Publishing; Anne Irza-Leggat, Library and School Manager, Marketing, Candlewick; RasShahn Johnson-Baker, School and Library Marketing Coordinator, Hyperion Books for Children; Karolina Nilsson, Marketing, HarperCollins Children's Publishing; Lisa Tedesco, Publishing Assistant, Kids Can Press; Jason M. Wells, Publicity and Marketing, Abrams Books for Young Readers/Amulet Books; Lucille Rettino, Director Advertising and Promotion, Adult & Books for Young Readers, Henry Holt and Company; Jeanne McDermott, Marketing Director, Farrar Straus & Giroux Books for Young Readers; Lisa DeGroff, Marketing, Penguin Group; Molly O'Neill, Marketing Assistant, Clarion Books; Kim Biggs, Marketing, Houghton Mifflin; Kathleen Morandini, Marketing, Holiday House; Jennifer Rees, Associate Editor, Scholastic; Kathy Tucker, Editor-in-Chief, Whitman; and Cecile Goyette, Senior Editor, Dial Books.

Even more enjoyable than reading all the books, however, was spending time in the vibrant classrooms; book-loving, kid-friendly libraries; and literate homes of some of the best models middle graders could hope for. For their warm welcome, special thanks go to Merle J. Bacon, teacher at Maple East Elementary School, Williamsville, New York; Lynn Fritzinger, principal at Dodge Elementary, East Amherst, New York, who, from the first, embraced this project with immense enthusiasm; Cathleen Ratzel and Ellen

Glaser, teachers with heart at Country Parkway School, Williamsville, New York; Joanne Magavern, Librarian and Media Specialist at Dodge Elementary, and Gayle Kerman, Librarian and Media Specialist at Country Parkway, whose marvelous spaces beckon and nurture readers; teachers Deborah O'Neill, Carolyn Mansell, and Barbara Santoro of Dodge Elementary; Dennis Stanley, a most accommodating custodian with true spirit at Country Parkway; and Ron, Sandy, and Matthew Shank, whose support of this project and love of books and reading is abundantly apparent and most appreciated.

This project continues to be a joy due to the efforts and support of the people with whom I interact at Libraries Unlimited/Greenwood Publishing. There are many, but special thanks go to my editor, Sharon Coatney, and Erin Durkin and Melissa Mazzarella in marketing and publicity respectively. Without their attentiveness and efficiency, this series would not be what it is.

Finally, it is with heartfelt gratitude that I thank those who are closest to me, who watch this project evolve (and overtake the house), offer suggestions, help with simple as well as odious tasks, and provide overwhelming support. They are Kelsey, my beloved daughter and soul mate; and Gene, the man with the camera, the computer expertise, and my heart in his hands.

# Introduction

This resource book contains 25 read-aloud plans for outstanding books to read with children in the third and fourth grades. Hundreds of related titles are highlighted alongside the read-aloud plans and in the Book Notes section. Fiction as well as nonfiction titles are represented. Look for holiday selections, books on popular themes and content area subjects, biographies, poetry, and books reflecting a spectrum of genres. Thought-provoking books, funny stories, illuminating studies, history, mystery, and math, as well as issues such as death, divorce, school and family conflicts, and the trials of friendship, are addressed.

These books celebrate reading by the very excellence they bring to the advanced picture book, early chapter book, and intermediate chapter book. As examples of the best there is to offer in literature for children in the middle grades, they nourish and sustain the independent reader while encouraging the reluctant reader to embrace the wonderful world of books. A variety of interests and a range of levels of reading difficulty are represented here. The plans offer instruction in all four strands of language arts: reading, listening, writing, and speaking.

In addition to read-aloud plans, you will find Tips and Techniques for Teachers and Librarians and Parent Pull-Out Pages intended to be sent home on a regular basis throughout the year. An extensive Book Notes section lists hundreds of children's books, categorized by the subjects they address and briefly summarized. Finally, consult the subject, title, author, and illustrator indexes to help you find just the right book for a special group or a particular child.

## How Were the Choices Made About Which Books to Include?

In deciding which children's books to include in this resource, several criteria were used to determine whether a book would be highlighted with a read-aloud plan, listed in the Book Notes section, mentioned on a Parent Pull-Out Page, or not included in the resource at all. The determination was based upon several factors, the most important of which was whether the book told an original story in an appealing way or approached a nonfiction topic in a memorable and fresh fashion *for the middle grade child*. In the case of a picture book, how the subject was handled and if the text and art created a package suitable for the middle grade child was essential for selection for inclusion. I strived to introduce worthy titles, both new and older, that teachers, librarians, and parents might not be familiar with, rather than well-known classics or popular children's titles. However, a list of titles and authors middle graders should be familiar with is included in the Parent Pull-Out Pages. These books and authors ought to be the foundation of a read-aloud program and the cornerstone of every middle grade classroom and school library, as well as fully represented in the children's collections of public libraries. Similarly, there is an extensive list of chapter books in the Tips and Techniques for Teachers and Librarians section of this resource. These books encourage and stimulate young readers and are ideal for reading aloud or for youngsters to read independently.

## What Do I Need to Know to Find the Book?

Publication information is provided on each book for which there is a read-aloud plan. This reflects the most up-to-date information available on the book at the time of the printing of *Children's Book Corner.* As there are a number of editions available for most titles, from hardcover to softcover to library binding, I have listed the hardcover edition publication information unless the book is not available in hardcover. By referring to the title information and looking up its listing in library catalogs, online bookstores, or publishers' catalogs or Web sites, you can access information on the edition that best suits your needs.

## Which Edition Should I Get?

There are typically several editions available for each of the titles presented here. The edition you choose will be based upon your needs, budget, and purposes. If you are a classroom teacher trying out a book, planning to use it just once, or if you have a limited budget, consider borrowing the title from the public library. If the school library owns it, you're in luck! Should you decide to purchase the book, consider which edition will work best for you.

Hardcover editions are the most common and most durable for use in the classroom library. Although they cost more initially than softcover copies, they will last longer and will not need to be replaced as often.

Library binding editions are especially designed for longer shelf life as in library settings, but these sturdy editions can be perfect for the classroom library as well. As they tend to be a bit more expensive, you may want to choose this edition for those books you think will see the most use over an extended length of time.

Softcover editions are ideal for schools with limited budgets and for multiple-copy purchases for classrooms in which a library lending program for students and their families will be instituted. Special printings of books are arranged by school book clubs and appear in softcover or specially priced hardbound editions.

Each edition bears its own ISBN, so be sure to note the correct one when ordering books for purchase.

## How Do I Know What the Books Featured in Read-Aloud Plans Are About?

In addition to publication information you will find a subject category listed for each book. Use this handy reference when you are trying to find just the right title to augment a unit of study, a particular season, or an issue you want to explore. The subject index provided at the back of the book will help with this search as well.

Books included in the Book Notes section are listed in all subject categories to which each book relates.

## How Does the Read-Aloud Plan Work?

Each plan follows the same format. At the beginning is the publication information and an estimate of the actual time it ought to take to read the book aloud (*not* including questions and follow-up activities, as these are used at the reader's discretion and the time spent on them will vary). Next you will find a brief summary of the book. The teaching plan itself consists of three parts.

The read-aloud session begins with a **Pre-Reading Focus**. The plan suggests ways to introduce the book. This is an important step because it focuses children on the book, its format, and its subject. Discussion before reading aids in building prediction skills and nurtures experiential background by enabling children to draw upon their personal experiences to bring meaning to the story. As children discuss and answer questions, they verbalize thoughts and feelings and relate their experiences. Each read-aloud plan launches the reading of the book with a **Let's read to find out** focus for listening to the story.

In the **While Reading** portion of most read-aloud plans, you will find questions to pose as you read the book aloud. Answers are given in parentheses for even the simplest and most obvious questions for ease in following the plan while preparing in advance for the read-aloud session. Suggestions for reading the book aloud that are specific to that title also will be found in this section.

> **Write Away!** suggestions offer writing activities related to the theme, plot, characters, student responses to events in the story, or personal reflections.

The **Follow-Up Discussion** offers ideas for bringing the read-aloud session to a meaningful close. Questions that relate to the outcome of the story are posed. Discussion is encouraged. On some of the plans there is additional information and related titles. Some of the suggested follow-up activities extend beyond a simple follow-up. "Book words," such as *setting*, or terms important to the story, are often presented. Introduce these words in context rather than as isolated vocabulary words.

The **Up Close and Personal** segments contain comments submitted by the book's author or illustrator, or both, on the making of the book that you may want to share with children as an extension activity.

It is advisable to become familiar with the read-aloud plan as well as the *entire* book prior to presenting it to children. This will ensure that the book's theme, plot, and vocabulary are appropriate for your students.

*Note:* Plan to have an easel with chart paper or a chalk or dry-erase board available in the read-aloud area. Many of the read-aloud plans suggest follow-up activities that make use of these.

## How Do You Recommend I Use the Questions Provided in the Plans?

Use questions at your discretion as time and student needs permit.

When asking the suggested questions, rephrase children's answers into complete sentences. Reinforce responses by beginning with an affirmative. If a response is incorrect or not what you are after, accept the answer and rephrase the question. Avoid negative responses ("No, that's not right."). Encourage and reinforce appropriate group discussion dynamics.

When asking children to relate personal experiences, be flexible within reason and allow for variance. Encourage complete-sentence answers rather than single-word responses whenever appropriate. When you are fishing for a specific response, allow children to throw out answers and prompt with, "Yes, anything else?" or "I hadn't thought about that! Any other ideas?" Bring a discussion to a close with, "I'll take one more answer and then we will go on with the story."

Several questions are suggested in each part of the read-aloud plan. You are encouraged to use some or all according to your schedule, the attention span of your listeners, and their needs as you perceive them.

## How Should I Use the Tips and Techniques for Teachers and Librarians Section of the Book?

This portion of the book is designed to provide practical suggestions for professionals who work with newly independent and developing readers. Resources, tips, and techniques are outlined and explained with the hope that teachers and librarians will utilize this section of the book as needed and find it to be a handy reference tool.

## What Is the Purpose of the Parent Pull-Out Pages?

In this section of the book you will find material developed especially for parents or caregivers responsible for the children with whom you work. Permission is granted to reproduce the Parent Pull-Out Pages for distribution. It is recommended that these pages be sent home on a regular basis throughout the year. Their purpose is to reinforce the importance of reading aloud to children and to provide useful techniques and information about books and reading to parents and caregivers. It is essential to reinforce the key role adults play in fostering a lifelong love of reading in children.

## What Will I Find in the Book Notes?

This section of the book offers hundreds of additional titles listed under the subject(s) the book addresses and briefly summarized. Brief bibliographic information is also included.

## Why So Many Indexes?

Subject, title, author, and illustrator indexes are provided at the back of the book for your convenience in locating the information you need on just the right book quickly and with ease. Use these indexes when you need to locate information on any book included in this resource.

## What If I Have Questions, Comments, or Feedback?

I'd love to hear from you! If you have information you'd like to share with me or would like to arrange a school visit, parent program, or teacher in-service training, send an e-mail to my attention at judyreads@bluefrog.com. Place "Children's Book Corner" in the subject line, please, so you'll be sure it reaches me. For information on other books in the Children's Book Corner series or this author, visit www.lu.com.

# Read-Aloud Plans

*Cover from THE HERO OF THIRD GRADE by Alice DeLaCroix. Illustrated by Cynthia Fisher. Copyright © 2002. Reprinted with permission of Holiday House.*

| Title | THE HERO OF THIRD GRADE |
|---|---|
| Author | Alice DeLaCroix |
| Illustrator | Cynthia Fisher |
| Publisher | Holiday House |
| Copyright Date | 2002 |
| Ages | 8 and up |
| Read-Aloud Time | 6–8 minutes per chapter |
| Read-Aloud Sessions | 10 |
| Subject | New school, self-image, friendship, trees, carnival fund-raiser |

Randall's life is ruined. We find out about it in the first chapter, on the first page. His parents are newly divorced, he's moved to a new school in a new town, and it's April. Ruined, ruined, ruined.

**PRE-READING FOCUS**: Introducing the book: Show the cover and read the title. Ask: What do we know about this book from the title? (The main character, a boy, is in third grade. He is imagining himself as a hero.) What might a third grader do that would make him a hero?

## Chapter One: "Mrs. Hubbard's Cupboard"

*Pre-reading:* Ask: What does it mean to "get knots in your stomach?" Discuss personal experiences. **Let's read to find out** who this boy is on the cover of the book.

*Follow-up:* Ask: Who is the main character? (Randall.) Why does Randall feel his life is ruined? (He has moved to a new town in April when school is nearly over. It is the second day in his new school.) Why is it hard to move to a new school in the spring? Discuss. What else has happened recently? (Randall's mom and dad have divorced. Dad stayed in their old house in their old town.) What was the movie about that Randall watched with his mom the night before? (The Scarlet Pimpernel was a person who did brave things in secret. He signed his notes with a red flower.) What does Randall collect? (Rubber stamps.) What other characters do we meet in Chapter One? (Gordo, the bully; Max, a quiet classmate.) What does Randall do that helps get rid of the knots in his stomach? (He saves Max's homework and passes a secret note to Max.) How is Randall feeling at the end of the chapter? (Much better!) How do you know? (He grins inside.)

**Write Away!** Write a report on a "pet tree." (Refer to the last chapter of the book for examples of what to include in this project.)

*Note: In preparation for the next chapter, have a copy of the nursery rhyme "Old Mother Hubbard" on hand. An illustrated copy would be even better! Consider conducting a class pet tree project similar to the one described in the story. Plan to introduce it following the reading of Chapter 2.*

## Chapter Two: "A Pet What?"

*Pre-reading:* Ask children to guess what this chapter might be about based on its title. **Let's read to find out** what the title means.

*Follow-up:* Ask: What does the title mean? (Each class member must choose a "pet" tree: one he or she will get to know well.) Today we met more characters in the story. Mrs. Hubbard is the teacher. Read the nursery rhyme to the class for the benefit of those children who may not be familiar with "Old Mother Hubbard." Ask: Describe Mrs. Hubbard. (She is kind, thoughtful, wise, and fair.) We also met a few classmates. Which one does Randall send a secret note to? (Tara.) Why? (She feels bad that she doesn't get to have the biggest tree as her pet. He likes the way she holds her chin high.) What do you think a "runty" tree looks like? (Small, twiggy.) What does "Keep your chin up" mean? (Don't lose heart; don't give up.) How do you think Tara will feel when she reads the note? (Better.) The story gives us clues about what the word *scarlet* means. Can anyone tell me? (Red. We know because Randall feels his face turning red when he doesn't know what is going on in class.) Begin your own class "pet tree" project.

## Chapter Three: "Who Wrote This?"

*Pre-reading:* Read the title. Ask: Who do you think is asking this question? **Let's read to find out.**

*Follow-up:* Ask: What did you learn about the Scarlet Pimpernel in this chapter? (He was romantic.) Randall does something tricky to hide his identity as the Scarlet Pimpernel. What does he do? (He asks Max what his note said.)

## Chapter Four: "The Scarlet Pimpernel to the Rescue"

*Pre-reading:* Ask: How do you think the Scarlet Pimpernel might come to the rescue? **Let's read to find out.**

*Follow-up:* Ask: When Gordo hands the Beanie Baby to Jenna, Randall wishes he could have done so. But he feels that is impossible. Why? (It may reveal him as the Scarlet Pimpernel.) What does Randall figure out by watching Gordo? (He likes Jenna, and that's why he hid her stuffed animal and then found it.)

## Chapter Five: "The Scarlet Pimpernel Foiled"

*Pre-reading:* Ask children if anyone knows what *foiled* means. (Defeated; thwarted.) **Let's read to find out** how the Scarlet Pimpernel is foiled.

*Follow-up:* Ask: What do you think of Randall's idea of a carnival for a fund-raiser? What do you think the class will say about it? How was the Scarlet Pimpernel foiled? (Tara was watching him, so he couldn't write a Scarlet Pimpernel note.)

*Note: In preparation for the next chapter, consider having your own class carnival. Formulate preliminary plans to present to the class.*

## Chapter Six: "Who Is the Secret Hero?"

*Pre-reading:* Read the chapter title. Ask: What do you think will happen in this chapter? **Let's read to find out.**

*Follow-up:* Ask: How does Randall feel when his idea is chosen? (Great!) Yesterday we read how the Scarlet Pimpernel was foiled. Ask: Who was foiled today? (Gordo.) How? (Tara realizes the flower is made with a marker and the handwriting belongs to Gordo.) Begin to plan your own class carnival to raise funds for a worthy cause!

## Chapter Seven: "In the Game at Last"

*Pre-reading:* Read the chapter title to the class. Ask: What do you think this means? (Randall is beginning to be accepted by his new classmates.) **Let's read to find out.**

*Follow-up:* Ask: How does Randall feel when he is part of the kickball game? (Great!) Why does Randall disguise his handwriting? (So Tara won't guess that he is the Scarlet Pimpernel.) Continue working on plans for your class carnival!

## Chapter Eight: "Monkey Business"

*Pre-reading:* Read the chapter title to the class. Ask children to predict what this chapter is about. **Let's read to find out.**

*Follow-up:* Ask: What does the title mean? (Someone has done something he or she shouldn't have. Money is missing from the cash box.) Ask children to predict who might have taken the money.

## Chapter Nine: "A Hero for Real"

*Pre-reading:* Read the chapter title. Ask what it might mean. **Let's read to find out.**

*Follow-up:* Ask: What does the title mean? (Randall was a hero being just plain Randall.) What did you think when Randall didn't take the money out of Slick's pocket? What did we learn about Gordo in this chapter? (He is honest.) Why is Randall so happy at the end of the chapter? (He didn't have to tell on Slick. This was the best day he had had in his new school.) In a way, Gordo is a hero, too. Why? (He does the right thing.)

## Chapter Ten: "General Ali Baba"

*Pre-reading:* Ask: What can you tell from this title? (It is a combination of the names of Randall and Max's pet trees put together.) Why do you think the chapter is titled "General Ali Baba?" What do you think will happen in this last chapter of the book? **Let's read to find out.**

*Follow-up:* Ask: Do you think Tara knows who the Scarlet Pimpernel is? (Yes.) How do you know? (She slips when talking with Randall.) What are three good things that happen at the end of May? (The trees got planted, Tara doesn't tell who the Secret Pimpernel is, and Randall discovers that Max lives in his apartment complex.) Do you think Randall will keep on being the Scarlet Pimpernel? (Probably not. He is happy just being himself.) If time permits, consider reading the tale of Ali Baba. Enjoy the class carnival. Collect and share pet tree projects!

*See also THIRD GRADE STINKS!, written by Colleen O'Shaughnessy McKenna and illustrated by Stephanie Roth (Holiday House).*

*For other suggestions of great realistic fiction for third-grade readers about third-grade life, refer to THAT COULD BE ME! in the Parent Pull-Out Pages.*

## Notes:

# Up Close and Personal

## *A Note from the Author, Alice DeLaCroix*

### *On where the idea for the book came from:*

My daughter was teaching science in a local elementary school when I decided to write THE HERO OF THIRD GRADE. I loved hearing her tales of classroom antics and the students' excitement over science projects, so I was inspired to create my own classroom. Also, I live in a part of the country that is stricken with terrible ice storms every so often. These events do wipe out or damage large numbers of trees, so I liked the idea of a class working together to earn money which would provide a few new trees to an ice storm-clobbered town. My "hero" has a problem which is hard for any child to work through—moving to a new school near the end of the school year, and I wanted him to find his own clever ways of fitting in.

### *On writing:*

Kids are full of original ideas, and most love a good story. That covers two important requirements for becoming a writer. Reading a great deal and writing, writing, writing probably takes care of the rest. If you grumble about rewriting, remember that published authors grumble, too. But they know a story that is polished with thoughtful rewriting shines brighter than the original draft.

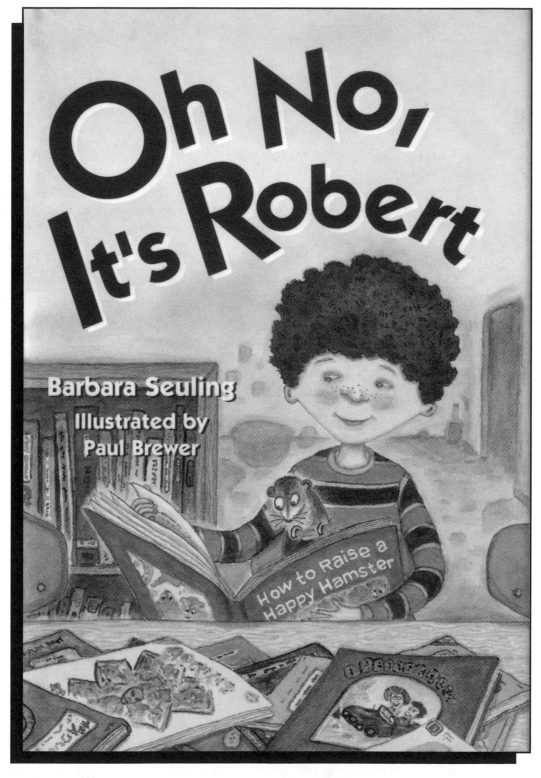

*Cover from OH NO, IT'S ROBERT written by Barbara Seuling, illustrated by Paul Brewer. Reprinted by permission of Carus Publishing Company. Illustration copyright © 1999 by Paul Brewer.*

| | |
|---|---|
| **Title** . . . . . . . . . . . . . . . . . . . . . . . . . . . . . . . . . . . . . . . . . OH NO, IT'S ROBERT |
| **Author** . . . . . . . . . . . . . . . . . . . . . . . . . . . . . . . . . . . . Barbara Seuling |
| **Illustrator** . . . . . . . . . . . . . . . . . . . . . . . . . . . . . . . . . . . . Paul Brewer |
| **Publisher** . . . . . . . . . . . . . . . . . . . . . . . . . . . . Front Street/Cricket Books |
| **Copyright Date** . . . . . . . . . . . . . . . . . . . . . . . . . . . . . . . . . . . . 1999 |
| **Ages** . . . . . . . . . . . . . . . . . . . . . . . . . . . . . . . . . . . . . . . . . 8 and up |
| **Read-Aloud Time** . . . . . . . . . . . . . . . . . . . . . . 8–10 minutes per chapter |
| **Read-Aloud Sessions** . . . . . . . . . . . . . . . . . . . . . . . . . . . . . . . . 12 |
| **Subject** . . . . . . . . . . . Self-esteem; character, friendship, school, mystery |

*Note: This story takes place around Thanksgiving.*

Robert's not good in math and his father is a math teacher. Robert's in the low reading group and there's a classroom contest in which the more books you read the better. Robert feels like a dodo bird around Susanne Lee. He'd like to talk to his mom about things, but she's busy with her new job. Good thing there are friends like Paul and wise teachers who value someone who cares. Oh yes, that's Robert.

> **PRE-READING FOCUS:** Introducing the book: Show the cover and read the title. Ask: What do you think this book is about? What do we know about this book from the cover? (Robert is the main character; a hamster figures somewhere in the story; we can infer from the title that Robert is not the most "with it" child in the classroom; and we can guess that Robert is about 9 or 10 years old.)

## Chapter One: "The Pig Stamp"

> *Pre-reading:* Ask: Why might this chapter be titled "Pig Stamp?" (Robert has a messy paper.) Clue on the cover: school setting. **Let's read to find out** what the title means and meet our main character.

> *Follow-up:* We've met Robert in this first chapter. Ask: What do we know about him so far? (Robert hates math and loves to ride his bike. His mom is away on business for the first time. Robert's dad calls him Tiger. Robert's older brother is Charlie. In the living room there are shelves of sports trophies that Charlie has won and plaques on the wall with his mother's and father's names on them. Robert has never won anything. Robert's best friend is Paul.) Describe Robert's mom. (She is wise and kind.) How do we know this? (She always makes him feel good about something.) Can you give me an example? (Robert draws a spaceship that she thinks is a cucumber and she puts it up on the refrigerator!) What happens when Robert gets help from his dad with his math homework? (Dad gets exasperated. Robert erases so much he makes a hole in his paper.) Robert's dad tells him "Always hand in neat work. Even if you have to do it over ten

times. It tells what kind of person you are. It shows you care." Discuss. Ask: What is the pig stamp and how does Robert feel about it? (The stamp says COULD BE NEATER! and the teacher uses it when papers are messy. Robert hates it. His homework almost always has this stamp on it.) Tell students that the next chapter is titled "Paper Keys" and it takes place in school.

*Note: In preparation for the next chapter, collect information on dodo birds to share with students. Prepare for your classroom contest.*

## Chapter Two: "Paper Keys"

*Pre-reading:* Today we are going to read about Robert in school. Ask: What do you think a chapter titled "Paper Keys" might be about? **Let's read to find out!**

*Follow-up:* Ask: Whom have we met in this chapter? (Mrs. Bernthal, the teacher; Susanne Lee Rodgers, Ms. Smarty Pants; Paul Felcher, Robert's best friend.) What can you tell me about these characters? (Susanne Lee is a very good student and Robert's reading buddy. She makes Robert feel like a dodo bird. Paul is a good artist and new to the school. Mrs. Bernthal is warm, fair, and kind.) Share information on dodo birds with the class. Ask: What did we learn about the paper keys? (Mrs. Bernthal is having a contest. A paper key will be placed on the bulletin board with the child's name on it for each item that he or she accomplishes. The student with the most keys after three weeks will earn the gold chest with his or her name engraved on it.) Do you think the contest would be fun? Review the tasks on the list. Ask: How does Robert feel about them? (Robert thinks three out of five will be just about impossible for him to achieve.) Why? (He is in the slow reading group, he hates math, he is a bad speller, and he makes holes in his homework papers.) Even so, Robert tries. He checks out a book. Ask: Which item on the list do you think Robert will work on to earn a paper key? At the end of the chapter Robert opens his book and finds that someone has scribbled in it with bright green marker. Ask: What do you think Robert will do? Begin your classroom contest!

*Note: In preparation for the next chapter, if you are brave and adventurous, offer samples of goat cheese!*

## Chapter Three: "The Five Food Groups"

*Pre-reading:* Read the title. Ask: Can anyone tell me what the five food groups are? (Meat, grains, fruits, vegetables, and fats.) Ask: If you were going to contribute food for a basket for the poor, what would you donate? **Let's read to find out** what Robert brings in.

*Follow-up:* In this chapter we met Lester. Ask: What does Robert think of him? (He's a bully and a tease, and there's no point in messing with him.) How many keys does Robert have? (Two.) What are they for? (Helping in the classroom.) How many does Susanne have? (Two.) What are they for? (Helping in the classroom and reading a book.) How many does Paul have? (One, for reading a book.) What do you think of Paul's idea that Robert advertise? Is Paul a good friend?

(Yes.) How do you know? (He helps Robert come up with ideas and offers to make flyers.) Who do you think will win the contest? Show a package of goat cheese so students can see why Robert mistook it for cream cheese. Pass out samples!

# Chapter Four: "Super Helper"

*Pre-reading:* Ask: What would a super helper do? **Let's read to find out** what jobs Robert does to be a super helper.

*Follow-up:* Ask: Which of Robert's jobs would you like best? Robert is glad to be the library monitor. Why? (Mrs. Bernthal says she needs someone who cares and Robert remembered his father's words.) What do you think of Charlie's suggestion to Robert about the invention he should talk about? (A toilet.)

# Chapter Five: "Pink Underwear"

*Pre-reading:* Ask: Whose underwear do you think this chapter is about? **Let's read to find out!**

*Follow-up:* Ask: What are some of the things bothering Robert? (His invention talk was a fiasco, he got beat up by Lester, he's wishing his home was like Paul's.) Discuss. Robert doesn't mention Lester's underwear. Why? What does that tell us about Robert? (He is kind and thoughtful.) What does Robert see in Paul's room that really impresses him? (The set of markers.) Let's remember that as we read more of the story tomorrow.

*Note: In preparation for the next chapter, if you are brave and artistically inclined, have fresh fish on hand for your own art project!*

# Chapter Six: "The Scribbler Strikes Again"

*Pre-reading:* Ask: Who do you think the scribbler might be? **Let's read to find out** who Robert thinks it might be.

*Follow-up:* Ask: Why does Robert think the scribbler might be Paul? (He has all those markers. The hamster book is scribbled in, and Paul was the last one to check it out.) How can Robert figure out who the scribbler is? Robert was offered another super helper job. How do you think he did cleaning up the art room for Miss Valentine? Does anyone have a hamster? What are some important facts Robert might learn about caring for Trudy from the book about hamsters that he checked out of the classroom library?

> **Write Away!** Who do you think the scribbler is? Support your opinion by listing reasons why and giving evidence from the story.

## Chapter Seven: "The Other Side of Town"

*Pre-reading:* Read excerpts from a few of the children's compositions. List "suspects" on chart paper. Tell children who received the most "votes" as the likely scribbler. **Let's read to find out** if Robert gets any more clues about who the scribbler is.

*Follow-up:* Ask: Why do you think Robert slunk down in his seat so Lester wouldn't see him? (He doesn't want to embarrass Lester.) Would Robert make a good friend and classmate? (Yes.) Discuss.

## Chapter Eight: "Charlie to the Rescue"

*Pre-reading:* Read the title. Ask: What do you think it means? **Let's read to find out** how Charlie helps out.

*Follow-up:* Ask children to recall times when a sibling or other family member came to their rescue.

## Chapter Nine: "Something Fishy"

*Pre-reading:* Read the title. Ask: What do you think this chapter might be about? Recall when we read about fish before in the story. **Let's read to find out** what the title means.

*Follow-up:* Ask: What did Robert learn about reading books? (Some books don't have to be read cover to cover from front to back.) We learned a big word in this chapter: fumigate. What do you think it means? (To apply smoke, vapor, or gas for the purpose of disinfecting or destroying pests) What kind of a day is Robert having? (A bad one!) Discuss.

## Chapter Ten: "Getting Warmer"

*Pre-reading:* Read the title. Yesterday we read about Robert's horrible day. This chapter is about Robert "getting warmer" about who the scribbler is. What does that mean? (Robert is getting closer to a solution to the mystery.) **Let's read to find out** what Robert learns.

*Follow-up:* Robert doesn't make fun of Lester for reading a "baby" book. Ask: How do you think Lester feels when Robert offers to sign out the book for him? Discuss Robert's character. Cross Lester's name off the class list of suspects. Robert thinks Paul is the "prime suspect." What does that mean? (The most likely person to have committed the crime.) Read the next chapter's title for added suspense and intrigue!

**Write Away!** What do you think Robert should do? Explain.

## Chapter Eleven: "Caught in the Act"

*Pre-reading:* Read the title. **Let's read to find out** what this title means!

*Follow-up:* Put a big red circle around Nick's name if it is listed on the class list of suspects. If not, write it in and circle it! At the beginning of the chapter Robert feels as if there is a rock in his stomach. Write this on chart paper. Ask: Why does Robert feel this way? What else could you say to show that you are upset? Write suggestions class members offer on the chart paper. At the end of the chapter Robert is very relieved. What could you say to show that? Write responses on the chart paper. What did you notice about Lester's lunch? (The cookies he eats are the ones Robert donated to the food basket.)

## Chapter Twelve: "Treasure Chest Day"

*Pre-reading:* Read the title. Ask: Who do you think will win? Write names down. Cast votes. **Let's read to find out** who the winner is!

*Follow-up:* Put a circle around Susanne Lee's name. Then put a circle around Robert's name. Ask: Why do you think Robert felt he had to tell Paul that he suspected him of being the Scribbler? (Honesty.) Complete your classroom contest!

*For more about Robert and his misadventures, refer fans to the other titles in the Robert Series, incluidng ROBERT TAKES A STAND, ROBERT AND THE BACK-TO-SCHOOL SPECIAL, ROBERT AND THE LEMMING PROBLEM, ROBERT AND THE WEIRD & WACKY FACTS, ROBERT AND THE GREAT PEPPERONI, and ROBERT AND THE GREAT ESCAPE. For more information about these books, visit the publisher's Web site at www.cricketbooks.net.*

Notes:

# Up Close and Personal

## *A Note from the Author, Barbara Seuling*

### *On how experiences turn into stories:*

When my niece, Gwenn, was 13, she came to visit me one summer in Vermont. As a special treat, I bought fresh trout, which I sautéed for breakfast. When breakfast was finished, Gwenn wanted to clean up, and I let her—she was so eager to help. Days later, after she went back to Brooklyn, there was a funny smell coming from the pantry. I investigated, thinking a mouse had come in and died there. But no, it was the leftover trout! Instead of putting it in the refrigerator, Gwenn had put the fish in the pantry where, in the hot summer weather, it soon became rank.

That experience was the basis of my first story about Robert. It was a scene that showed my readers the kind of boy Robert was—eager to please, but someone whose good intentions often got him into trouble. Robert's character would be the core of any story I wrote, so this was important to establish early in the process.

In OH NO, IT'S ROBERT, I turned the smelly fish episode into a school scene, but the basic intention and result is the same. From that scene, I was able to weave an entire story around my character. From the very beginning, I had to show that he was a good kid who wanted to do the right thing, but someone who always managed to do it in ways that backfired. That could be funny, and I wanted to write a funny story. And since every good story has to have a problem for the main character to solve, why couldn¹t the problem in some way relate to this feature of Robert's personality?

### *On getting a book published:*

It wasn't that easy selling the story of Robert. It took nine years before someone wanted to publish it. It had gone to many publishers, but nobody offered to buy it. I swallowed my pride, revised it, and sent it out again. Still nobody wanted it, although I got some very nice comments along the way. I put it away, but I couldn't forget it. Then one day at a workshop, someone read from her manuscript about a boy who was funny. He reminded me of my own Robert, who was languishing on a shelf. I took the story out and read it again. I still thought it was good. I sent it to a writer friend for an opinion. She liked it and made a few minor suggestions. Just as I was about to send it out again, I heard that a new publisher was starting up. I sent it there. That was Cricket Publishing, and they bought it for their first list of books. That was 1998, and now there are more than eight ROBERT books.

*To learn more about Barbara Seuling, visit her at www.barbaraseuling.com.*

| | |
|---|---|
| **Title** | LEONARDO: BEAUTIFUL DREAMER |
| **Author/Illustrator** | Robert Byrd |
| **Publisher** | Dutton |
| **Copyright Date** | 2003 |
| **Ages** | 8 and up |
| **Read-Aloud Time** | 5–8 minutes per 2 spreads |
| **Read-Aloud Sessions** | up to 10 |
| **Subject** | Leonardo da Vinci, curiosity, observation, experimentation, inventions, journals |

This illustrated biography is chock-full of intriguing details and detailed drawings depicting the life and personality of the well-known genius of the Renaissance period. Laid out so that each spread addresses a subject that was of interest to da Vinci, this picture book intended for older children offers myriad opportunities to delight, entrance, and teach children about the power of observation. It can be read from cover to cover over a number of days, or the reader may choose to highlight specific aspects of da Vinci's life and accomplishments to delve into. Each spread is divided into main text, "sidebars" that add another layer of understanding, and award-winning illustrations that extend and enhance the text. Da Vinci's personal notebooks inspired the format of the book, and quotations from it are peppered throughout the book. A perfect example of how far nonfiction for children has come, this book is an excellent introduction to a unit on inventions and exemplifies the important role curiosity plays in how inventions can come to be.

*Note: The Write Away! activities progress as students experience da Vinci's style of exploration of ideas through the use of a notebook or journal. Consider making personal notebooks before beginning the reading of this book.*

**PRE-READING FOCUS:** Read the first paragraph of the Introduction. Ask: Have you ever tried to do something that was really hard? Discuss. What did it feel like when you finally were able to do it? Refer back to the word, *exhilarating*, in the text. Leonardo da Vinci felt *exhilarated* when he figured something out. Show illustration of da Vinci. Ask students to list facts about da Vinci's life. Write them on chart paper. For more information about the Renaissance period, read aloud the rest of the Introduction.

## "The Omen of the Kite"; "The Wonder of All Things"

*Pre-reading:* Ask: What is a kite? **Let's read to find out** where the word kite comes from. (A bird.)

*Follow-up:* Da Vinci kept many notebooks, or journals, and it is from these that the author of this book knows about da Vinci's life, his thoughts, his ideas, and his plans. Da Vinci was very curious. He asked questions about all sorts of things in nature. What questions do you have about things in nature that you would like answered?

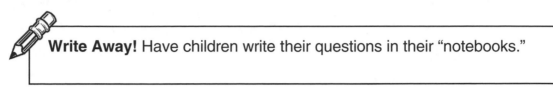

**Write Away!** Have children write their questions in their "notebooks."

## "The Pool of Water"; "The Cave of Bones and Shells"; "Florence"

*Pre-reading:* When da Vinci went into a cave for the first time as a young boy, he was frightened. Ask: If you were frightened by a place, what would you do? **Let's read to find out** what da Vinci did.

*Follow-up:* Do you think da Vinci was happy to be in Florence? Discuss.

**Write Away!** Highlight the one question in your notebook that you most would like to learn the answer to. Write about how you might find out more about this if you were da Vinci.

## "In the Workshop of the Master"; "In the Court of Ludovico"

*Pre-reading:* Explain what an *apprentice* is. (One who serves another in exchange for learning an art or trade.) Ask: What do you think da Vinci learned from the master artist? **Let's read to find out** what da Vinci worked on in his years with Verrocchio.

*Follow-up:* Explain what a *patron* is. (One who financed the living expenses and work of an artist.) Ask: How did da Vinci convince Ludovico to be his patron? (Da Vinci wrote a letter to Ludovico filled with details about his talents and how he could be of service to him.)

## "Paradiso and the Great Horse"; "The Dining Hall of the Great Monks"

*Pre-reading:* Have you ever worked on something for a very long time before you finished it? Discuss. **Let's read to find out** how da Vinci worked and what made him famous.

*Follow-up:* Discuss da Vinci's advice for a painter. Ask: When are the opinions of others important? When are they not? Discuss when da Vinci listened to others and when he did not. (He would not be rushed to finish a project.) Continue working on finding the answers to individual questions from personal notebooks. Update the chart of facts about da Vinci's life.

## "Strange Animals, Mythical Beasts"; "The Fantastic Notebooks"

*Pre-reading:* Why do you think da Vinci kept a notebook? **Let's read to find out** some of the odd things found in da Vinci's notebooks. (Da Vinci wrote from right to left, crammed lots of ideas and thoughts on a page, and was disorganized.)

*Follow-up:* Use a mirror to read entries. Take a vote on which notebook entry is the most interesting. Discuss.

**Write Away!** In your notebook, create a mythical beast! Use words first, then illustrate.

## "Grand Plans and Visions"; "The Makeup of All Life"

*Pre-reading:* Ask: What words would you use to describe da Vinci? Da Vinci believed man should "consult nature in everything." What does this mean? **Let's read to find out** how he did that.

*Follow-up:* Continue working on finding the answers to individual questions, da Vinci-style.

## "As Far As the Eye Can See"; "Muscle and Marvelous Machines"

*Pre-reading:* Ask: Which part of the body do you think da Vinci would consider the most remarkable? (The eye.) **Let's read to find out** what it is and why he felt that way.

*Follow-up:* Discuss the marvelous machines da Vinci invented. See books listed at the end of this plan for additional follow-up ideas.

## "The Eternal Birdman"; "Water, the Driver of Nature"

*Pre-reading:* Why do you think da Vinci studied birds so much? (He believed that humans might fly.) When da Vinci wanted answers to a question, how did he go about trying to find out? (He observed and experimented.) **Let's read to find out** what da Vinci believed to be the four elements of nature. (Earth, air, fire, and water.)

*Follow-up:* Ask: What words would you use to describe da Vinci? Ask children to support their answers with information from the text. Add to the list on the chart.

## "The Vault of Heaven"; "The Smiling Lady"

*Pre-reading:* **Let's read to find out** what the "vault of heaven" is. (Our view of the moon, planets, sun, and stars.)

*Follow-up:* Show a picture of the *Mona Lisa*. Discuss why the painting is so famous, using the points highlighted in the text.

## "Fanciful Fabrications"; "The Perfect Patron"; "The Endless Mystery"

*Pre-reading:* Review what a patron is. **Let's read to find out** who was the perfect patron and why.

*Follow-up:* Discuss the fanciful fabrications! Use back material at your discretion to extend your study of da Vinci. Finalize notebook entries.

*For more fanciful fabrications, see HERE'S WHAT YOU CAN DO WHEN YOU CAN'T FIND YOUR SHOE: INGENIOUS INVENTIONS FOR PESKY PROBLEMS, written by Andrea Perry and illustrated by Alan Snow (Atheneum), for which a read-aloud plan can be found in Children's Book Corner, Grades 1–2. For a fanciful, factual account of the man who invented the ice- cream cone as well as an accounting of many others who believed they did, read ICE-CREAM CONES FOR SALE!, by Elaine Greenstein (Scholastic). Finally, don't miss SO YOU WANT TO BE AN INVENTOR?, written by Judith St. George and illustrated by Caldecott Award winner David Small (Philomel).*

## Notes:

# Up Close and Personal

## A Note from the Author/Illustrator, Robert Byrd

### On how he chose to write about Leonardo da Vinci:

I wanted to do a book about a famous person, and during the "countdown" for the most influential people of the last millennium, Leonardo da Vinci seemed the most exciting to me. The main difficulty in writing about Leonardo was that there was too much information!

Leonardo da Vinci was incredibly diverse and involved in so many things. I thought it would be best to have every spread in my book show a different facet of his life and work, and I wanted them in chronological order. The larger pictures show the theme of each spread—the smaller art shows specific information relating to the main theme. The larger type describes the main story, the smaller type describes related material and Leonardo da Vinci's actual words.

I wanted my book to be imaginative, fanciful, and for it to show some of Leonardo's life that people may not know about. But at the same time, I wanted it to be absolutely accurate. Everything in the book is based on Leonardo's own drawings and his written notebooks.

### Tips on writing a biography, or a story about a real person's life:

• Really know your subject. Find out if you have the slightest doubt about anything.

• Decide what you really want readers to know about your subject, and then think about the best and most interesting way to tell your story.

• Above all, a biography must never be dull; make it exciting and informative!

*For more about Robert Byrd and his books, go to the Penguin Web site: http://www.penguinputnam.com/nf/Author/AuthorPage.*

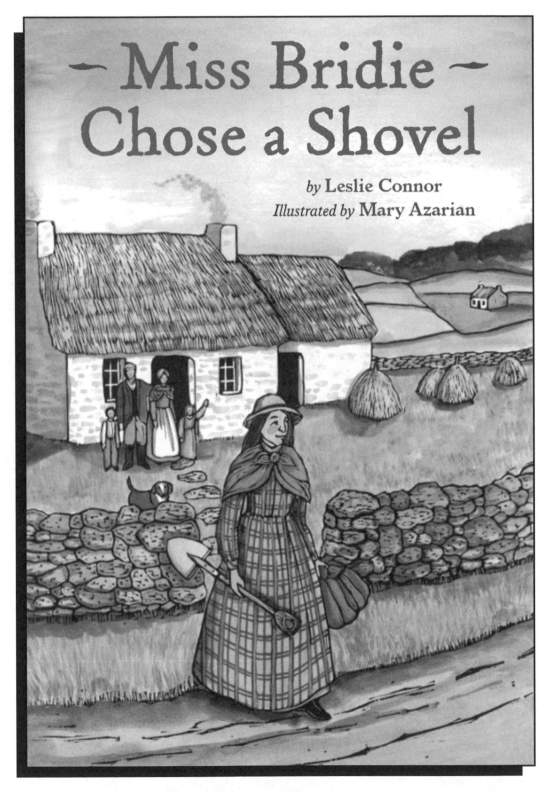

Cover from MISS BRIDIE CHOSE A SHOVEL by Leslie Connor. Jacket art
© 2004 by Mary Azarian. Reprinted by permission of Houghton Mifflin Company.
All rights reserved.

| | |
|---|---|
| **Title** . . . . . . . . . . . . . . . . . . . . . . . . . . . . . . . . MISS BRIDIE CHOSE A SHOVEL | |
| **Author** . . . . . . . . . . . . . . . . . . . . . . . . . . . . . . . . . . . . . . . . . Leslie Connor | |
| **Illustrator** . . . . . . . . . . . . . . . . . . . . . . . . . . . . . . . . . . . . . Mary Azarian | |
| **Publisher** . . . . . . . . . . . . . . . . . . . . . . . . . . . . . . . . . . . Houghton Mifflin | |
| **Copyright Date** . . . . . . . . . . . . . . . . . . . . . . . . . . . . . . . . . . . . . 2004 | |
| **Ages** . . . . . . . . . . . . . . . . . . . . . . . . . . . . . . . . . . . . . . . . 7 and up | |
| **Read-Aloud Time** . . . . . . . . . . . . . . . . . . . . . . . . . . . . . . . 5–7 minutes | |
| **Read-Aloud Sessions** . . . . . . . . . . . . . . . . . . . . . . . . . . . . . . . . 1 | |
| **Subject** . . . Strength of character, immigrant experience, farm life, time line | |

As the story opens, Young Miss Bridie, straight of back and sure of self, steps on board a ship bound for America with her prized possession, a shovel. With this shovel Miss Bridie faces challenges and joys as she builds a life in her new homeland. Through spare text accompanied by evocative woodcuts created by Caldecott medalist Mary Azarian, the reader is treated to the unfolding of the life of one immigrant who represents millions who came to America from Europe in the mid-1800s.

*Note: If you have a sturdy garden shovel, plan to display it during the read-aloud of this book.*

**PRE-READING FOCUS:** Do not show the cover of the book or read the title. Ask: If you were going to move far away and could take only one thing with you besides your clothing and other basic necessities, what would you choose? Read the title of the book and show the cover. Ask children to make predictions about the time and setting of this story. (1850s; Ireland to America.) Pull out the shovel. Ask: Why do you think Miss Bridie chose a shovel to take with her to her new home in America? **Let's read to find out.**

**WHILE READING:** After reading the first page, note the time period. (1856.) Read through the page on which Miss Bridie gets her first job. Ask: What is millinery? Use illustration clues to define the word. (Hat maker.) Note the term "to let." Ask children to guess what that means. (For rent.) Ask: What do you think is in Miss Bridie's blue bundle? Consider its size. Discuss. As you continue reading through the end of the story, note details of the seasons of Miss Bridie's life on the farm and the part the shovel plays in her experiences.

**FOLLOW-UP DISCUSSION:** Ask: Do you think Miss Bridie was wise to choose a shovel? Now that we have read the story of Miss Bridie's life, what else might she have taken and put to good use? Discuss Miss Bridie's character strengths. Create a time line of Miss Bridie's life, using an outline of a shovel handle as the base for the time line. Illustrate key events.

*Related stories include SO FAR FROM HOME: THE DIARY OF MARY DRISCOLL, AN IRISH MILL GIRL, by Barry Denenberg (Scholastic), and THE ST. PATRICK'S DAY SHILLELAGH, written by Janet Nolan and illustrated by Ben F. Stahl (Whitman), in which a shillelagh and its history are handed down through the generations.*

*See also ORANGES ON GOLD MOUNTAIN, written by Elizabeth Partridge and illustrated by Aki Sogabe (Penguin), in which a Chinese boy makes his home on the California coast in the 1850s.*

## Notes:

# Up Close and Personal

## *A Note from the Author, Leslie Connor*

### *On where the idea for the story came from:*

The idea for MISS BRIDIE CHOSE A SHOVEL came to me years ago when my husband and I were building our house into the side of a hill. I remember looking around our property and thinking, I'm going to need a good shovel. Compared to the people who immigrated to America centuries ago, our life was easy. Imagine moving far, far away and only being able to take what you could carry! You'd have to make wise choices and leave some things behind. As I built my gardens with my new shovel, I realized what a handy tool it was. I thought about a character, a woman, breaking new earth on a hillside farm and began to hear the line that became my title: Miss Bridie chose a shovel . . .

One line wasn't enough for a story but I began to put the imagined events of Miss Bridie's life in an order (or sequence) that made sense to me. My story started taking shape. But everything seemed to go along a little too smoothly for Miss Bridie. Life isn't always easy. I knew that if I really wanted her to come alive for my readers, I had to give her some troubles. I added the passage about the drought and the barn fire. Then I let her react to that problem in a way that I felt was true to her character.

After my work on the book, the writing, was done, it was Mary Azarian's turn to make the art for the book. I enjoyed seeing her loose sketches and then her beautiful, hand-colored woodcuts. Mary said she began to think of Miss Bridie as an ancestor. I love the way she filled in so many details that I could not have taken the space to write about. Did you see how many children Miss Bridie had? Did you notice the way the dogs at the farm change over the years? Did you see the new barn going up in the background?

| | |
|---|---|
| **Title** | THE KING'S CHESSBOARD |
| **Author** | David Birch |
| **Illustrator** | Devis Grebu |
| **Publisher** | Dial |
| **Copyright Date** | 1988 |
| **Ages** | 7 and up |
| **Read-Aloud Time** | 10–12 minutes |
| **Read-Aloud Sessions** | 1–2 |
| **Subject** | Math (doubling), pride, wisdom, chess |

This prideful king will not take no for an answer, and when he doesn't know the answer, he won't admit it. It takes a wise man and a chessboard to teach the king that pride can make a fool of anyone, even the mighty. And while readers glean that important lesson from this entertaining tale, they are also learning the concept of doubling in a memorable and meaningful way.

*Note: Have a chessboard and a bowl with a pound of raw white rice in it on display for the reading of this book. Also, have available plastic bags of various sizes.*

**PRE-READING FOCUS:** Show the chessboard. Ask the children what they know about chess/chessboards. Note how many squares there are. (Do the math! 8 x 8 = 64.) Show the book. Read the title. Ask: Where might this story take place? (India.) Is it a present day story? (No.) Why do you think this? (Dress of characters.) Who do you think the man in red and green is? (King.) Why do you think this? (The other man is bowing before him.) Ask children what they think this story might be about. **Let's read to find out** about the king's chessboard.

**WHILE READING:** After reading the wise man's request, study the chessboard. Discuss the request. Review the king's reasoning: "[O]ne, two, four, eight, sixteen. . . . There were sixty-four squares. Would that be a pound of rice in all?" Allow students to make predictions about the amount of rice that this would be in all. Read the queen's suggestion. Ask: Do you think the king will ask the wise man? (No.) Why? (Pride.) Read on through the delivery of the first grain of rice. Take a grain and place it on the chessboard. Continue reading, adding grains of rice to the chessboard until no more can be added. Then put rice in the plastic bags until they are full. Do the math as the story progresses. Ask: What do you think the wise man will do with all this rice? (Give it to the poor and hungry.) Read on. When the Grand Superintendent realizes what's happening, do the math to determine how many pounds are in "over half a ton." (1,024.) When the king summons the mathematicians to calculate the number of tons he has promised, write the number on the board. (274,877,906,944.) Or, have the children compute it! (Possibly, this could be given as an extra credit homework assignment, in which case you may want to continue reading the story on the following day.) Read to the end of the story.

**FOLLOW-UP DISCUSSION:** At the end of the story, the king smiled "not a happy smile perhaps, but a genuine smile." Discuss. The king tells the wise man that he has done yet another service for his majesty. What does he mean? (The wise man has taught the king humility: "how easy it is for pride to make a fool of any-one, even a king.")

*For a list of fables and tales, refer to the Book Notes section of this resource.*

<u>Notes:</u>

*Cover from SEESAW GIRL by Linda Sue Park. Jacket illustration copyright © 1999 by Jean and Mou-Sien Tseng. Reprinted by permission of Clarion Books/Houghton Mifflin Company. All rights reserved.*

| | |
|---|---|
| **Title** . . . . . . . . . . . . . . . . . . . . . . . . . . . . . . . . . . . . SEESAW GIRL |
| **Author** . . . . . . . . . . . . . . . . . . . . . . . . . . . . . . Linda Sue Park |
| **Illustrator** . . . . . . . . . . . . . . . . . . . . . . . . . . Jean and Mou-Sien Tseng |
| **Publisher** . . . . . . . . . . . . . . . . . . . . . . . . . . . . . . . . . . . . Clarion |
| **Copyright Date** . . . . . . . . . . . . . . . . . . . . . . . . . . . . . . 1999 |
| **Ages** . . . . . . . . . . . . . . . . . . . . . . . . . . . . . . . . . . . 8 and up |
| **Read-Aloud Time** . . . . . . . . . . . . . . . . . . . . 6–8 minutes per chapter |
| **Read-Aloud Sessions** . . . . . . . . . . . . . . . . . . . . . . . . . . . . 14 |
| **Subject** . . . . . . 17th-century Korea, resourcefulness, fulfilling one's dreams |

This is the story of an independent-minded girl hemmed in by tradition and the constraints of her culture in seventeenth-century Korea. We learn not only about that culture and the deep division between what girls and boys were allowed to do, but also about strength of spirit and the power of dreams. As 12-year-old Jade tries to find a way to see the world outside her courtyard while remaining obedient to her elders, readers will cheer her on and revel in her resourceful nature and her ultimate triumph.

*Note: The Author's Note at the end of the book serves to explain and extend many of the factual aspects of the story.*

**PRE-READING FOCUS:** Read the title. Show the cover. Ask: What do you think this story might be about? Explore what children know about Korea.

## Chapter 1: "Brushes and Ashes"

*Pre-reading:* In this first chapter we meet the main character of the story. As I read, listen to learn about her *character traits*. **Let's read to find out:** What is the character like? What does this main character like to do? How old is the main character? Think about how you would describe the main character. We will also learn a bit about the *setting* of the story, or where and when it takes place.

*Follow-up:* Who is the main character? (Jade.) What did we learn about Jade in this chapter? (She is 12 years old; she likes to play pranks; she has brothers; her cousin and friend is Willow.) Can you guess where this story takes place? (Korea.) Do you think it takes place in the present, the future, or the past? (Seventeenth century.) What are some customs we learn about in this chapter? (Boys learn from a schoolmaster; girls embroider. Male and female roles and expectations are clear and rigid.) Begin a chart of what boys and girls are allowed to do. You will add to this throughout the story. Show the illustration. Ask: Which girl do you think is Jade? Why? (The one on the right is Jade.)

## Chapter 2: "Laundry Sticks"

*Pre-reading:* Today we will learn how laundry was done in seventeenth-century Korea, the *setting* of our story. **Let's read to find out** what Jade's job was on laundry day.

*Follow-up:* Discuss the laundry procedure. In this chapter the friends have a difference of opinion. At the end of the chapter, Jade decides to go along with Willow. Why? What would you have done? Re-read the last sentence of the chapter. Ask what clue this might be giving the reader about what might happen later in the story. Introduce the term, *foreshadowing.*

*Note: You will need a map of Korea for the next read-aloud session.*

## Chapter 3: "Within the Walls"

*Pre-reading:* Find Seoul on the map. This is where Jade lives. **Let's read to find out** more about Jade's home and the customs of her time.

*Follow-up:* How is Jade's life different from yours? Discuss. What does Jade treasure more than anything else? (A carved ivory ball.) Explain what ivory is. Why does Jade value this ball? (Because it reminds her of the large ivory ball nesting smaller balls that the king gave as a gift to her father.) What do you think Willow's news is? For a clue, read the title of the next chapter. Make a map of Jade's home. Add to the chart.

## Chapter 4: "A Goose for the Wedding"

*Pre-reading:* Ask: What do you think this title means? (Willow is getting married.) **Let's read to find out** about the wedding ceremony.

*Follow-up:* Ask: Why did Jade put a brush on the back of the purse instead of a Chinese symbol? (To recall their prank in Chapter 1.) Discuss the similarities and differences between modern American weddings and Willow's wedding. Add to the chart. Discuss how Jade feels. Recall the foreshadowing from Chapter 2. Ask: What do you think will happen next?

*Note: Have a spool of thread on hand for the reading of this next chapter.*

## Chapter 5: "Thread with No End"

*Pre-reading:* Read the chapter title. Unravel a length of thread from the spool. Ask: If a thread has no end, what does that mean? (It goes on forever.) **Let's read to find out** what this title has to do with the main character, Jade.

*Follow-up:* Ask: How does Jade feel now that she is the oldest girl in the household? (She does not relish this role.) Discuss. Why does Jade stand in the same spot in the center of the garden every day? (She wants to see the mountain peaks.)

What do you think Jade wishes for? (To be able to see and experience things beyond the courtyard; to reunite with Willow.)

## Chapters 6 and 7: "Baskets to Market"; "The Road to Willow"

*Pre-reading:* Recall Jade's wishes. Today we will read more about Jade's determination to see the world beyond her courtyard and to reunite with her cousin and friend, Willow. Ask the children to predict how Jade might accomplish these goals. **Let's read to find out.**

*Follow-up:* Ask: What part of Jade's plan are you wondering about? (How will she get back home? What will her mother and Elder Aunt say when they see her clothing? What will be Willow's reaction to seeing Jade?) Re-read the sentence describing the young boy as *voluble.* Ask the children to use context to figure out what this big word means. (Talkative.) What do you think will happen next? Have the children draw a map to Willow's home following Chang's directions. Add to the chart.

## Chapters 8 and 9: "Prisoners"; "The Gatekeeper"

*Pre-reading:* Jade sees and hears many things she has never experienced before as she continues her adventure outside the courtyard. **Let's read to find out** about her experiences.

*Follow-up:* How is Jade feeling? (Sad.) What is making her sad? (She did not get to see Willow. She longs to walk in the mountains.) What about the mountains do you think appeals to Jade? What do you think Jade's mother will say and do?

## Chapter 10: "A Willing Heart"

*Pre-reading:* **Let's read to find out** what the title means.

*Follow-up:* Review Jade's mother's explanation for why Willow refused to see Jade. Discuss the punishment. Ask: Do you think that Jade will be able to do the laundry with a willing heart? Update the chart.

## Chapter 11: "Different Rules"

*Pre-reading:* Jade has many questions about the things she experienced outside the courtyard. Whom do you think she will ask? (Tiger.) What questions do you think she might ask? **Let's read to find out** what Jade asks Tiger.

*Follow-up:* Ask: What do you think bothers Jade most about what she has learned about life outside the courtyard? Discuss. Jade asks Tiger to give her share of sweets to Chang. What does this tell you about Jade's character?

## Chapter 12: "A Humble Request"

*Pre-reading:* Read the chapter title. Ask the children to predict who will make the humble request and what it might be. **Let's read to find out.**

*Follow-up:* Jade speaks up on behalf of Servant Cho. Ask: What does this tell us about her qualities or traits? Discuss Jade's father's comments about the prisoners. List the Five Virtues (Right behavior, good form, wisdom, faith, and love.) on the board. Discuss. At the end of their conversation, Jade's father says, "I do not forget, Daughter, that right behavior is only one of the Five Virtues." Ask the children why he said this. (He forgives Jade for her bad behavior. He realizes she possesses other virtues.)

> **Write Away!** Of the five virtues, Jade's father says, "They are small words, but they hold all that is good about men." Explain what you think he means by that. Use details from the story and/or your own experiences with reference to one or more of the virtues.

## Chapter 13: "Royal Decision"

*Pre-reading:* In this chapter the king will decide the fate of the prisoners. Ask: What do you think he will decide? What would you decide if you were king? **Let's read to find out** what the king's decision is.

*Follow-up:* Discuss the king's decision. For insight on the prisoners and additional information concerning the factual basis for this aspect of the story, go to Park's Web site, www.lspark.com, and click on SEESAW GIRL.

> **Write Away!** Jade's father says, "The path to wisdom lies not in certainty, but in trying to understand." Explain what he means by this.

## Chapters 14 and 15: "A Mountain of Stitches; Brushes and Scrolls"

*Pre-reading:* In Jade's time, girls were not allowed to embroider on silk panels until their work was deemed worthy enough. Ask: What do you think Jade would choose to embroider on a silk panel? (The mountains.) **Let's read to find out.**

*Follow-up:* At the end of this chapter, Jade is joyful. Why? (Jade is learning to paint the mountains and Cho has been given a position with another family.) Update the chart.

## Chapter 16: "Yut Sticks"

*Pre-reading:* Ask: What does Jade want more than anything else? (To see the mountains again.) Do you think she will? Discuss, reminding the children of the limits on what Jade is allowed to do and the disaster of her escape to the outside world. **Let's read to find out** what Jade does about that.

*Follow-up:* Ask children to make predictions about what Jade's invention might be, based on clues in the chapter.

## Chapter 17: "Beyond the Walls"

*Pre-reading:* Read the title. Ask the children what they think will happen in this final chapter. **Let's read to find out!**

*Follow-up:* Discuss how Jade has made her dream come true within the limits of her culture and society. In the end she recalls her mother's words to her. Discuss. Note the meaning of the title of the book.

*See also THE KITE FIGHTERS, by Linda Sue Park (Clarion), set in fifteenthcentury Korea, and the picture book story THE FIREKEEPER'S SON, written by Linda Sue Park and illustrated by Julie Downing (Clarion), set in Korea in the 1800s.*

*For a list of other books about world cultures, refer to the Book Notes section of this resource.*

## Notes:

# Up Close and Personal

### *A Note from the Author, Linda Sue Park*

#### *Tips for young people who want to become writers:*

READ! If you want to be a writer, you have to read A LOT. Reading is training for writers the same way that working out is training for athletes!

That's the most important tip, READREADREADREADREADREAD! And here are some ideas for writing:

• Keep a "list journal." Lists are great! Get a notebook and make lists of your favorite songs, foods, baseball players, books (of course). The ten things that bug you the most. Fifty things you want to do in the future. Five things you've done once but never want to do again. The thinking process that goes along with keeping a list can sometimes lead to more writing-you might end up writing a poem or a story about how you happened to eat a caterpillar and why you'll never do it again . . .

• Publish a family newspaper. Write stories about your family's activities-extended family too. (If you have access to e-mail, this is an easy way to get in touch with relatives who don't live nearby.) You can have sections for news and sports; a recipe exchange; a birthday corner. You can interview a different family member for each issue. Photocopy your newspaper and mail it to everyone in your family. Or send it by e-mail. I know families who make this a regular activity once or twice a year. The kids started the idea, and the adults enjoyed it so much that they ended up pitching in!

• Experiment with different kinds of writing. Do you like writing stories? Try a poem once in a while. Are you a poet? Write a sports article about your last soccer game!

• Start a swap journal. For this you need a partner-preferably a good school friend. Get a regular spiral notebook. Write something in it-a poem, a letter, a list. Give the notebook to your friend. He or she can add to your list, respond to your letter, write something of their own. But-here's the secret-you have to 'swap' the journal back within a set amount of time, like two or three days. It can help to have a friend's encouragement to get you writing! I got this idea from my daughter-she and her friend kept their swap journal going for nearly a whole school year.

Happy reading and writing to all!

*For more information about Linda Sue Park and her books, visit her fabulous Web site: www.lspark.com.*

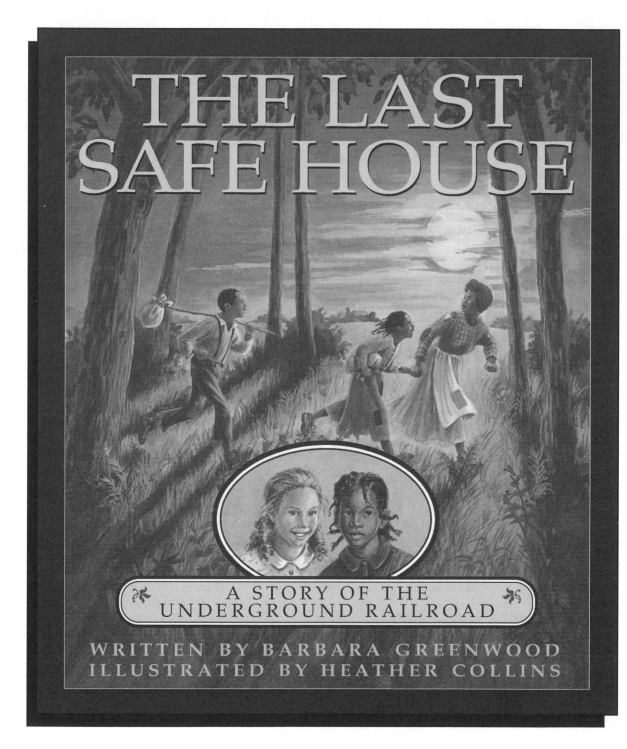

Cover from *The Last Safe House* written by Barbara Greenwood and illustrated by Heather Collins is used by permission of Kids Can Press Ltd., Toronto. Cover illustration © 1998 Heather Collins.

| | |
|---|---|
| **Title** | THE LAST SAFE HOUSE: A STORY OF THE UNDERGROUND RAILROAD |
| **Author** | Barbara Greenwood |
| **Illustrator** | Heather Collins |
| **Publisher** | Kids Can Press |
| **Copyright Date** | 1998 |
| **Ages** | 8 and up |
| **Read-Aloud Time** | 8–10 minutes per chapter |
| **Read-Aloud Sessions** | 12 |
| **Subject** | Underground Railroad, 1850s, period crafts, friendship, helping others |

In this combination fictional story/historical perspective, we learn about the escape of a fictional family from a plantation in Virginia to freedom in Ontario, Canada, via the Underground Railroad. Alternating with the story are extended "sidebars" that offer factual information about various aspects of the times, the troubles, the culture, and the handicrafts of America in the 1850s, especially as they relate to the issue of slavery. A list of possible report topics that could be assigned to students before, during, or after the reading of the book can be found at the end of the read-aloud plan.

*Note: Have available a map of North America with the Canadian–U.S. border clearly depicted.*

**PRE-READING FOCUS:** Read the title of the book. Show the cover. Ask what the children know about the Underground Railroad. Discuss.

## "Introduction"; "Midnight Guest"; "The Road to Freedom"

*Pre-reading:* Read the first paragraph of the Acknowledgments. On a map, find where St. Catherines, Ontario, Canada, is located. Review what *fictional* means. **Let's read to find out** who the characters are in this story.

*Follow-up:* Ask: How does Johanna feel when she first finds Eliza? (A bit put out; not very empathetic.) Why? (Eliza has Johanna's china doll. She is worried that her neighbors and friends will find out they are harboring a runaway slave. Not all of them are sympathetic to the cause. She must share her clothing with Eliza.) How do you know her sentiments have changed as a result of her conversation with Eliza? (She hands her the doll when Eliza starts to cry.) Discuss the range of feelings Johanna is experiencing.

Read the factual information following the chapter on pages 16–17. Review the map.

### "A Woman Called Moses"; "Sold into Slavery"

*Pre-reading:* Review some of the code words and phrases we learned in the previous reading. Ask: Who was Moses? (In the Bible, Moses led the Israelites out of slavery in Egypt to freedom in the Promised Land.) **Let's read to find out** about a woman with the code name, Moses.

*Follow-up:* Ask: How would you describe Harriet Tubman? What traits or skills did she possess that helped her be successful? Discuss. Ask for support from the material of opinions offered. List the answers on chart paper. For more information on Harriet Tubman, refer to the bibliography; see also the picture book AUNT HARRIET'S UNDERGROUND RAILROAD IN THE SKY, by Faith Ringgold (Crown).

> *Note: Following this next chapter is a recipe for making gingerbread cookies. Consider making them with the class following the read-aloud of Eliza's story.*

### "Eliza's Story"; "A Cotton Plantation"; "Working in the Big House"

*Pre-reading:* Today we return to the *fictional* story. We will hear Eliza's story. Eliza lived on a plantation in the South. What is a plantation? (A large farm.) **Let's read to find out** about her life on the plantation.

*Follow-up:* Ask: Why does Eliza cower in the corner after she breaks the bowl? (She is fearful that she will be beaten.) Johanna's mother says, "You can always tell if a dog's been mistreated." What does she mean? (A mistreated dog will often cower.) Read and study the pictorial map of a plantation. Review the duties of working in the big house. Make a batch of gingerbread cookies!

> *Note: Following this next section you may want to make lanterns to put in windows. See directions and a list of necessary materials on pages 60–61.*

### "Deciding to Run"; "The Abolitionists"; "Ben on the Run"

*Pre-reading:* Ask: What might make a slave decide to run, or try to escape? **Let's read to find out** why Eliza's family decided to run.

*Follow-up:* Review the meaning of *abolitionist*. How did Ben throw the dogs off his scent? (He trailed a dead skunk on a rope behind him.) What did he look for as he traveled? (Lanterns in upper windows.)

Make lanterns to put in windows.

> **Write Away!** Ben wonders why strangers care what happens to him. What would you tell him?

## "Life on a Plantation"; "The Cotton Gin"; "A Freed Slave"; "The Swamp Ghost"; "Bold Escapes"

*Pre-reading:* **Let's read to find out** interesting facts about life as a slave in the 1850s.

*Follow-up:* Which bold escape did you like best? Why?

## "The Outsiders"

*Pre-reading:* Think back to when you learned to print your name. Did you enjoy learning to write? Discuss the children's experiences. **Let's read to find out** how Eliza learned to write her name even though slaves were not allowed to learn to read and write.

*Follow-up:* Before she runs her errand, Johanna is frustrated. Why? (She is tired of having guests.) What changes her outlook? (Caroline's behavior.) Why do you think Johanna decides to teach Eliza to read?

## "Freedom to Read and Write"; "Frederick Douglass"; "Storytelling"

*Pre-reading:* Why do you think slaves were not allowed to learn to read and write? **Let's read to find out**.

*Follow-up:* Review the steps to sharing a story successfully. Have children work on a story they will share with their classmates.

## "Slave Catcher!"

*Pre-reading:* Read the chapter title. Ask the children to predict what will happen next in the story. **Let's read to find out.**

*Follow-up:* Ask: What is *planing*? (To make smooth or even; level.) What did the girls do that was wise as they dealt with the slave catcher? (Johanna bit his hand. They forced him out of the house. They latched and bolted the doors. They escaped out the front door. They ran!) Look at the diagram of the Reids' house on page 90. Ask: What do you think will happen next?

## "Slave Catchers"; "Alexander Ross"; "Songs"

*Pre-reading:* **Let's read to find out** more about slave catchers.

*Follow-up:* If you are musically inclined, play the spirituals and teach the words to the children. Discuss where the word *spirituals* came from.

> **Write Away!** Write your own words to a spiritual.

*Note: To make cornhusk dolls following the reading of this next section, refer to the list of materials and instructions found on pages 108–109.*

## "Friends"

*Pre-reading:* Ask: How would you describe a friend? Throughout the story Johanna has had mixed feelings about Eliza. She is very disappointed about the way her friends treated her. Would you say Eliza and Johanna are friends? Johanna and Caroline? **Let's read to find out** how true a friend Johanna is to Eliza.

*Follow-up:* Ask: Why is Eliza smiling when Caroline dashes off, even though she has been insulted? (She is happy Johanna called her a friend.) How do we know how Eliza feels about Johanna? (She leaves her the cornhusk doll.)

To make cornhusk dolls, follow the instructions on pages 108–109.

## "Six Months Later"; "The Rescue"; "Finding Work"; "Learning to Be Free"; "Freedom for All"

*Pre-reading:* **Let's read to find out** what happened when Eliza and Ben reunited with their mother.

*Follow-up:* If you were a freed slave and you were able to return to America from Canada after the Civil War, would you? Discuss.

### Report Topics:

| | |
|---|---|
| • Plantation Life | • Swamp Ghosts |
| • Cotton Gin | • Harriet Tubman |
| • The North Star | • Levi Coffin |
| • Abolitionists | • Frederick Douglass |
| • Spirituals | • Alexander Ross |
| • Swamps | • Mary Ann Shadd |

• Book reports on resources listed in the bibliography

*For a meaningful follow-up to this story, read PINK AND SAY, by Patricia Polacco (Philomel), for which a read-aloud plan can be found elsewhere in this resource. See also the picture book AUNT HARRIET'S UNDERGROUND RAILROAD IN THE SKY, by award winner Faith Ringgold (Crown), for more about Harriet Tubman. Don't miss the recipient of the 1994 International Reading Association's Children's Book Award, SWEET CLARA AND THE FREEDOM QUILT, written by Deborah Hopkinson and illustrated by James E. Ransome (Knopf), and its companion, UNDER THE QUILT OF NIGHT, by the same author/illustrator team (Atheneum).*

*For a list of other books about moments in American history, refer to the Book Notes section of this resource.*

# Up Close and Personal

## A Note from the Author, Barbara Greenwood

### On where the idea for the story came from:

I got the idea for this story when I visited the Wellington County Museum near Niagara Falls. One whole room was devoted to the history of black people in the area. I knew that many slaves fleeing on the Underground Railroad had crossed into Canada near Niagara Falls, but I had assumed that free and safe, they lived happily ever after. Studying the display in the museum, I was astounded to learn that even though they were free, often they weren't safe. So much money had been offered for their return that slave catchers crossed into Canada intent on kidnapping them. My interest was caught. I wanted to write a story about the Canadian part in the Underground Railroad.

The story of Eliza and Johanna is fiction but it was inspired by the lives and adventures of real people who fled to freedom in Canada as well as the people who gave them refuge along the way. In the library I found first person accounts by many slaves telling of their escapes. All the events in Eliza's life are "borrowed" from actual events.

Once I had my research, I had to decide what form to use to tell the story. One way would be to write the story as a novel, then add an historical note to explain the background. Instead I decided I could give more interesting details by adding information pages after each section. With the help of Heather Collins' wonderful illustrations I was able to show what had happened to Eliza and her family before the story began—such information as why slaves were brought to American, how they lived and worked on plantations, and what they and many other people did to achieve, at last, freedom for all.

| | |
|---|---|
| **Title** . . . . . . . . . . . . . . . . . . . . . . . . . . . . . . . . . . . . . . PINK AND SAY |
| **Author** . . . . . . . . . . . . . . . . . . . . . . . . . . . . . . . . Patricia Polacco |
| **Publisher** . . . . . . . . . . . . . . . . . . . . . . . . . . . . . . . . . . . . . Philomel |
| **Copyright Date** . . . . . . . . . . . . . . . . . . . . . . . . . . . . . 1994 |
| **Ages** . . . . . . . . . . . . . . . . . . . . . . . . . . . . . . . . . . . . . . 8 and up |
| **Read-Aloud Time** . . . . . . . . . . . . . . . . . . . . . . . . . 15 minutes |
| **Read-Aloud Sessions** . . . . . . . . . . . . . . . . . . . . . . . . . . . . 1 |
| **Subject** . . . . . . . . . . . . . . . . . . Civil War, friendship across race, reading |

This account is based on the true story of Pinkus Aylee, a Union soldier who fought in the colored army during the Civil War, and his friendship with Sheldon Russell Curtis, a white Union soldier who deserted and then rejoined the army to fight for the cause.

*Note: Have a map of the United States available.*

**PRE-READING FOCUS:** Look at the cover and read the title. Discuss what the boys are doing and what this illustration might be depicting. Show the back cover. Ask: When do you think this story takes place? (Civil War.) **Let's read to find out** what the title means.

**WHILE READING:** Read the first two spreads. Show the illustrations. Ask: Which boy is the *narrator*? (The one lying down.) Where is he from? (Ohio.) Where is he now? (Georgia.) Look at the map. Which side of the Civil War would he be fighting for? (North.) Read the next page. Ask: What does the boy mean when he says, "Not bad if it don't go green?" (His leg will be all right if it doesn't become infected.) From context, ask the children to define *marauders*. (Those who roam about and raid or plunder.) Read through the next three spreads. Tell the children that this story is based on true events. Pinkus Aylee was a real person, as was the narrator, Sheldon Russell Curtis. Ask the children to imagine what Sheldon must be thinking and feeling. Explain the "Forty-eighth Colored." (This was a division of the Northern army that was composed of black men.) Read the next spread. When Moe Moe Bay asks Pinkus if he is planning to stay with her, he doesn't answer and he "looks troubled." What do you think Pinkus is planning? (To return to the war effort.) Explain what a "root cellar" is. (A pit used for the storage of root crops, or vegetables, such as turnips.) Read the next spread. Now we understand the meaning of the title. **Let's read to find out** more about what's shown on the cover.

Read the next two spreads. Ask: What are *vittles*? (Food.) Discuss how Pink got his last name. (From his master.) Ask: What does Pink mean when he says that it's "his fight?" (He is fighting to be free from slavery.) Discuss Say's feelings about going back. Read the next spread. Ask: What does Pink mean when he says that after he learned to read, "nobody, ever, could really own me?" Look again at the cover illustration and compare it with the inside illustration. Read the next two spreads. Ask: What does Moe Moe mean when she refers to paper talking? (Reading.) Are you surprised that Say can't read? Look at the cover again. Ask: What do you think is happening here now? What words does Pink use to describe slavery? ("The sickness.") Discuss. What do you think Say wants to tell Pink? **Let's read to find out.** Read the next spread. Discuss Moe Moe's words: "[B]ein' brave don't mean you ain't afeared." Show the next illustration. Ask the children what is happening. (The boys are hiding in the root cellar.) **Let's read to find out.** Read the next three spreads. Ask: Why are Say's steps "as sure now as they had ever been since the war started?" (He wants to fight in the Civil War in Moe Moe's honor. He now feels strongly about the cause.) Ask: Why did Pink give his spectacles to Say? (So the soldiers wouldn't know he could read.) What do you think will happen next? **Let's read to find out.** Read to the end.

**FOLLOW-UP DISCUSSION:** Discuss how Polacco came to know this story and tell it here. Repeat the line, "Touch the hand that shook the hand of Abraham Lincoln." Discuss why that would have meant so much to Pink.

*Did you know that Patricia Polacco has written and illustrated many books, but she does not use a computer? To learn more about Patricia Polacco and her books, visit her Web site at www.patriciapolacco.com, where you can even find a quiz on this book!*

*For another absorbing account of the Civil War from a child's perspective, read RED LEGS: A DRUMMER BOY OF THE CIVIL WAR, by Ted Lewin (HarperCollins). The spare text and rich illustrations tell the story of a Civil War battle. It is based on true accounts of the life of Stephen Benjamin Bartow, who fought in the 14th Regiment, Company E, otherwise known as the Red-Legged Devils, "because of the color of their uniform and their tough fighting spirit." See also the magnificent picture book WALT WHITMAN: WORDS FOR AMERICA, written by Barbara Kerley and illustrated by Brain Selznick (Scholastic), in which readers learn how the Civil War shaped this beloved American poet's work.*

*For a list of other books about American history, refer to the Book Notes section of this resource.*

## Notes:

*Cover of STARRY MESSENGER: GALILEO GALILEI © 2004 by Peter Sís.
Used with the permission of Farrar Straus Giroux.*

| | |
|---|---|
| **Title** | STARRY MESSENGER: GALILEO GALILEI |
| **Author/Illustrator** | Peter Sís |
| **Publisher** | Farrar, Straus & Giroux |
| **Copyright Date** | 1996 |
| **Ages** | 7 and up |
| **Read-Aloud Time** | 15 minutes |
| **Read-Aloud Sessions** | 1 |
| **Subject** | Biography of Galileo Galilei, questioning, curiosity, the Renaissance period |

This picture book "depicting the life of a famous scientist, mathematician, astronomer, philosopher, and physicist," as the subtitle tells us, won the Caldecott Honor Award. It brings to life for children, in an accessible and meaningful manner, the amazing accomplishments of a genius who changed the way we view our place in the vast universe because he dared to question accepted beliefs.

**PRE-READING FOCUS:** Look at the cover, drawing attention to the telescope, and read the title. Ask: What is Galileo doing? (Looking at the stars.) Why do you think the author/illustrator named his book about Galileo STARRY MESSENGER? **Let's read to find out.**

**WHILE READING:** Throughout the reading of this book, pay particular attention to the bountiful information provided in the illustrations. Read the first page. Discuss what the word *tradition* means. (An established pattern of thought or behavior.) Read the next three spreads. Find Galileo in the illustration. Read the next two spreads to learn about the time in which Galileo lived. Examine the illustrations. Ask: What is the author/illustrator telling us with his illustrations? (Galileo questioned what most people believed to be true.) Find Galileo in the illustration. Read the next spread. Ask: What is this "new instrument?" (Telescope.) Read Galileo's quote and note that the word *telescope* was not coined until two years later. Examine the map. Find Italy. Read the next spread (Here is the answer to where the title of book came from.) After the next spread, discuss Galileo's comment: "[I]t [is] harder for me to discover the truth than to refute what is false." Read the next spread. Discuss what a patron was in Galileo's time. (A wealthy or influential person who financed the living expenses and work of another.) Read the next three spreads. Ask: What do you think happened when Galileo appeared before the Pope? **Let's read to find out.** Read the next spread. Explain what *heresy* is. (Holding an opinion contrary to church belief.) Ask: What does the author mean when he writes, "the stars had left his eyes?" Read the next spread. Note that Galileo's quotations are placed by the author/illustrator in the shape of an eye. Discuss why he might have done that. Read the final spread.

**FOLLOW-UP DISCUSSION:** Have the children read about and report to the class on one of the topics touched upon in this biography of Galileo's life. Topics might include Ptolemy, Aristotle, Copernicus, the Italian Renaissance period, Galileo's Law of the Pendulum, the Law of Falling Objects, the Law of Floating Objects, the invention of the telescope, Cosimo de Medici, the Medici Court, the Galileo spacecraft, Galileo's book, STARRY MESSENGER. For extensive suggestions on how to approach research after reading STARRY MESSENGER: GALILEO GALILEI, visit the publisher's Web site, http://www.fsgkidsbooks.com/teachersguides/starrymessenger.htm.

*For another standout picture book biography by Peter Sís, see THE TREE OF LIFE, about naturalist and geologist Charles Darwin (Farrar, Straus & Giroux). Listen to Sís discuss THE TREE OF LIFE in an audio interview on writtenvoices.com. For more about the author and his books, visit his Web site, www.petersis.com.*

*For a list of other picture book biographies suitable for grades 3 and 4, refer to the Book Notes section of this resource.*

## Notes:

Cover from THE AMAZING IMPOSSIBLE ERIE CANAL written and illustrated by Cheryl Harness. Copyright © 1986. Used with permission of Simon & Schuster Books for Young Readers, an imprint of Simon & Schuster Children's Publishing

| | |
|---|---|
| **Title** | THE AMAZING IMPOSSIBLE ERIE CANAL |
| **Author/Illustrator** | Cheryl Harness |
| **Publisher** | Simon & Schuster |
| **Copyright Date** | 1995 |
| **Ages** | 7 and up |
| **Read-Aloud Time** | 12–15 minutes |
| **Read-Aloud Sessions** | 1 |
| **Subject** | The Erie Canal, transportation, maps |

This picture book explains the development of the Erie Canal, depicting clearly the path it took and the means of construction utilized to complete this amazing engineering feat in the early 1800s. It focuses on a giant step taken to improve transportation across our young nation by a man with foresight and true grit.

*Notes: The first journey on the Erie Canal began in late October 1825.*

*If you are reading this book aloud to a large group that may not be able to view the details of the illustrated maps, have a large map of New York State available to trace the routes described in the book*

*Lyrics and music for the song "Low Bridge, Everybody Down" can be found at the end of the book.*

**PRE-READING FOCUS:** Look at the cover, drawing attention to the details found there. Note the horses pulling the barge and the activities taking place on it. Ask children why they think the author/illustrator chose this title. **Let's read to find out.**

**WHILE READING:** Read the first page. Find the Appalachian Mountains on the map. Then find the Mississippi River. Read the next page. Trace the Mohawk Trail. After reading the next page, ask what an *obstruction* might be. Use context to define. (Some thing or condition that blocks.) Why did George Washington like the idea of canals? (They would hold a young country together.) Why did the people of the time think the project of constructing a waterway that went 363 miles was impossible? Discuss. Read the next spread. Ask: How do you think the Romans felt at dawn on the Fourth of July, 1817? (Excited, optimistic.) Read and study the next spread. Note how the locks work. Explain what *aqueducts* are. (Bridges that carry water.), and trace the path of the Erie Canal. Ask: What is a *toll*? (A fee paid for the privilege of traveling along the canal.) Read the next two pages. Ask the children to listen for the definition of what a *packet* is. (Horse-drawn passenger boat.) Ask: What did the Erie Canal accomplish? (The waters of the East and the West were now connected.) Read the next page and study the diagram. Why was the Erie Canal amazing? (A feat of engineering, especially in the locks.) Read the next three pages. Discuss how De Witt Clinton must have felt going from "ditch" to "amazing." Read the next spread. Ask: What was the hope of the people who lived along the canal? (More trade would occur now that the waterway was complete.) Read the next five pages and discuss what the Erie Canal meant to our young nation. (It was the longest canal in the world, built with the least experience and know-how for the least money; shipping costs would drop; it would take less time to travel.) Read the final spread. Ask: What took the place of the canal? (Trains, cars, and eventually airplanes.)

**FOLLOW-UP DISCUSSION:** As a follow-up to this book, students can trace the history of the development, rise, and fall of trains as a preferred means of transportation. The advent of airplane travel can be compared to the advent of train travel. Compare and contrast. What might be next?

*See also THE ERIE CANAL, by Peter Spier (Doubleday).*

*For a list of other titles about moments in American history,
refer to the Book Notes section of this resource.*

<u>Notes:</u>

*Cover from THE EMPTY POT written and illustrated by Demi. Copyright © 1990. Reprinted with permission of Henry Holt Books for Young Readers.*

| | |
|---|---|
| **Title** | THE EMPTY POT |
| **Author/Illustrator** | Demi |
| **Publisher** | Holt |
| **Copyright Date** | 1990 |
| **Ages** | 6 and up |
| **Read-Aloud Time** | 8–10 minutes |
| **Read-Aloud Sessions** | 1 |
| **Subject** | Honesty, effort, taking pride in trying your hardest |

This Chinese tale exemplifies the value of telling the truth and the wisdom in being proud when you've tried your hardest and done your best. This is recommended reading to set the tone for your classroom at the beginning of the school year or when esteem and self-confidence are flagging. It is an IRA-CBC Children's Choice and an *American Bookseller* "Pick of the Lists" with detailed illustrations that evoke the setting of the simple, well-crafted tale.

*Note: Have seeds, small pots, and planting medium available for the Follow-up activity.*

**PRE-READING FOCUS:** Before reading the title of the book, read the first page. Ask: What is the setting of this story? (China.) Who is the main character? (Ping.) Turn back to the cover and read the title. Ask the children to predict what this story might be about. **Let's read to find out.**

**WHILE READING:** Read through the page on which the Emperor needs to choose a successor to the throne. Ask the children to guess what a *successor* might be. Use the context. (One who follows.) Ask: What qualities do you think the Emperor will look for in the successor to the throne? Read the next two pages. Ask: What would you do with your seeds if you were given some by the Emperor? Read the next six pages. Nothing grew in Ping's pot. Ask: What should Ping do? Read the next six pages. Ask: Why do you think Ping's seeds are not growing? What do you think will happen next? Read the next two pages. Note the illustrations. Read the next two pages. Ask: How is Ping feeling? (Frustrated.) Read the next two pages. Ask: What did Ping's father mean when he said, "You did your best, and your best is good enough to present to the Emperor?" Do you think it is good enough? What do you think the emperor will say? Read the next two pages. Ask: Why is the emperor frowning? Read to the end. Ask: Will Ping make a good Emperor? Discuss.

**FOLLOW-UP DISCUSSION:** A natural follow-up to this story is a discussion of the value in trying our hardest and being proud of what we achieve regardless of the outcome. Honesty can also be discussed. This book can set the tone for the classroom atmosphere and set expectations regarding individual achievement.

Pass out seeds and assist students in planting and labeling pots. Care for plants over the next several weeks. Re-read this story when plants have sprouted and again when they are grown and ready to be taken home.

*For a list of additional tales, refer to the Book Notes section of this resource.*

## Notes:

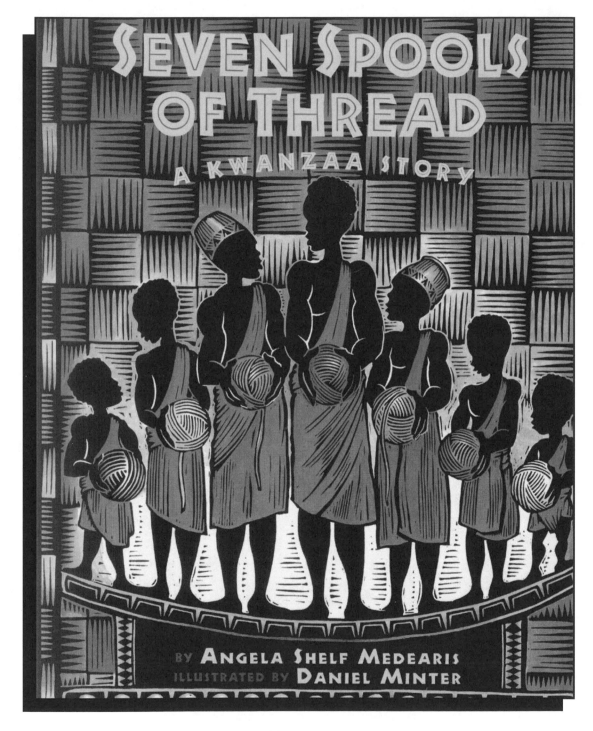

*Cover from SEVEN SPOOLS OF THREAD: A KWANZAA STORY by Angela Shelf Medearis, illustrated by Daniel Minter. Copyright © 2000. Reprinted with permission from A. Whitman & Co.*

| | |
|---|---|
| **Title** | SEVEN SPOOLS OF THREAD: A KWANZAA STORY |
| **Author** | Angela Shelf Medearis |
| **Illustrator** | Daniel Minter |
| **Publisher** | Whitman |
| **Copyright Date** | 2000 |
| **Ages** | 6 and up |
| **Read-Aloud Time** | 8–10 minutes |
| **Read-Aloud Sessions** | 1 |
| **Subject** | Teamwork, family, principles of Kwanzaa |

This tale about teamwork among brothers exemplifying the principles of Kwanzaa is memorable for its simple language, authentic art, craft idea, and supplemental material. Although it is a story based on the principles of Kwanzaa, it would be suitable to read-aloud at any time of the year.

*Note: Use the introductory material on the history of the cultural holiday, Kwanzaa, as you wish. A writing opportunity based on the descriptions of the seven principles of Kwanzaa as described in this book is included in this plan. Also, at the back of the book you will find a craft activity related to the story. Consider having materials on hand so you can weave cloth to make belts using this simple technique following the read-aloud of this story.*

**PRE-READING FOCUS:** After reading the title of the book, read the African proverb that precedes the introductory material. ("Sticks in a bundle are unbreakable.") Discuss how this might relate to the story. **Let's read to find out.** Ask the children to think about that as you read the story.

**WHILE READING:** Read through the first page. Ask: Why is the father disappointed in his seven sons? (They quarrel.) Read the next three pages, using expression for the words of the quarreling sons. Ask: What do you think the father can do about all this quarreling? Read the next two pages. Review what the father decreed in his will and ask for predictions about what will happen next. Read the next few pages. What do you notice? (The brothers are not quarreling.) Read to the end of the story. Ask: Why were the brothers successful? (They worked together.) Which brother do you feel has learned the most? (Perhaps the youngest since he shows compassion for the poor villagers. Perhaps the oldest because he formulates a plan that will help the villagers prosper.)

**Write Away!** Read about the seven principles of Kwanzaa. (A simple summary is provided at the beginning of the book.) Ask each child to choose one of the seven principles and write how he or she might follow it. Sit in a circle and read responses beginning with the first principle and moving through all seven. If possible, light candles to signify each principle.

**FOLLOW-UP DISCUSSION:** Ask: Do you think the brothers are happier at the end of the story? Why? Discuss. Ask: Thinking about the story, what can we do to make our classroom a better place? Directions for making simple looms children can use to weave cloth to make belts can be found at the back of the book. Weave and wear!

*See also IT'S KWANZAA TIME!, written by Linda Goss and Clay Goss and illustrated by a number of award-winning artists (Penguin), in which five folk tales exemplify this cultural holiday.*

*For the titles of additional holiday books and tales suitable for this grade level, refer to the Book Notes section of this resource.*

## Notes:

*Cover from THE JANITOR'S BOY by Andrew Clements, illustrated by Brian Selznick. Copyright © 2000. Used with permission of Simon & Schuster Books for Young Readers, an imprint of Simon & Schuster Children's Publishing.*

| Title | THE JANITOR'S BOY |
|---|---|
| Author | Andrew Clements |
| Publisher | Simon & Schuster |
| Copyright Date | 2000 |
| Ages | 9 and up |
| Read-Aloud Time | 6–8 minutes per chapter |
| Read-Aloud Sessions | 20 |
| Subject | Peer pressure, stereotyping, family and school relationships |

Jack, a fifth grader, is the son of the school janitor. Although he loves his dad, he is ashamed of his father's job and angry that because of it his peers are taunting him. How Jack comes to know what kind of person his dad is makes for a memorable, absorbing story complete with a range of emotions from anger, despair, and righteous retaliation to panic, terror, and love. And all in 21 chapters that ring true. Now what beats that?

*Note: As a follow-up to the reading of the first chapter, consider having samples of various bubble gum, including Bazooka and watermelon Bubblicious, available. The latter flavor plays a part in a pivotal scene at the end of the book.*

**PRE-READING FOCUS**: Introducing the book: Show the cover and read the title. Note the details in the cover art. Ask students to predict what the story is about.

## Chapter 1: "The Perfect Crime"

*Pre-reading:* Ask the children to take a deep breath through their noses. Ask: What do you smell? What are some common smells in a school building? **Let's read to find out** what the main character, a fifth-grade boy named Jack Rankin, smells in his school.

*While Reading:* Read the entire chapter with the exception of the last three paragraphs. Ask: Who is the *someone* who would normally clean up the mess? (The janitor.) Read the final three paragraphs.

*Follow-up:* Ask: What have we learned about our main character in this chapter? Discuss. Why has Jack come up with this "perfect crime?"

**Write Away!** Why do you think kids put gum under desks or do other damage to school property?

## Chapter 2: "What Do You Want to Be?"

*Pre-reading:* Discuss what *vandalize* means. (Damage.) **Let's read to find out** what might be provoking Jack to behave as he does.

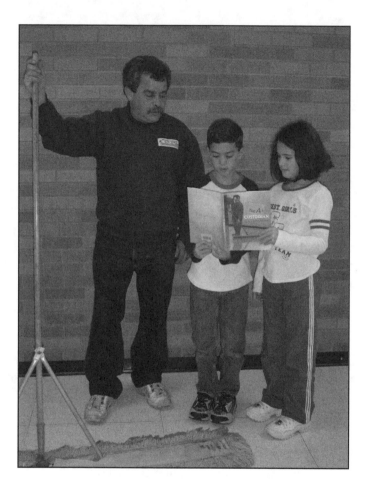

*Follow-up:* On the last page of the chapter are the words, "laughter from kids is more powerful than words from teachers." Discuss. Would Jack have felt differently about his dad's job if he had not had this experience in second grade? If time permits, read the picture book THE A+ CUSTODIAN, written by Louise Borden and illustrated by Adam Gustavson (McElderry), for an appreciative look at the role of the school custodian.

**Write Away!** Write about a time when laughter from other kids made you feel ashamed. Give details and try to recall the exact words that were said. Tell how you felt inside. What did you do? Or, have you ever teased someone about something he or she could not change? Why? How do you think your teasing made the person feel? How did it make *you* feel?

## Chapter 3: "L Is for Loser"

*Pre-reading:* Read the title of the chapter. Ask: Whom do you think this chapter title is describing? (Jack.) Why does Jack feel this way? **Let's read to find out** more about why Jack put gum underneath the desk.

*Follow-up:* Discuss how Jack is feeling. Explore ways he might handle his anger. Discuss how we hurt other people's feelings and the effect our actions have.

## Chapters 4 and 5: "The Sweet Smell of Victory"; "School Justice"

*Pre-reading:* Read the title of Chapter 4. What do you think this is referring to? (The bubble gum.) **Let's read to find out.**

*Follow-up:* Ask: What do you think of Jack? Discuss.

Read the title of Chapter 5. **Let's read to find out** what it means.

*Follow-up:* Discuss the principal's reaction and punishment. Was it fair? What would you have given Jack as punishment? What would you have done in that office if you were Jack? What do you think will happen when Jack gives the note to his parents? What do you think it says?

 **Write Away!** Write a letter to Jack's parents as if you were the principal.

## Chapter 6: "Reporting for Duty"

*Pre-reading:* **Let's read to find out** what happens when Jack reports for duty.

*Follow-up:* What do you think Jack's father was feeling as he stared out the window? Discuss.

## Chapter 7: "Gum Patrol"

*Pre-reading:* Ask: How long does Jack have Gum Patrol? (Three weeks.) What do you think will happen in those three weeks? **Let's read to find out** how the first day goes.

*Follow-up:* Why do you think Jack wants his mom to read the note by herself first? What do you think his mom will do?

## Chapter 8: "Hung Jury"

*Pre-reading:* Ask: What is a *hung jury*? (A jury that is unable to reach a decision or verdict.) **Let's read to find out** how Mrs. Rankin reacts to the letter.

*Follow-up:* What do you think will happen when Mr. Rankin gets home from work? Compare the letters your students wrote to the one Principal Ackerby wrote.

## Chapter 9: "Boy Territory"

*Pre-reading:* **Let's read to find out** what "Boy Territory" means.

*Follow-up:* Make a list of predictions about what might happen over the next three weeks. Keep it to refer to for the duration of the read-aloud of this book.

## Chapter 10: "Rumors"

*Pre-reading:* Ask: What is a rumor? (A statement or report without a known source to prove it.) Play the rumor game: Line the children up or sit in a circle. Whisper a statement in the first child's ear. Do not repeat. Ask each child to pass along what he or she hears to the next child. No repeating allowed. The last child repeats the "rumor" out loud. Compare it to what you whispered to the first child. **Let's read to find out** about the rumor spreading around Jack's school.

*Follow-up:* Is Pete a good friend? Discuss. What do you think is in the cabinet? Do you think Jack will look inside? Should he?

## Chapter 11: "Open Sesame"

*Pre-reading:* Read the title. Ask: Do you think Jack will look inside the cabinet? **Let's read to find out**.

*Follow-up:* Look at the cover of the book. Discuss why the illustrator may have chosen this scene to illustrate for the cover of the book. (Its importance to the story.) Review the predictions.

## Chapter 12: "Chewology"

*Pre-reading:* Read the title. What does it remind you of? (Science, as in *biology* and *zoology*.) Explain what the suffix *-ology* means. (The study of.) Ask what *chewology* might be. (The study of chewing gum.) **Let's read to find out** if you are right.

*Follow-up:* Ask: What has Jack learned about chewing gum? Do you think Jack should go to the bell tower? Discuss.

# Chapter 13: "Altitude"

*Pre-reading:* Read the chapter title. Ask: What is *altitude*? (Height; elevation.) Why do you think the author named this chapter "Altitude?" (The bell tower is high in the building.) **Let's read to find out.**

*Follow-up:* Discuss what we learned about Jack in this chapter.

**Write Away!** In this chapter, Jack lists the ways he is not like his father. Write a four-paragraph essay about the ways that you are similar to and different from a member of your family. Paragraph one: Introduction; Paragraph two: three to four similarities with an example or two, or a brief memory that explains one similarity; Paragraph three: three to four differences with an example or two, or a brief memory that explains one; Paragraph four: Conclusion: Overall, are you more the same as or different from this family member?

# Chapter 14: "Homeward"

*Pre-reading:* Today **let's read to find out** more about Jack's dad.

*Follow-up:* Ask: Why do you think Jack didn't tell his dad how upset he is by the kids who tease him about his father's job? At the end of the chapter it says Jack wants to learn more about his dad. Why? The next chapter is entitled "Discoveries." Do you think we'll learn more about Jack's dad?

# Chapter 15: "Discoveries"

*Pre-reading:* Read the title of the chapter. Ask: Why do you think this chapter is titled "Discoveries?" **Let's read to find out** what "discoveries" we make in this chapter.

*Follow-up:* What has Jack learned about himself in this chapter? (He is not as ashamed of his dad as he was at the beginning of the story.) Why? (He is learning how big his father's responsibilities are.) What was your reaction to how Jack handled Luke? Discuss the last line in the chapter, in which Jack repeats his father's words from a few chapters back when he cleaned up the vomit in Mrs. Lambert's room.

## Chapter 16: "Behind the Curtain"

*Pre-reading:* In this chapter, Jack finds something behind the curtain in the auditorium. Ask the children for predictions of what it might be. (A door.) **Let's read to find out** what Jack finds behind the curtain.

*Follow-up:* Discuss where the smell of watermelon bubble gum could be coming from and what it might mean.

## Chapter 17: "One Way Ticket"

*Pre-reading:* Ask: What is a one way ticket? (A ticket that takes you to a destination, but does not bring you back.) What do you think will happen in this chapter? **Let's read to find out.**

*Follow-up:* What do you think will happen next? Discuss what Jack has with him and how those items might help him in his predicament. (Sword, spool of nylon string, baseball cap, backpack, flashlight.) What words would you use to describe how Jack must be feeling? (Panic, terror, trapped.)

## Chapter 18: "Underground"

*Pre-reading:* Ask: What can Jack do? **Let's read to find out**.

*Follow-up:* Discuss the things Jack has done so far to try to solve his problem.

## Chapter 19: "Walk into the Light"

*Pre-reading:* In this chapter we meet a new character. Who or what do you think it might be? **Let's read to find out.**

*Follow-up:* What has Jack learned about his dad? (He helps others in need.) Who else in the story did that? (Jack's grandfather.) Discuss what Jack used and didn't use as he navigated the underground. In teams, illustrate scenes from this chapter. Label and display.

## Chapter 20: "Two Plus Two"

*Pre-reading:* Read the title of the chapter. Discuss what it might mean. (Someone is figuring something out.) **Let's read to find out** who has figured out what.

*Follow-up:* How would you describe Jack's dad?

## Chapter 21: "Something Permanent"

*Pre-reading:* Read the title. Ask: What does *permanent* mean? (Lasting; enduring.) What are some things that are permanent? **Let's read to find out** what's permanent in this chapter. (Love.)

*Follow-up:* Discuss what Jack has learned about his father. Ask: How has Jack changed since the beginning of the story? Review the predictions chart.

**Write Away!** Interview a parent, grandparent, clergy person, or staff member in the school building (janitor, secretary, cafeteria worker, bus attendant, crossing guard, principal) about his or her life. Brainstorm questions to ask and interviewing techniques. Questions might cover details of the job, why the person chose his or her career, a childhood anecdote, his or her hobbies, favorite books, and a piece of advice based on experience. Write short biographies of the people interviewed or a "feature" article for a class newspaper (for a related story, see THE LANDRY NEWS, by Andrew Clements; Simon & Schuster).

*Andrew Clements is the author of several books suitable for middle graders. See especially the award-winning, million-copy best seller, FRINDLE, about a boy who coins a new name for the pen. Visit the official Web site for the book: www.frindle.com. Other titles by Clements include THE LANDRY NEWS, THE REPORT CARD, and THE LAST HOLIDAY CONCERT, all of which approach subjects important to children in this age group with skill and heart. All titles listed are published by Simon & Schuster. See also the JAKE DRAKE titles in Aladdin's Ready-for-Chapters line of books.*

*See the read-aloud plan for THE JACKET, by Andrew Clements (Simon & Schuster) elsewhere in this resource.*

*See also the Parent Pull-Out Pages for information to send home to parents on Andrew Clements and other authors popular with students in grades 3 and 4.*

*For books by Andrew Clements referenced in this resource, refer to the author index.*

## Notes:

#  Up Close and Personal

## *A Note from the Author, Andrew Clements*

**On where the idea for the book came from:**

From my years as a teacher and as a parent of school age children, I noticed that the janitor at a school does important work, day in and day out—a lot like the school secretary and the librarian. And the janitor's work is sometimes not appreciated by kids who have not yet realized that all honest work is valuable, that a good gardener or a good receptionist can take just as much pride in doing careful work as a good doctor or a good lawyer does. I've also known boys and girls whose moms or dads were school custodians, and sometimes those kids were teased about it. So I thought that would be an interesting situation to explore. I wanted Jack to see his dad more clearly, to see life and work and family more clearly. And I especially wanted him to see himself with more understanding.

I spend a lot of time describing the school building itself, the old high school. Every school building has a personality and a history of its own, certain elements that make it unique. In a way, the school itself is one of the main characters in The Janitor's Boy, and I had a lot of fun trying to make the place feel real to the reader. Jack comes to realize that the school is the way it is because of the hard work and care and pride his dad takes in his job. And schools are like that. Every school reflects the work of the custodian, the principal, the teachers, the kids, the parents, everyone. We're all in it together.

*Cover from THE LANDRY NEWS by Andrew Clements, illustrated by Brian Selznick and Salvatore Murdocca. Copyright © 2000. Used with permission of Simon & Schuster Books for Young Readers, an imprint of Simon & Schuster Children's Publishing.*

*Cover from THE REPORT CARD by Andrew Clements. Copyright © 2004. Used with permission of Simon & Schuster Books for Young Readers, an imprint of Simon & Schuster Children's Publishing.*

| | |
|---|---|
| **Title** | THE BOY ON FAIRFIELD STREET: HOW TED GEISEL GREW UP TO BECOME DR. SEUSS |
| **Author** | Kathleen Krull |
| **Illustrators** | Steve Johnson and Lou Fancher |
| **Publisher** | Random House |
| **Copyright Date** | 2004 |
| **Ages** | 8 and up |
| **Read-Aloud Time** | 8–10 minutes |
| **Read-Aloud Sessions** | 1 |
| **Subject** | Biography of the childhood of Dr. Seuss |

With fabulous illustrations by Johnson and Fancher that hearken back to a magical time—the childhood of a child's hero—this biography of the man who opened the door to reading for millions of youngsters is enchanting. Decorative illustrations throughout are by Geisel himself and help to unfold the story of how Geisel came to be Dr. Seuss.

*Note: It may be interesting to students if you have on display several of Dr. Seuss's books. Those referred to in the end material (AND TO THINK I SAW IT ON MULBERRY STREET, THE 500 HATS OF BARTHOLOMEW CUBBINS, HORTON HATCHES THE EGG, MCELLIGOT'S POOL, BARTHOLOMEW AND THE OOBLECK, IF I RAN THE ZOO, THE CAT IN THE HAT, HOW THE GRINCH STOLE CHRISTMAS!, GREEN EGGS AND HAM, THE BUTTER BATTLE BOOK, YOU'RE ONLY YOUNG ONCE!, and OH, THE PLACES YOU'LL GO!) will be helpful for the extended follow-up activity.*

**PRE-READING FOCUS:** Read the title of the book and show the cover. Ask: If you had Dr. Seuss here today, what questions would you like to ask him about how he became a children's author? List questions on chart paper or the board. **Let's read to find out** if any of these questions are answered in this biography, or the true story of Dr. Seuss's life.

**WHILE READING:** As you read the book, refer back to the chart of questions often. Check off those that are answered by the text as you progress through the book. After reading about the happy times of his childhood (through page 15), ask: How do you think Ted's childhood helped him write stories when he was older? After reading about the tough times of his childhood (through page 17), ask the same question again. After reading page 20, pause to take a look at some of the characters found in Dr. Seuss's books. After reading page 22, discuss how Ted must have felt when he was guided offstage. After reading page 27, discuss how Ted Geisel became Seuss. Predict why he later became *Dr.* Seuss. (It was his mother's dream that he become a doctor.) Ask: Why do you think that classmates voted Ted "least likely to succeed?" Read through the end.

**FOLLOW-UP DISCUSSION:** Finally Ted is sure what he wants to do with his life. Ask: What helped him make that decision? (His classmate at Oxford encouraged him, his work was being bought by magazines, and the fan letter he received from a 12-year-old boy.) Ask: Why do you think the author chose to end her biography where she did? To learn more about the facts presented in this biography, read the back material, "On Beyond Fairfield Street." What other sources could we check for more information on Dr. Seuss?

**Write Away!** Become Seuss experts! Assign one book written by Seuss to each student. Gather information about the books from various sources and prepare reports. Have students read excerpts of the book as part of their presentation to the class.

*For other biographies, refer to the Book Notes section of this resource.*

*For other books by Kathleen Krull referenced in this resource, refer to the author index.*

## Notes:

# Up Close and Personal

## *A Note from the Author, Kathleen Krull*

### On why she chose to write about Ted Geisel:

Like a lot of other people, I felt as if I'd somehow lost a personal friend when Ted Geisel died in 1991. I've always found him inspirational as a writer who literally changed his world. I was moved to write a tribute to him for a local San Diego magazine. I actually got to meet him once, in 1982, at a reception in his honor. In person, he confirmed just what you might think about him—wise, but a little silly too, gentle, with such integrity that you stood up a little straighter. I have to add that he was very handsome.

When I moved from the Midwest to San Diego, the vegetation, especially around La Jolla (a part of San Diego) was strangely familiar—extravagant flora as seen in his books (I'm not the only one to have noticed this). I was always aware that I was living in his city, and it tickled me to look for things we might have in common. For example, he lived on the top of Mount Soledad in La Jolla, and by coincidence I lived at the bottom. In the event of an earthquake, the same Rose Canyon fault that ran underneath his house would do equal damage to my apartment. . . . He had a 180-degree view of the Pacific Ocean from his home office, and if I stepped into my alley and stood on tiptoe, I could glimpse the same ocean. . . . Okay, these were little things.

I'm sure I was a reader thanks to Dr. Seuss books. In all the years since, I have seen so many kids—nieces and nephews and others—read aloud their first book ever, and it's always GREEN EGGS AND HAM or another one of his books. Kids still adore his plots with their inner logic and wickedly limited vocabulary.

Kids tend to think that artists and writers are hatched fully formed. But Ted wasn't born Dr. Seuss; it was a long process of development and finding a focus, not all of it comfortable. In many ways he didn't fit in, even where he grew up, on Fairfield Street. At 22 all he had to show was a knack for fooling around. He'd been named "Least Likely to Succeed" in college, and there was some doubt as to whether he'd ever be able to move out of his parents' home on Fairfield. But the "Lives of" series has taught me that it's often the ones who don't fit in who grow up to become the geniuses. As one more example, I hope his story offers comfort to "misfits" today.

*For more about Kathleen Krull and her books, visit her Web site: www.kathleenkrull.com*

| | |
|---|---|
| **Title** | SCIENCE VERSE |
| **Author** | Jon Scieszka |
| **Illustrator** | Lane Smith |
| **Publisher** | Penguin |
| **Copyright Date** | 2004 |
| **Ages** | 9 and up |
| **Read-Aloud Time** | 1 minute (reading one poem at a time is suggested) |
| **Read-Aloud Sessions** | 21 |
| **Subject** | Humor; science topics treated in humorous verse |

From the creators of MATH CURSE comes this hilarious collection of poems that poke fun at serious and other befuddling concepts in science while "emulating" more famous verses (listed in "Observations and Conclusions" at the back of the book). From evolution to anatomy and astronomy, these poems, framed in a story that could be construed as a sequel to MATH CURSE, make science FUN! A CD of the book read by the author and illustrator is tucked into the back cover of the book. Even MORE FUN!

*Note: This book can be read in one sitting as a hilarious read-aloud. However, consider reading these poems one at a time as poetry pauses (see Tips and Techniques for Teachers and Librarians) either alone or matched up with the poem from which each is derived (see back of book). Fun, FUN! FUN!!*

**PRE-READING FOCUS:** Show the cover of the book. Ask: What do you think this book might be about? What topics might a poetry book about science cover? What would make a science poem fun to read? Who has read a book by Jon Scieszka (pronounced: SHESS ka) and Lane Smith? Titles include MATH CURSE, the Time Warp Trio series, THE TRUE STORY OF THE 3 LITTLE PIGS!, and THE STINKY CHEESE MAN AND OTHER FAIRLY STUPID TALES. Discuss the books the children are familiar with. **Let's read to find out** what this duo has to say about science.

**WHILE READING:** Use poems as poetry pauses. Once all the poems have been read, read aloud the entire book so the story's framework can be enjoyed.

**FOLLOW-UP DISCUSSION:** Discuss the last page of the book. Brainstorm ideas for a book about art that follows this format. Read MATH CURSE by the same wacky author/illustrator team (Penguin).

**Write Away!** Consider having a contest in which children write their own verses modeling those found in this book. Ask the children to cite the original poems from which theirs are derived.

*For more fun while learning, this time about various historical events, refer to Scieszka and Smith's Time Warp Trio series (Penguin). See the Book Notes section of this resource for titles and summaries.*

*For other books by Scieszka and Smith referenced in this resource, refer to the author and illustrator indexes.*

*For other science-related read-aloud titles, refer to the Book Notes section of this resource.*

## Notes:

# **U**p Close and Personal

## *About the Author, Jon Scieszka*

Jon Scieszka lives in Brooklyn, New York. He is married and has one daughter and one son. His wife designed the jacket for his books, THE FROG PRINCE, CONTINUED and THE BOOK THAT JACK WROTE. Their cat, Potvin, is named for the goalie, Felix "The Cat" Potvin, of the Toronto Maple Leafs. Scieszka was an elementary school teacher for ten years. He says he gets his ideas for his books from those years of teaching, and from "reading books, being a dad, listening to music, staring out the window, thinking, staring out the window some more, and then writing stuff down." He claims that the three boys in the Time Warp Trio series are like the kids he used to teach in the fourth and fifth grades.

Scieszka says it was letters from kids asking for a SCIENCE CURSE after MATH CURSE was published that got him thinking about writing a science book. Scieszka says it took nine years and between 10 and 20 versions before he thought of science poetry as the basis for SCIENCE VERSE. When he decided to write different kinds of poems that were takeoffs of famous poems, he knew he was onto something. He says he wrote all different kinds of verse. Then he spent lots of time speaking them and singing them aloud to himself to get them just right. He also wanted to cover as much true science as he could because he loves science.

Scieszka has done many books with Lane Smith, the illustrator. He feels Smith has done some of his best work ever on SCIENCE VERSE. It was Smith's idea to tie the story together by putting the narrator in every illustration. Smith's wife is a book designer and she also worked on bringing even more details to the project. "It was all just so much fun to work on every detail!" says Scieszka.

*For more information about Scieszka and Lane Smith, visit the publisher's Web site: http://us.penguingroup.com at Go to Young Readers and look for Scieszka's name in the Author Spotlight.*

*Cover from CHIMP MATH: LEARNING ABOUT TIME FROM A BABY CHIMPANZEE by Ann Whitehead Nagda and Cindy Bickel. Copyright © 2002. Reprinted with permission of Henry Holt Books for Young Readers.*

| Title | CHIMP MATH: LEARNING ABOUT TIME FROM A BABY CHIMPANZEE |
|---|---|
| **Authors** | Ann Whitehead Nagda and Cindy Bickel |
| **Publisher** | Holt |
| **Copyright Date** | 2002 |
| **Ages** | 8 and up |
| **Read-Aloud Time** | 15 minutes |
| **Read-Aloud Sessions** | 1 |
| **Subject** | Math, time, time lines, graphs, charts, calendars, record keeping, chimps, zoos |

This true story of a chimp named Jiggs, who was raised by professionals in two different zoos, chronicles his life with the use of a variety of time records. Photographs of Jiggs and his keepers appear with the story on the right-hand side of the book. Clear examples of charts, graphs, and time lines appear on the left-hand side. Together they are successful at holding the interest of even those children who may not relish math. The math concepts and record-keeping methods presented here are straightforward, with an eye toward the connection of math to the keeping of scientific records.

*Note: Read this book in one sitting and then refer to it as you complete the extended follow-up activities listed below or to illustrate the various math concepts when they are presented in class throughout the year.*

**PRE-READING FOCUS:** Ask: If you were going to observe a wild animal from birth and you wanted to keep records on what happened as it grew, how would you do that? Write answers on the board or chart paper. Show the cover of the book. Read the introduction. **Let's read to find out** more about Jiggs.

**WHILE READING:** Take time to fully explore the time records provided on the left-hand side of the book throughout the story. Discuss why the zookeepers may have used these time records. Consider other ways records may have been kept. Pay close attention to the photographs. Read the captions. Reflect on how important photographs, diagrams, and charts are in science, math, and social studies books.

**FOLLOW-UP DISCUSSION:** Ask: Which was your favorite time record? Discuss. Brainstorm other situations in which the various time records presented here might be used. Note these on the board or chart paper as students make suggestions. Have students keep time records on something of their choosing using one of the means described in the book. Encourage students to make the time record interesting and easy to understand with use of color, captions, and other visual aids. Have students present their time records to the class. Display.

*For an amazing true story related in theme, read KOKO'S KITTEN, written by Dr. Francine Patterson with photographs by Ronald H. Cohn (Scholastic), about a gorilla and her kitten.*

*See also the related titles POLAR BEAR MATH: LEARNING ABOUT FRACTIONS FROM KLONDIKE AND SNOW and TIGER MATH: LEARNING TO GRAPH FROM A BABY TIGER, by Nagda and Bickel (Holt).*

*For other science and math-related books, refer to the Book Notes section of this resource.*

## Notes:

# Up Close and Personal

## A Note from Author, Ann Whitehead Nagda

### How the book came about:

In 1994 my agent had suggested that I consider writing math books for children because of my background in math—I studied math in college and worked as a computer programmer for nearly 20 years. In November, 1994, Klondike and Snow, two baby polar bears, were born at the Denver Zoo and had to be hand-raised in the zoo hospital because their mother abandoned them. I was fascinated by the baby bears and thought they'd be a great subject for a math book. I hung out at the zoo for hours at a time watching them and got to know Cindy Bickel, a zoo veterinary technician, who had raised hundreds of baby animals. Cindy said she used math all the time in her job and offered to help me with the book. I had written several drafts of the book before I learned that the zoo had signed an exclusive agreement with a local publisher to do their own book about Klondike and Snow. So Cindy showed me photographs of T. J. the tiger and Jiggs the chimpanzee and told me about them. Several elementary teachers helped me with the math for the books. While I was working on CHIMP MATH, a teacher lent me KOKO'S KITTEN, which she said kids loved. I loved it too, and had Cindy look for photographs she had taken of Jiggs interacting with her cat and dog at home. I chose time as the subject for CHIMP MATH because my daughter had struggled with time concepts in third grade. (She also struggled with graphing, the math concept for TIGER MATH, and with fractions, the math concept for POLAR BEAR MATH.)

*For more information on Ann Whitehead Nagda and her books, visit her Web site, www.AnnNagda.com.*

*Cover from THE JACKET by Andrew Clements, illustrated by McDavid Henderson. Copyright © 2002. Used with permission of Simon & Schuster Books for Young Readers, an imprint of Simon & Schuster Children's Publishing.*

| | |
|---|---|
| **Title** | THE JACKET |
| **Author** | Andrew Clements |
| **Publisher** | Simon & Schuster |
| **Copyright Date** | 2002 |
| **Ages** | 9 and up |
| **Read-Aloud Time** | 6–8 minutes per chapter |
| **Read-Aloud Sessions** | 6 |
| **Subject** | Prejudice, stereotyping |

Phil, a sixth grader, has an active imagination. When he sees a boy down the hall with a jacket just like his brother's, he jumps to conclusions and accuses the boy of stealing the jacket. This boy, who came by the jacket honestly, happens to be black. When Phil learns the truth, he begins to questions his motives and whether he is prejudiced.

**PRE-READING FOCUS**: Introduce the book by showing the cover and reading the title. Note the details in the cover art. Ask students to predict what the story is about.

## Part I: "Collision Course"

*Pre-reading:* Ask the children what a collision is. (A clash or encounter resulting in an exchange of energy.) Judging from the cover, what do you think the title means? (The boys will clash with one another.) **Let's read to find out** who these boys on the cover are and what the collision is about.

*Follow-up:* Before Phil approaches Daniel, he is thinking about some things. What is he worried about? (Getting in trouble; failing.) What happens as he continues to look for his brother? (His imagination runs wild and he gets more and more frustrated and irritated.) What happens when he realizes that the boy wearing the jacket is not his brother? (He jumps to conclusions and overreacts.) How do you think Daniel felt when Phil grabbed him? (Intimidated, angry, upset.) As Mrs. Cormier read the label on the jacket, what were you thinking? (Possibly that Daniel had indeed stolen the jacket.) Explore this. Chances are the students jumped to conclusions, too. We know how Daniel feels at the end of part I. How do you think Phil feels? (Ashamed, embarrassed.)

## Part II: "Friends with Everybody"

*Pre-reading:* Ask: What does it mean to be friends with everybody? Discuss. What does it mean to be somebody's friend? Discuss. Are the two different? In this part Phil does a lot of thinking. **Let's read to find out** what's going on in his mind.

*Follow-up:* Ask: If you were Phil, would you have accepted the quarter? Discuss.

**Write Away!** What is a friend? Describe the qualities of someone who is your friend. Give specific examples. Describe how you are a friend to someone else. Be specific.

## Part III: "Close to Home"

*Pre-reading:* Ask: What does the word *prejudiced* mean? (Having attitudes, opinions, or judgments formed without just grounds about the characteristics of a group, race, or individual.) Is Phil prejudiced? Is Daniel? **Let's read to find out** what Phil thinks about as he continues to work out his feelings about what he did.

*Follow-up:* Discuss Phil's mom's reaction and comments to Phil about his feelings.

**Write Away!** Do you think you are prejudiced? Support your answer with examples just as Phil has done as he thought about his actions toward Daniel.

## Part IV: "Forget About It"

*Pre-reading:* Read the part title. Ask: Do you think Phil will be able to "forget about it" as his mother suggested? **Let's read to find out.**

*Follow-up:* Phil's imagination runs wild again in part IV. What happens? (He imagines Daniel will die of an illness he caught as a result of not wearing the jacket in the cold weather.) At the end of the part, Phil takes the jacket from the coat stand in the main office. What do you think will happen next?

## Part V: "Something in the Tone"

*Pre-reading:* Ask: What can you tell from the tone of voice a person uses? Discuss and ask volunteers to demonstrate! **Let's read to find out** why this part is titled, "Something In The Tone."

*Follow-up:* Ask: What does the title mean? Discuss. What do you think Phil intends to do?

## Part VI: "Round-Trip"

*Pre-reading:* Review what the children think Phil intends to do. What do you think Daniel will do? **Let's read to find out** if your predictions are correct.

*Follow-up:* Discuss how both boys feel at the end of the book. Both boys have learned and grown from this experience. Discuss. Ask: If you were going to write one more part for this book, what would happen?

*For a moving follow-up read-aloud on the topic of prejudice, see the picture book based on a true story, THE CHRISTMAS MENORAHS: HOW A TOWN FOUGHT HATE, written by Janice Cohn and illustrated by Bill Farnsworth (Whitman).*

*See the read-aloud plan for THE JANITOR'S BOY, by Andrew Clements (Simon & Schuster), elsewhere in this resource.*

*Andrew Clements is the author of several books suitable for middle graders. See especially the award-winning, million-copy bestseller, FRINDLE, about a boy who coins a new name for the pen. Visit the official Web site for the book: www.frindle.com. Other great titles by Clements include THE LANDRY NEWS, THE REPORT CARD, and THE LAST HOLIDAY CONCERT, all of which approach subjects important to children in this age group with skill and heart. All titles listed above are published by Simon & Schuster.*

*See the Parent Pull-Out Pages for information to send home to parents about Andrew Clements and other authors popular with students in grades 3 and 4.*

*For other books by Andrew Clements referenced in this resource, refer to the author index.*

## Notes:

*Cover from FRINDLE by Andrew Clements, illustrated by Brian Selznick. Copyright © 1996. Used with permission of Richard Jackson Books/Atheneum Books for Young Readers, an imprint of Simon & Schuster Children's Publishing.*

# Up Close and Personal

## A Note from the Author, Andrew Clements

### On why he wrote this story:

In 1990 *The Boston Globe* newspaper asked me to write a story that would appear six Mondays in a row on their Student Newsline page, and they said I could write about anything. I began to think about Boston, and I recalled the ugly racial divisions that happened when the city schools were ordered by the courts to become more integrated. A lot of mean, hateful thinking bubbled up and exploded into unkindness and even violence. Boston's not like that these days, at least not on the surface. But underneath, there are still prejudices to be healed, and of course, it's not just in Boston. People everywhere need to be more loving and more tolerant, more appreciative of the differences among their fellow Americans and all humanity.

But back to 1990: Thinking about race relations and Boston made me remember an incident in my own life. When I was in fifth grade, I saw my big brother grab a kid, an African American boy, who was wearing a jacket that looked like his. And it turned out that the boy had gotten the jacket in the same way I write about in the book. Sitting there with the Globe writing assignment in front of me, I looked back at this incident and wondered, 'If that boy had been white instead of black, would my brother have accused him of stealing?' So this story grew out of my own experience—which is true of most of my books.

| | |
|---|---|
| **Title** | RUMPELSTILTSKIN'S DAUGHTER |
| **Author/Illustrator** | Diane Stanley |
| **Publisher** | Morrow |
| **Copyright Date** | 1997 |
| **Ages** | 7 and up |
| **Read-Aloud Time** | 12–15 minutes |
| **Read-Aloud Sessions** | 1 |
| **Subject** | Fractured fairy tale, greed, hope |

In this fractured fairy tale, we meet Rumpelstiltskin's feisty and wise daughter, who teaches the king who once snared her mom a thing or two about wealth. The style is witty and light, and the opportunities to learn while being entertained are as bountiful as the king's gold.

**PRE-READING FOCUS:** Read the title of the book and show the cover. Note the expression of the king. Read the title. Review the story of Rumpelstiltskin. Read the two post cards on the inside cover. Rumpelstiltskin's daughter signed her cards "H." What might her name be? **Let's read to find out** what Rumpelstiltskin's daughter has planned.

**WHILE READING:** Read from the recap of the fairy tale through the distribution of the gold coins throughout the kingdom. Ask : What is a *portcullis*? Use the context and illustrations to define. (A grating of iron lowered between grooves to prevent passage.) Ask: What do you think will happen next? Read with expression the words of the king as you continue through *"Time for phase two."* Ask: What do you think will happen next? Read to the end of the story.

**FOLLOW-UP DISCUSSION:** Discuss why the author chose the name she did for Rumpelstiltskin's daughter. Ask: How would you describe Hope? What are her character traits? What parts of this tale are funny? What parts of this tale are wise? Why do you think Hope wanted to be the prime minister instead of the queen? Do you think she would make a good leader? Why? List her leadership qualities.

*For a list of fractured fairy tales, consult the Book Notes section of this resource.*

Notes:

| | |
|---|---|
| **Title** | MRS. BIDDLEBOX |
| **Author** | Linda Smith |
| **Illustrator** | Marla Frazee |
| **Publisher** | HarperCollins |
| **Copyright Date** | 2002 |
| **Ages** | 6 and up |
| **Read-Aloud Time** | 6–8 minutes |
| **Read-Aloud Sessions** | 1 |
| **Subject** | Having a bad day, overcoming a bad mood |

Mrs. Biddlebox wakes up in a "dreary little funk" and her day begins with gloom and fog. What she does to take control of her day and whip it into shape makes for a delightful tale told in jaunty rhyme. Winner of the Golden Kite Award, author Linda Smith is said to have been "Mrs. Biddlebox" during her two-year battle with breast cancer, which she lost in June 2000, prior to the publication of this book.

**PRE-READING FOCUS:** Read the title of the book and show the cover. Note the expression on Mrs. Biddlebox's face and the "cloud" of hair over her head. Ask: Who do you think this is on the cover? (Mrs. Biddlebox.) What do we know about her from the expression on her face? (She is not in a good mood; she is determined.) Ask: What is a bad mood? How does a bad mood feel? Have you ever been around another person in a bad mood? How does a bad mood make those around you feel? What can you do to get yourself out of a bad mood? What do you think Mrs. Biddlebox is doing on the cover? **Let's read to find out.**

**WHILE READING:** Read through the first page. Ask: Have you ever heard the expression, "He/she got out on the wrong side of the bed?" What does that mean? (Woke up in a bad mood.) What words does the author use to describe a bad mood? (Dreary little funk.) Read the next page. Ask: How has the illustrator shown Mrs. Biddlebox's bad mood? (She used grays and browns and swirly strokes.) Read the next page. Ask: What do you think Mrs. Biddlebox is going to do? Read the next three spreads. Refer back to the cover. Discuss what Mrs. Biddlebox is doing. (Twirling the fog like spaghetti.) Read the next several pages, through welcoming in the night. Ask: What do you notice is different about Mrs. Biddlebox in this illustration? (Her "cloud" of hair is under her nighty cap.) Read to the end.

**FOLLOW-UP DISCUSSION:** Ask: How did Mrs. Biddlebox get rid of her bad mood? (She didn't let it get the best of her.) What can you do the next time you're in a bad mood? Discuss. The illustrator uses color and brush strokes to give you the feeling of Mrs. Biddlebox's mood. Make a list of "moods" and allow students to choose one to illustrate in the style of Marla Frazee. Display the pictures around the room.

# Up Close and Personal·················

## *A Note from the Illustrator, Marla Frazee*

### *A story about the story:*

I didn't have the opportunity to get to know Linda Smith in person, but we did speak on the phone a few times. I called her to see if there was anything she might want to share with me about the book. This is not the way it typically works between authors and illustrators. Usually discussions about the development of a book go through the editor. But I knew that there was a chance Linda would never get to see the finished book and I felt it was important for me to hear what she might want to say. (Linda died of cancer before I started working on the illustrations.) She was very professional and didn't want to influence my thinking, but finally Linda did share some of her thoughts. One was that Mrs. Biddlebox should have a pet of some kind, and she suggested a mangy dog or a skinny cat or something. In the initial sketches, I drew Mrs. Biddlebox with a dog and a cat and then a goat and I even tried a raccoon. Finally I settled on the goose. It seemed just right to me. It turns out that Linda used to have a goose named Gabby that would follow her around and bite her through her jeans. Linda's family felt she would have been delighted with Mrs. Biddlebox and her goose. This convinced me that I was taking good care of Linda's brilliant story.

### *About illustrating a book:*

A picture book has two simultaneous stories being told—one in the words, and one in the pictures. Sometimes those stories say the same thing at the same time, and sometimes they diverge. It is this dance between the word story and the picture story that I find so fascinating as an illustrator of picture books. What I hoped to show in this picture story is that there is a light side and a dark side to everything. At the end of the book, Mrs. Biddlebox is still in the same world as she was before—it just looks different now. There are twinkly stars and swirly flowers, as well as shadows. We all have a bad day once in a while, and this book not only says that's okay, it says that it's within our power to do something about it.

I spent a lot of time thinking about what it feels like to be in a bad mood and then trying to translate those feelings into a visual medium. I drew the pictures with a black grease pencil, which provided a very dark line, but were also incredibly messy. I wanted to express Mrs. Biddlebox's bad mood in a tangible way. I wanted the emotion to come through in the color. I think that's one of the wonderful things about picture books: the illustrations can operate in a similar way to a soundtrack in a film. They can swell the emotion of the text. I love the questions that have been posed about the black cloud of hair that hovers over her head. I did want it to represent her mood—the black cloud that descends upon us at certain times. I have the same head of hair. It has been suggested that Mrs. Biddlebox is a self-portrait, and I wouldn't disagree. I just hope that when I am Mrs. Biddlebox's age, I will be dancing around my stove, too.

*For more information about Marla Frazee, her childhood, her workspace, and her books, visit her Web site: www.marlafrazee.com.*

## Notes:

| | |
|---|---|
| Title | IF NOT FOR THE CAT |
| Author | Jack Prelutsky |
| Illustrator | Ted Rand |
| Publisher | Greenwillow |
| Copyright Date | 2004 |
| Ages | 7 and up |
| Read-Aloud Time | 6–8 minutes |
| Read-Aloud Sessions | 1 |
| Subject | Haiku |

This picture book collection of first-person haiku offers a wonderful introduction to the formula poetry that often opens the door to an appreciation of poetry in young people. The illustrations, beautifully simple themselves, extend the inherently spare text and enhance the focused image of the words with close-up depictions of the subjects achieved with a variety of media. My favorite poem/illustration of them all is the title piece. This book was awarded a 2004 Parent's Choice Gold Award.

**PRE-READING FOCUS:** Begin with an introduction of haiku: its origin, its formula (three lines; five syllables, seven syllables, five syllables.), its style, and its allure, as well as its usual subject, which is some aspect of nature. Ask what specifically one might write haiku about. **Let's read to find out** what subjects Jack Prelutsky chose for his haiku. Show the cover of book. Read the title. Count the syllables in this first line. (Five.) Predict what the rest of the poem might be about.

**WHILE READING:** Read through the poems in one sitting. Enjoy them and the accompanying illustrations.

**FOLLOW-UP DISCUSSION:** Ask: Which haiku did you like best? Discuss. Note the poet's word choices: the powerful verbs, adjectives, and adverbs Prelutsky chose to give readers sensory details about the animals while creating one powerful image. Ask: What other aspects of nature would you like to see Prelutsky write about?

Consider re-reading these poems one at a time during poetry pauses. (See the Tips and Techniques for Teachers and Librarians section of this resource book.)

**Write Away!** Choose a theme in nature, such as animals, flowers, trees, or seasons. Write a haiku and illustrate it. Allow students to present their haiku to the class and then display them.

*For additional poetry suggestions, refer to the Tips and Techniques for Teachers and Librarians section of this resource.*

*For a list of poetry books written by Jack Prelutsky, refer to the author index.*

Notes:

| | |
|---|---|
| **Title** | KITES SAIL HIGH: A BOOK ABOUT VERBS |
| **Author/Illustrator** | Ruth Heller |
| **Publisher** | Grosset & Dunlap |
| **Copyright Date** | 1988 |
| **Ages** | 8 and up |
| **Read-Aloud Time** | 5–7 minutes |
| **Read-Aloud Sessions** | 1 |
| **Subject** | Verbs |

One in Ruth Heller's inviting World of Language series in which parts of speech are explained by way of lively, vivid word choices accompanied by bold illustrations in the style for which this author/illustrator is famous. These books, written in rhyme, enliven that part of language arts that is often shunned because of its dry and intimidating aspects. Fear no more! Perky parts of speech books exist! But don't be fooled by the package; these books pack a punch. You'll find higher level skills between the covers. Learn about mood, tenses, and irregular verbs as well as passive and active voices in this book.

*Note: An excellent introductory book about parts of speech is the interactive THE AMAZING POP-UP GRAMMAR BOOK, by Jennie Maizels and Kate Petty (Dutton), a book that definitely lives up to its name. Consider using it to introduce each part of speech before turning to Heller's World of Language series (see titles below).*

**PRE-READING FOCUS:** Ask: What is a verb? (Word that expresses action; also, state of being, linking, and helping.) Ask for examples and list them. Encourage vivid verb choices: jogged instead of ran, lumber instead of walk, wept instead of cried. **Let's read to find out** more about verbs.

**WHILE READING:** Choose to read the entire book or just specific sections. For each topic covered in the book, pause to ask the children for additional examples. Refer to the first page of the book (before the title page) for an excellent list of vivid action verbs.

**FOLLOW-UP DISCUSSION:** Add to your list of verbs. Consider sharing Denise Fleming's IN THE SMALL, SMALL POND and IN THE TALL, TALL GRASS (Holt) with children for a wonderful look at vivid verbs at work. Spectacular.

*Other titles in Heller's World of Language series include MINE, ALL MINE: A BOOK ABOUT PRONOUNS; BEHIND THE MASK: A BOOK ABOUT PREPOSITIONS; A CACHE OF JEWELS AND OTHER COLLECTIVE NOUNS; MANY LUSCIOUS LOLLIPOPS: A BOOK ABOUT ADJECTIVES; MERRY-GO-ROUND: A BOOK ABOUT NOUNS; UP, UP AND AWAY: A BOOK ABOUT ADVERBS; and FANTASTIC! WOW! AND UNREAL!: A BOOK ABOUT INTERJECTIONS AND CONJUNCTIONS (Grosset & Dunlap).*

*For additional writing-related titles, refer to the Books Notes section of this resource.*

## Notes:

*Cover from SEURAT AND LA GRANDE JATTE: CONNECTING THE DOTS by Robert Burleigh. Copyright © 2004. Reprinted with permission of Abrams Books for Young Readers/Amulet Books.*

| | |
|---|---|
| **Title** | SEURAT AND LA GRANDE JATTE: CONNECTING THE DOTS |
| **Author/Illustrator** | Robert Burleigh |
| **Publisher** | Abrams |
| **Copyright Date** | 2004 |
| **Ages** | 8 and up |
| **Read-Aloud Time** | 12–15 minutes |
| **Read-Aloud Sessions** | 1-3 |
| **Subject** | Art appreciation, in-depth look at this famous piece of artwork |

This book not only delves into a study of the painting, the subject of which is a Sunday afternoon in a park on an island in the Seine River (pronounced Sane) in Paris in 1884, but also offers insight into the artist who created this life-sized (approximately 11-by-7-foot) masterpiece. Readers are guided through an investigation of the details of the painting. They note subjects and their stances, their dress, and what they might be gazing at. Georges Seurat (pronounced Zhorzh Sirrah) is the father of pointillism (painting with dots), and this was his major work, the study of which is memorably brought to young people by a painter himself.

*Note: This book can be read in a single sitting or spaced over several days. If it is possible to find other copies of this painting and other works of art by Seurat, have them handy for the investigative portions of this read-aloud.*

**PRE-READING FOCUS:** Ask: Can a painting tell a story? (As the author says, it can tell many.) Read page 2. Show the painting. Note the actual size. Read page 3. Answer the question posed on page 3. Count the people (about 50), dogs (3), and monkies (1). Is it sunny? (Yes.) How do we know? (Shadows, parasols.) **Let's read to find out** more about La Grande Jatte.

**WHILE READING:** Read pages 4–5. Answer the question posed. (What are they doing?) Read pages 6–7 and complete the "find" exercise. Read page 8 and note the details Burleigh points out. Read page 9. Read pages 10–11.

*Note: This would be a good point at which to stop reading. Ask the children to sketch this "single moment in time" to freeze it so others would be able to see everything exactly as it is right now. They should produce sketches only.*

Continue reading pages 12–13. Observe the effect in the painting. Read pages 14–15. Note points the author makes. Read pages 16–17. Discuss what the word *impulse* means (Sudden, spontaneous movement.) and why Seurat was not entirely an Impressionist. Read pages 18–21.

*Note: You may want to stop reading here to continue working on student scenes. Add dots and use colors to highlight and accentuate.*

Read pages 22–23. Ask: How would you describe Seurat's personality? (Patient, introspective, hardworking, polite, mannerly.) How do we know this? (From the clues in how he worked and behaved in his everyday life.) Read pages 24–25. Discuss the colors he used to give his work a mood or feeling. Read to the end.

**FOLLOW-UP DISCUSSION:** Study other pieces of art by Seurat (See those on page 31.) Add finishing touches to the "masterpieces." Display them around the room.

*For additional art-related titles, refer to the Book Notes section of this resource.*

*For other books written and/or illustrated by Robert Burleigh suitable for grades 3-4, refer to the author and illustrator indexes.*

## Notes:

# Up Close and Personal

## *A Note from the Author, Robert Burleigh*

### *How and why the book came to be:*

SEURAT AND LA GRANDE JATTE: CONNECTING THE DOTS was different in certain ways from other books I've done. It was really a very collaborative effort between myself, the editor at Abrams, Howard Reeves, and the publications department people and various consultants at the Art Institute of Chicago. There was much back and forth between the people mentioned above and myself throughout the project.

The main reason for the book, beyond the excellence of the painting, was the show the Art Institute put together last summer on Seurat's making of the Grande Jatte. Because this was the primary reason for the book, and also because there is not a lot known about his daily life, it was pretty much a given that the painting be featured up front, as it is, with biographical details on Seurat being in the background.

I suppose the main thing I found out in researching the book was how careful and diligent Seurat was, with his numerous studies paving the way for the final picture. I spent a good bit of time sitting in front of the painting at the Art Institute on a bench that is placed in front of the work for that purpose, and which was often filled to the max. It was fun listening to the various people there talk about the painting that I was in the process of writing a book about!

Now it's your turn to study the painting and talk about it. I hope this book helps!

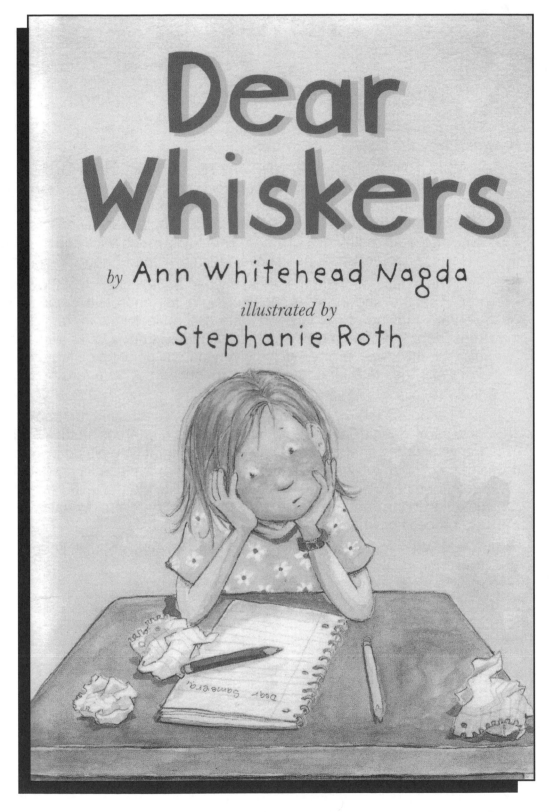

*Cover from DEAR WHISKERS by Ann Whitehead Nagda. Illustrated by Stephanie Roth. Copyright © 2000. Reprinted with permission of Holiday House.*

| Title | DEAR WHISKERS |
|---|---|
| Author | Ann Whitehead Nagda |
| Illustrator | Stephanie Roth |
| Publisher | Holiday House |
| Copyright Date | 2000 |
| Ages | 7–10 |
| Read-Aloud Time | 5–7 minutes |
| Read-Aloud Sessions | 11 |
| Subject | Letter writing, Saudi Arabia, ESL students |

*Note: Have a friendly letter form handy for the reading of Chapter 1.*

*Consider beginning a pen pal program to dovetail with the reading of this book. Introduce it following Chapter 1. Possibilities include children in lower grades, older students in another building (i.e., high school students), children in a sister school, a grandparent, or mystery pen pals from another classroom of the same grade in your school.*

**PRE-READING FOCUS:** Read the title of the book and show the cover. Ask: What can you tell me about this book from the cover? (Girl is main character; she is writing a letter; she is having difficulty.) Whom is she writing to? (Whiskers.) Who might Whiskers be?

## Chapter 1

*Pre-reading:* Ask: What do you call a person you correspond with, or write letters back and forth to? (A pen pal.) Have you ever had a pen pal? Discuss. **Let's read to find out** about this character's pen pal assignment.

*Follow-up:* Ask: What do we know so far? (The main character is Jenny. Other characters are Richard, Susan, Kevin, and Mrs. Steele. The children are in fourth grade. Susan is a great writer; Jenny is not. Jenny is writing to her pen pal, a second grader named Sameera.) What is the *setting* of the story? (Fourth-grade classroom.) What can you tell from the end of the chapter? (Jenny is frustrated. She erased until she almost tore her paper and she broke the point on her pencil from pushing down so hard.)

**Write Away!** Review the friendly letter form. If you are going to institute a pen pal program, "introduce" pen pals. Write a first letter.

## Chapter 2

*Pre-reading:* Ask: What kind of letter would you like to get from a pen pal? Not like to get? **Let's read to find out** what kinds of letters Jenny and her classmates get from their second-grade pen pals.

*Follow-up:* Discuss the letters the children receive. Ask: Why is Jenny so upset with Sameera's response? How would you feel if you were Jenny? Why do you think Sameera wrote what she did? What should Jenny write next? Consider having students take turns drawing Mrs. Steele's outfits as described in the story.

## Chapter 3

*Pre-reading:* What do you think Jenny will write to Sameera? **Let's read to find out.**

*Follow-up:* What do you think of Jenny's letter? Discuss.

## Chapter 4

*Pre-reading:* Ask: What do you think Sameera's second letter will say? **Let's read to find out.**

*Follow-up:* Ask: What did we find out about Sameera in this chapter? (She is new to the school. She has moved here from Saudi Arabia. Jenny does not feel Sameera is very friendly.) What do you think? Discuss. What do you think will happen next?

## Chapter 5

*Pre-reading:* Ask: What do you remember about Sameera? What do you think will happen when Jenny visits the second-grade classroom again? **Let's read to find out.**

*Follow-up:* Discuss Jenny's reactions and what alternatives she has. Discuss what it must feel like to be a student from another country who does not understand the language of the new country.

## Chapter 6

*Pre-reading:* Ask: What is an adjective? (A modifier of a noun; a word that describes time, quality, quantity, or distinction.) **Let's read to find out** what adjectives have to do with this chapter.

*Follow-up:* Ask: What could Jenny have put in her letter?

> **Write Away!** Continue working on letters to pen pals. Ask students to use lots of adjectives in their next letters.

*Note: For the reading of the next chapter, consider having available a copy of IF YOU GIVE A MOUSE A COOKIE, written by Laura Joffe Numeroff and illustrated by Felicia Bond (HarperCollins), and ALEXANDER AND THE WIND-UP MOUSE, by Leo Lionni (Knopf), to show to students.*

# Chapter 7

*Pre-reading:* Ask: If you had to read to Sameera, what books would you choose? Show the books Jenny chose (listed above). Ask: Do you think these are good choices? **Let's read to find out.**

*Follow-up:* Ask: Do you think Sameera had fun? Did Jenny?

*Note: Have four cookies available to "do the math" that Susan and Jenny do in this chapter.*

# Chapters 8 and 9

*Pre-reading:* Ask: If you wanted to help Sameera write a letter, what would you do? **Let's read to find out** what Jenny does.

*Follow-up:* Demonstrate the math problem using cookies, as Susan suggests. Mrs. Steele says, "Sometimes a hard job is a gift." What do you think this means? Discuss. What has Jenny learned about some of the other children in the story? What do you think will happen with the letter Sameera took with her?

*Note: Have information available on the Gregorian calendar and Islamic calendar to share with children following the reading of this chapter.*

# Chapter 10

*Pre-reading:* In this chapter Jenny comes up with some ideas to help Sameera. Ask: What would be a good idea? **Let's read to find out** what ideas Jenny came up with.

*Follow-up:* Discuss Jenny's ideas for acting out stories for Sameera. Jenny's mother says, "Easy isn't always better." What does she mean? Do you agree? Discuss. Review what Jenny learned about Sameera's culture. Ask: How did she learn these things? Where else could you find information about Saudi Arabia and Islamic ways? Review information on the calendars. Explain where the information came from.

**Write Away!** Brainstorm topics related to Sameera's culture to research. Assign mini-reports. Give guidelines.

*Note: Have a map of Saudi Arabia available for this chapter.*

## Chapter 11

*Pre-reading:* Ask: What do you think will happen when Jenny gets together with Sameera? **Let's read to find out.**

*Follow-up:* Discuss how Jenny feels at the end of the chapter.

## Chapter 12

*Pre-reading:* In this last chapter, another stack of letters comes from the second graders. **Let's read to find out** if there is one for Jenny.

*Follow-up:* Make a list of the things Sameera has learned from Jenny. Then make a list of the things Jenny has learned from Sameera.

*For a follow-up to this story, see the picture book HOME AT LAST, written by Susan Middleton Elya and illustrated by Felipe Davalos (Lee & Low), in which a Hispanic family assimilates into the United States. See the read-aloud plan found in Children's Book Corner, Grades 1–2.*

*The companion novel to DEAR WHISKERS is MEOW MEANS MISCHIEF, written by Ann Whitehead Nagda and illustrated by Stephanie Roth (Holiday), which features some of these same characters in a story about a new girl in class who is of Indian descent, and the stray kitten who is the subject of the title.*

*See also the read-aloud plan for CHIMP MATH: LEARNING ABOUT TIME FROM A BABY CHIMPANZEE, written by Ann Whitehead Nagda and Cindy Bickel (Holt), elsewhere in this resource.*

# Up Close and Personal

## A Note from the Author, Ann Whitehead Nagda

**Where the idea for the story came from and how the story developed:**

DEAR WHISKERS was inspired by a project my daughter did in fifth grade, where her whole class wrote "mouse letters" to second-graders. My daughter loved this project and her pen pal wrote wonderful letters to her. But one student's pen pal didn't cooperate, writing back, "Don't lie to me. There's no mouse in my desk." In the first version of the book, there was no Sameera, and no publishers were interested in it. Several years later I tutored a girl from Saudi Arabia who had just come to this country and didn't speak much English, and the character of Sameera was modeled after her. I had been an exchange student in Denmark and knew what it was like to sit in a classroom and not understand much at first. When I did the rewrite with the Sameera character, the whole book worked much better, and it sold right away.

MEOW MEANS MISCHIEF is a companion book to DEAR WHISKERS, and was inspired by my daughter's experience as a mixed-race child (my husband was born in India and my background is Irish and Welsh).

*For more information on Ann Whitehead Nagda and her books, visit her Web site, www.AnnNagda.com.*

# Up Close and Personal

## A Note from the Illustrator, Stephanie Roth

### About the story:

I have a very personal connection to the story DEAR WHISKERS. When I was almost 7 years old, we moved to the States from Belgium. I could speak English all right, but I definitely didn't fit in. My clothes were all wrong, for example. I remember being teased for wearing my favorite jacket: a yellow leather biker-style jacket. I had the wrong everything. All the kids in Burnsville, MN were pretty homogeneous and that was not like the community I came from. I was used to being with other international kids. Everyone was "different." To the kids in Burnsville, I spoke funny and dressed funny, and so I felt like a big disappointment. For this reason, I felt an affinity for Sameera, a girl who has been dropped into a culture that is so different and trying to fit in, trying to understand how to be in this new place. Everyone wants to be accepted: that's one of the most basic human needs, and I love the Jenny character because she has to be brave to reach out to Sameera. She has to learn how to connect in a more basic way, to think outside the box. She has to take a risk.

### About illustrating:

When I decide what to illustrate in a book, it's always the same process. I read the story and try to figure out in a very general way, what it is about and what the characters are feeling. My illustrations mirror the main emotional points of the story. I don't concentrate so much on what's happening as what's being felt. I also try my best to use every tool I have to emphasize the emotion in each picture. For example, when Jenny is reading her letter, she feels small, so I drew her small and holding the letter in front of her, as if she is trying to "hide" behind it. Susan is more confident, so I drew her bigger and in a more open body posture. I always draw a picture of my old cat, Dweezel, in the books I illustrate. He's on the couch in this story. Can you find him?

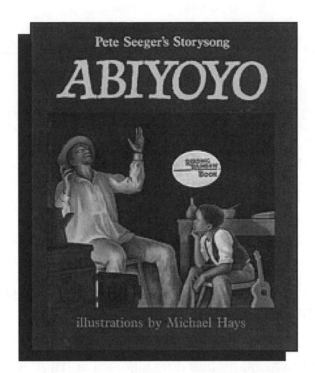

*Cover from ABIYOYO by Pete Seeger, illustrated by Michael Hays. Copyright © 1986. Used with permission of Simon & Schuster Books for Young Readers, an imprint of Simon & Schuster Children's Publishing.*

*Cover from ABIYOYO RETURNS by Pete Seeger and Paul DuBois Jacobs, illustrated by Michael Hays. Copyright © 2001. Used with permission of Simon & Schuster Books for Young Readers, an imprint of Simon & Schuster Children's Publishing.*

| | |
|---|---|
| **Title** | ABIYOYO; ABIYOYO RETURNS |
| **Author** | Pete Seeger; Pete Seeger and Paul DuBois Jacobs (sequel) |
| **Illustrator** | Michael Hays |
| **Publisher** | Macmillan; Simon & Schuster |
| **Copyright Date** | 1986; 2001 |
| **Ages** | 7 and up |
| **Read-Aloud Time** | 6–8 minutes |
| **Read-Aloud Sessions** | 2 |
| **Subject** | Lullaby, South African folktale |

This story is an adaptation of a South African folk tale that grew out of Seeger's experience telling his children a story one night in the 1950s when they refused a lullaby. He went on to perform the story on stage. In the foreword to ABIYOYO, Seeger encourages readers to feel free to change the story so the telling is theirs. The sequel, ABIYOYO RETURNS, was written several years later. Read the original story on the first day and the sequel on the following day.

*Notes: Prior to presenting the first book, read the foreword so you can provide a background to this folk tale to your students as part of the introduction to the read-aloud.*

*A tape of ABIYOYO is available. If you are able to locate it, consider playing it for listeners following the read-aloud of the first book.*

*Note the extended follow-up activity suggested below.*

## Day 1

***Pre-reading Focus:*** Ask: What is a *lullaby?* (A song to quiet children or lull them to sleep.) Can you name one? If you are so inclined, sing a bit of the more common ones as they are named. Read the title. Show the cover. Present the background to the story. Be sure to mention that Pete Seeger is a songwriter/performer. Explain the oral tradition of folk tales. **Let's read to find out** who Abiyoyo is. Ask listeners to think about how they might act out this folk tale and what parts they might change if they were retelling this tale.

***While Reading:*** As you read ABIYOYO, be sure to use expression, especially on the italicized words and the words of dialogue. After a few pages, encourage listeners to chorus *Zoop!* at the appropriate time in the story. Read through the page on which the son whips out his ukelele and sings to Abiyoyo. Before turning to the next page, ask: What do you think will happen next? Read and sing. Encourage listeners to sing along. When the father uses his magic on Abiyoyo, ask the children to recall the word *Zoop!* Before turning the page, ask: What do you think will happen next? Turn the page and *Zoop!* Read to the end.

*Follow-up Discussion:* If you have a copy of the tape of this story, listen to it. Re-read the description of Abiyoyo. Brainstorm what could be used to make a model of Abiyoyo that fits the description.

> **Write Away!** Rewrite this folk tale to make it your own. What will you change? How will it be different? What elements will you keep the same?

*Note: Gather art and craft materials for the follow-up activity prior to the read-aloud of the sequel.*

# Day 2

*Pre-reading Focus:* Review the story of Abiyoyo. Ask: What do you think happened to Abiyoyo? Read Seeger's comments on why he wrote the sequel, found on the back cover of the book. **Let's read to find out** what happened to Abiyoyo.

*While Reading:* Read ABIYOYO RETURNS, using expression and encouraging *Zoop!* in the spirit of the reading of the original story.

*Follow-up Discussion*: After reading the story, read the rest of Seeger's comments, found on the back cover of the book. Ask: What is something Pete Seeger seems very concerned about? (The environment.) Why do you think Pete Seeger says that Grandpa's rule is a good one? Discuss.

Re-read the description of Abiyoyo in the original story and in the sequel. As a group, create Abiyoyo, using craft and art materials you have gathered. Play the music throughout the creation and throughout the day! Listen to other songs by Pete Seeger, especially those listed on the book jacket of ABIYOYO RETURNS.

> **Write Away!** Research why forests are important. Write a paragraph summarizing what you have learned. Or: Pete Seeger says, "[E]very community must learn to manage its giants, whoever and whatever they might be." What giants do you think need managing? Choose one. Explain the "giant" and give specific examples. Do you have suggestions for how the giant might be managed?

*For additional folk tale suggestions, refer to the Book Notes section of this resource.*

| Title | PAUL BUNYAN |
|---|---|
| Author/Illustrator | Steven Kellogg |
| Publisher | Morrow |
| Copyright Date | 1984 |
| Ages | 7 and up |
| Read-Aloud Time | 8–10 minutes |
| Read-Aloud Sessions | 1 |
| Subject | Tall tale |

This Reading Rainbow Book selection is a charming and amusing retelling of the favorite tall tale about the likable lumberjack who traveled the countryside. Kellogg's illustrations are filled with delightful details. His Bunyan is an endearing giant among heroes who's sure to please young readers.

**PRE-READING FOCUS:** Ask: What can you tell me about Paul Bunyan? What is a tall tale? (A story with details and characters that are grossly exaggerated and larger than life in size, characteristics, and/or abilities.) Show the cover. Ask: What can you tell me from looking at this cover? (Note Bunyan's size: eagle, tigers, and oxen are small in comparison.) **Let's read to find out** more about Paul Bunyan.

**WHILE READING:** Be sure to take time to enjoy Kellogg's illustrations and the details you will find there that make this retelling special. Revel in the details of the language Kellogg uses as well, such as the names of Bunyan's lumbering crew. You'll never think of flapjacks in the same way again!

**FOLLOW-UP DISCUSSION:** After reading, review the tall tale aspects of this retelling. Brainstorm other feats one might attribute to Paul Bunyan.

**Write Away!** After reading several tall tales, compare and contrast the heroes. Ask students to use specific details from the tales to support their opinions.

*See also the companion tall tales, PECOS BILL, JOHNNY APPLESEED, and MIKE FINK, retold and illustrated by Steven Kellogg (HarperCollins). And for a twist on another classic, don't miss JIM AND THE BEANSTALK, by Raymond Briggs (Putnam), in which Jim earns gold coins by helping the old giant feel young again.*

*For additional suggestions of tall tales, refer to the Book Notes section of this resource.*

# Tips and Techniques for Teachers and Librarians

# The Case for Reading
# Aloud to Middle Graders

It seems that teachers and librarians abandon the practice of reading aloud to children who have advanced beyond the first few years of their education. Perhaps teachers and librarians find it more and more difficult to justify reading aloud to middle grade students in the face of standards and the increased push to perform well on local, state, and national measures. Then there's parental pressure. Reading aloud is often seen as a practice associated with younger students and primary grades. Teachers and librarians hesitate to read aloud novels, let alone introduce picture books, to middle graders because they are concerned about how administrators, colleagues, and parents, as well as students, might react. Is it time put to good use?

If a teacher or librarian who loves books and loves to read and share the wonders found between the covers of books firmly believes in the value of reading aloud to middle graders and is able to enumerate its merits , then justifying it to parents and administrators becomes easier. Winning over the children is a piece of cake. There are novels, nonfiction books, and short stories that students will beg you to keep on reading once you get started. And you will be amazed at how riveted fourth graders will be to the array of outstanding picture books written especially for older children that have graced bookshelves in the last few years.

So put these pointers in your pocket. Have them ready like a six-shooter to pull out when you need ammunition to support what you're doing and how you're satisfying all those goals and checklists placed before you on the first day of school. You are a reader, and if you instill a love of books in your middle graders, you will have passed on a legacy that will serve them well throughout their lives. And that ought to be at the tippy top of any list of professional objectives.

## WHY READING ALOUD TO MIDDLE GRADERS IS WORTHWHILE

Reading aloud to children is teaching. As you progress through a book using a read-aloud plan such as those found in this resource, you develop key skills in listeners. These skills are fundamental and the learning is nonthreatening. During the read-aloud session you build on the child's previous knowledge and expand his or her experiential knowledge (see the Prereading step in the read-aloud plans in the first part of this resource). When discussing a character's motives or an author's choice of names for characters, or when predicting what might happen next after a story is finished, there is no correct answer, but thinking skills are sharpened nonetheless. Beyond developing an appreciation for literature, the skills learned during read-aloud sessions include

- active listening;

- visualizing;

- answering questions on a continuum of levels from straightforward and literal to interpretive and critical;

- making predictions;

- thinking in new ways;

- speaking;

- interacting appropriately with peers;

- writing (see the Write Away! suggestions in the read-aloud plans in the first part of this resource);

- developing various discussion techniques;

- increasing listening, speaking, reading, and writing vocabularies;

- broadening interests;

- building concepts; and

- becoming familiar with a variety of genres and viewpoints.

As you pause to question, comment, or engage in a short discussion (see the While Reading step in the read-aloud plans in the first part of this resource); when you use the Write Away! suggestions; and when you share the Up Close and Personal notes from authors and illustrators or visit their Web sites, you are developing sustaining connections to books, to those who create them, and to each other. You extend into other curriculum arenas (see the Follow-up step in the read-aloud plans in the first part of this resource) when you engage in activities that relate the book and its theme to other strands in the curriculum. When you read aloud to your students you are developing valuable cumulative skills and shaping lifelong critical readers.

For students, the read-aloud experience is, as Mary Lee Hahn suggests in RECONSIDERING READ-ALOUD (Stenhouse), "learning without trying." It is teaching at its best.

# Reading Aloud to Middle Graders

## FROM THEORY TO PRACTICE

Teachable moments abound during read-aloud sessions. As you handle the book, read with expression, laugh out loud, or well up with emotion, you are modeling reading behaviors and demonstrating the power of the written word.

### Choosing What to Read Aloud

Choose books that are outstanding examples of literature. This is your chance to introduce children to the filet mignon or portobello mushrooms of books. Refer to the list of Web sites later in this section for handy references to award winners. Choose old nuggets that have withstood the test of time as well as new books that blaze trails. Read short stories (see suggestions listed later in this section), newspapers, and magazine articles. Build poetry pauses into every school day. (See the list of resources found elsewhere in this section.)

As you introduce historical fiction, fantasy, biography, and nonfiction books, you enrich your students' knowledge of and familiarity with the breadth of books available to them and give them a perspective on other cultures, other times, feelings, ethics, morals, and the strength of the human spirit. You enable children to visit other nations, see through a different set of eyes, and walk awhile in another's shoes. By choosing to read aloud books that enhance and extend your curriculum, you deepen students' understanding of key concepts and of themselves while developing and nurturing an interest in reading.

Know your students, their needs, their abilities, and their interests. Consider your curriculum and your long-range objectives. Also take into account the subject matter of the book. Be sure that it is suitable and age appropriate for your class or group. You must know a book in its entirety before choosing it as a read-aloud for your students.

### Strategies for Reading Aloud

Preview every book you intend to read aloud. Read it from cover to cover so you are confident that there is nothing in the book that is objectionable to you or may be unsuitable for your students. By reading the book first before presenting it, you will have an understanding of the overarching themes in the book, you will be able to decide on discussion points and pacing of the read-aloud, and you will be able to best fit the book into your overall teaching plan.

Begin read-alouds the first day of school. Establish a tradition and set expectations. Your behavior will give students the message that this is a place where books are honored and cherished; here is a teacher who loves to read. This place is a haven for those who love books and a nurturing environment for those who are reticent readers.

As you follow the read-aloud plans provided in this resource, note the three steps consistent in all of them. Preview the book with the children. With chapter books, review what happened in the last chapter as a warm-up to each subsequent read-aloud session. Build on prior knowledge and make predictions before reading. Keep the pre-reading segment short. Read with expression. Note vocabulary that is tough as you read through the text. Use context. Question or comment throughout the read-aloud, but do so judiciously. Don't lose the thread or momentum of the story. In the follow-up to fiction, consider the story elements, the author's techniques, the pacing of the story or book. In nonfiction, discuss the author's point of view, delve into his or her "expert" status, and consider the angle and what facts were/were not presented.

For additional read-aloud techniques, refer to the Parent Pull-Out Pages.

## Where to Read Aloud

Read-aloud sessions ought to take place in the most inviting space in the room. Consider gathering students around you rather than having them sit at their desks, if this is feasible.

## When to Read Aloud

Each and every day there are myriad opportunities to bring children and the written word together. Read to the group as part of your opening exercises. This offers a calming, focusing, affirming activity with which to start the day. Upon the conclusion of a difficult lesson that stretches your students' brain power, read a poem, a joke, or a riddle. For wonderful selections on all sorts of topics, see the "poetry pause" anthologies and collections listed in this section. Following lunch, read a news clipping or magazine article to reconnect your students to the classroom setting. Choose a specific time of the day that suits you to read daily from a great chapter book, such as those suggested in the read-aloud plans and in this section, and finally, strive to read aloud something every day that connects to curricular study. See the Book Notes section of this resource for suggestions cross-referenced by subject. End the day on a literary note by reading something warm and fuzzy or lighthearted and whimsical that will attract your students to ink on paper. Send them out the door eager to hear more tomorrow.

# Reading Aloud to Independent Readers

## PICTURE BOOKS FOR THE MIDDLE ELEMENTARY GRADES

Just as cartoons aren't only for kids, picture books aren't only for those fresh out of diapers.

In fact, there are shelves full of thought-provoking, complex tales and meaty nonfiction written for older children that also happen to be lushly illustrated. Picture books for older elementary students feature longer text, elaborate story lines, and heavier concept loads. Although illustrated, the text could stand alone, which distinguishes these books from those written primarily for the primaries, in which the text and illustrations are absolutely and justifiably dependent upon one another. Picture books aren't meant to be a steady diet for older children, but there's no question that they're deliciously appealing.

So enhance, enrich, and extend curricular study with selected picture books related to the theme of the unit. In 15 minutes or less, you can deepen understanding of a concept. And because well-executed picture books engage multiple senses, they make even the driest subject appealing. How can you resist a clearly drawn map in full color, an illustrated timeline of the Renaissance Period, or a jaunty portrayal of a character in history? And when the class needs a laugh to lighten a difficult situation, what's better than an uproarious picture book? The best of illustrated books make classroom study lively, accessible, and memorable. Lucky for kids, and lucky for adults who will have their audience snug in their hand from page one. It's a win-win situation.

Invest 15 minutes. Indulge your students' senses; tempt them with a luscious treat that's certain to make a tough subject easier to digest. Sit back, gather your listeners in, and clinch that concept with a picture book!

*In addition to the Read-Aloud Plans, see the Book Notes section of this resource for scores of books suitable for reading aloud to middle grade students, conveniently listed by subject according to content area themes. Subjects, titles, authors, and illustrators are also listed in the indexes found at the back of this resource.*

# Poetry Pauses

## GOT A MINUTE? GRAB A POEM!

If you remember poems as those dreaded eight lines you had to memorize, or if the word *poetry* conjures up Middle English and obscure, convoluted phrasing, stop gritting your teeth long enough to browse through the lighthearted, effervescent, and palatable offerings on today's poetry shelves. Fun, frivolity, rhythm, rhyme, and best of all, *connections* are in store for you and your listeners (not to mention imaginative, expansive, enlightening illustrations).

Take a minute now and then throughout the day to spark the energy of your students with these wonderful word packages. Yep, that's all you need: one minute or less once you have your favorites marked in the poetry books you shelve in a handy location. Browse the collections, choose your favorites, mark them according to subject, and then delight your students with **poetry pauses**. Pause throughout the day, week, month, and year when the children least expect it, when they've come to anticipate it, when they need a break to get them back in the mood to learn, or for closure on a topic. And don't forget those times when you need a poetry pause to restore your own flagging vigor. Recite a gem and you'll be snapping your fingers and tapping your toes in no time—in a minute or less, in fact.

### Recommended Poetry Anthologies and Collections

- LUNCH BOX MAIL AND OTHER POEMS by Jenny Whitehead (Holt); playful, lighthearted poems about myriad childhood experiences, from "I Loth My Tooth" to "Daddy's Spaghetti," these verses are easy to digest.

- LUNCH MONEY AND OTHER POEMS ABOUT SCHOOL, written by Carol Diggory Shields and illustrated by Paul Meisel (Dutton). From running to catch the bus and searching the house for lunch money to walking home from school, these are happy-go-lucky, humorous, and upbeat verses. My favorite is "Book Report," on the last page.

- LAUGH-ETERIA, poems and drawings by Douglas Florian (Penguin); delightfully catchy poems with lighthearted black and white drawings on subjects ranging from "Tragic Magic" to "Ogre Argument."

- ALMOST LATE TO SCHOOL AND MORE SCHOOL POEMS, written by Carol Diggory Shields and illustrated by Paul Meisel (Dutton). Lighthearted poems reflect on the "First Day," "Almost Late," "Gotta Go" (and we're talking wiggly, jiggling, crossed legs here), and much more that's all in a day's work at school.

- POCKET POEMS, selected by Bobbi Katz and illustrated by Marylin Hafner (Dutton); short delights.

*Cover from LUNCH BOX MAIL AND OTHER POEMS written and illustrated by Jenny Whitehead. Copyright © 2001. Reprinted with permission of Henry Holt Books for Young Readers.*

- NO MORE HOMEWORK! NO MORE TESTS! KIDS FAVORITE FUNNY SCHOOL POEMS, selected by Bruce Lansky and illustrated by Stephen Carpenter (Meadowbrook).

- KIDS PICK THE FUNNIEST POEMS: POEMS THAT MAKE KIDS LAUGH, selected by Bruce Lansky and illustrated by Stephen Carpenter (Meadowbrook).

- A PIZZA THE SIZE OF THE SUN, poems by Jack Prelutsky and illustrated by James Stevenson (Greenwillow).

- THE NEW KID ON THE BLOCK, poems by Jack Prelutsky and illustrated by James Stevenson (Greenwillow).

- SOMETHING BIG HAS BEEN HERE, poems by Jack Prelutsky and illustrated by James Stevenson (Greenwillow).

- GOOD BOOKS, GOOD TIMES!, selected by Lee Bennett Hopkins and illustrated by Harvey Stevenson (HarperCollins); poems that celebrate books.

- JOYFUL NOISE: POEMS FOR TWO VOICES, written by Paul Fleischman and illustrated by Eric Beddows (HarperCollins); poems for two to read aloud together; Newbery Medal winner.

- BIG TALK: POEMS FOR FOUR VOICES, written by Paul Fleischman and illustrated by Beppe Giacobbe (Candlewick); snappy poems for four or more to read aloud together; be sure to read the hints on "how to read this book" for utmost enjoyment.

- I LIKE BEING ME: POEMS FOR CHILDREN ABOUT FEELING SPECIAL, APPRECIATING OTHERS, AND GETTING ALONG, written by Judy Lalli with photographs by Douglas L. Mason-Fry (Free Spirit).

- DIRTY LAUNDRY PILE: POEMS IN DIFFERENT VOICES, selected by Paul B. Janeczko and illustrated by Melissa Sweet (Greenwillow). Animals and inanimate objects tell it like it is from their perspective, everything from a vacuum cleaner to a mosquito—and of course, the dirty laundry pile.

- I INVITED A DRAGON TO DINNER AND OTHER POEMS TO MAKE YOU LAUGH OUT LOUD, illustrated by Chris L. Demarest (Philomel); hilarious collection by a variety of poets.

- THE FROGS WORE RED SUSPENDERS, rhymes by Jack Prelutsky and illustrated by Petra Mathers (Greenwillow); zippy, zany poems and pictures about people and animals in places and spaces from here to there all over the world: from Minneapolis to Indianapolis, from the store to the pudding vat. Now how can you not laugh at that?

- TAKE SKY, written by David McCord and illustrated by Henry B. Kane (Little, Brown); a collection of 48 poems on everyday subjects such as a "Spelling Bee" and "The Importance of Eggs."

*Cover from NONSENSE! By Edward Lear, illustrated by Valorie Fisher. Copyright © 2004. Used with permission of Anne Schwartz Books/Atheneum Books for Young Readers, an imprint of Simon & Schuster Children's Publishing.*

- SING A SONG OF POPCORN: EVERY CHILD'S BOOK OF POEMS, selected by Beatrice Schenk de Regniers, Eva Moore, Mary Michaels White, and Jane Carr and illustrated by nine Caldecott Medal artists (Scholastic); in memory of Arnold Lobel.

- WHERE THE SIDEWALK ENDS, by Shel Silverstein (HarperCollins); zany, zippy, crazy fun, but thoughtful, too. A must-have collection.

- A LIGHT IN THE ATTIC, by Shel Silverstein (HarperCollins); more by the prince of poetry for children.

- LEWIS CARROLL'S JABBERWOCKY, illustrated by Jane Breskin Zalben with Annotations by Humpty Dumpty (Boyds Mills Press). Originally published in 1872 as part of THROUGH THE LOOKING GLASS AND WHAT ALICE FOUND THERE, the poem is imaginatively illustrated in this edition.

- NONSENSE!, written by Edward Lear and illustrated by Valorie Fisher (Atheneum); pure nonsense, pure rhythmical fun brought to you in a bright and jaunty picture book.

- A SWINGER OF BIRCHES: POEMS OF ROBERT FROST FOR YOUNG PEOPLE, illustrated by Peter Koeppen (Stemmer House).

- POETRY FOR YOUNG PEOPLE: RUDYARD KIPLING, edited by Eileen Gillooly and illustrated by Jim Sharpe (Sterling).

- POETRY FOR YOUNG PEOPLE: CARL SANDBURG, edited by Frances Schoonmaker Bolin and illustrated by Steven Arcella (Sterling).

- POETRY FOR YOUNG PEOPLE: LEWIS CARROLL, edited by Edward Mendelson and illustrated by Eric Copeland (Sterling).

- POETRY FOR YOUNG PEOPLE: EMILY DICKINSON, edited by Frances Schoonmaker Bolin and illustrated by Chi Chung (Sterling).

- POETRY FOR YOUNG PEOPLE: ROBERT BROWNING, edited by Eileen Gillooly and illustrated by Joel Spector (Sterling).

- OLD ELM SPEAKS: TREE POEMS, written by Kristine O'Connell George and illustrated by Kate Kiesler (Clarion); visually appealing in both words and text.

- FIREFLIES AT MIDNIGHT, written by Marilyn Singer and illustrated by Ken Robbins (Atheneum). Profiles of everyday, summery creatures told from their point of view include the otter, monarch, bat, red fox, horse, and spider. Delightful word play. Use as part of a more in-depth unit of study on animals.

- IF NOT FOR THE CAT, haiku by Jack Prelutsky and illustrated by Ted Rand (Greenwillow); a Parents' Choice Gold Award winner; see the read-aloud plan elsewhere in this resource.

- A CIRCLE OF SEASONS, written by Myra Cohn Livingston and illustrated by Leonard Everett Fisher (Holiday House). See also SKY SONGS, EARTH SONGS, SEA SONGS, and SPACE SONGS by this incredible team (Holiday House).

Cover from *OLD ELM SPEAKS: TREE POEMS by Kristine O'Connell George. Jacket illustrations copyright © 1998 by Kate Kiesler. Reprinted by permission of Clarion Books/Houghton Mifflin Company. All rights reserved.*

Cover from *TOASTING MARSHMALLOWS: CAMPING POEMS by Kristine O'Connell George. Jacket illustrations copyright © 2001 by Kate Kiesler. Reprinted by permission of Clarion Books/Houghton Mifflin Company. All rights reserved.*

- CREATURES OF EARTH, SEA, AND SKY, poems by Georgia Heard and illustrations by Jennifer Owings Dewey (Boyds Mills Press).

- THE REASON FOR THE PELICAN, written by John Ciardi and illustrated by Dominic Catalano (Boyds Mills Press); "35th Anniversary Edition" of this first book of poetry by a Hall-of-Famer among the best and finest poets for children.

- ANIMALS ANIMALS, selected and illustrated by Eric Carle (Philomel); a thick volume of poems about animals from the ant to the yak, richly illustrated by the master of collage.

- SCRANIMALS, poems by Jack Prelutsky and illustrated by Peter Sis (Greenwillow). This duo collaborates with successful results. These poems focus on scrambled animals and veggies: perfect fare for this age group. Sample "sweet porcupineapple/unflappable chap" and the "detested radishark" and more beastly creatures on Scranimal Island.

- TOASTING MARSHMALLOWS: CAMPING POEMS, written by Kristine O'Connell George and illustrated by Kate Kiesler (Clarion); from pitching the tent to pulling up stakes, the memorable adventures experienced when a family goes camping.

- DEAR WORLD, by Takayo Noda (Dial); Pause to celebrate details of our everyday world, from "dear snow" to "dear car," with these spare poems accompanied by bright, engaging, cut-paper collages. Perfect pauses.

- IF I WERE IN CHARGE OF THE WORLD AND OTHER WORRIES, written by Judith Viorst and illustrated by Lynne Cherry (Aladdin). Subjects of the poems range from "Wishes and Worries" to "Facts of Life" to "Thanks and No Thanks." One of my favorites is the one in which Cinderella takes a closer look at the prince and decides, "I think I'll just pretend that this glass slipper feels too tight."

- LET THERE BE LIGHT: POEMS AND PRAYERS FOR REPAIRING THE WORLD, compiled and illustrated by Jane Breskin Zalben (Dutton). Representing a cross section of faiths, these poems illustrated with collages offer hope and comfort.

- MY AMERICA: A POETRY ATLAS OF THE UNITED STATES, selected by Lee Bennett Hopkins and illustrated by Stephen Alcorn (Simon & Schuster). Outstanding illustrations accompany the work of well-known poets as well as newcomers.

- TALKING DRUMS: A SELECTION OF POEMS FROM AFRICA SOUTH OF THE SAHARA, edited by Veronique Tadjo (Bloomsbury); traces African history in stories in verse, arranged in chapters from the Animal Kingdom and People to Pride and Defiance. Some of the poems, such as "Friendship," transcend cultures to speak universally on common themes.

- NOT A COPPER PENNY IN ME HOUSE: POEMS FROM THE CARIBBEAN, written by Monica Gunning and illustrated by Frane Lessac (Boyds Mills Press); lyrical portrayal of a girl's life.

*Cover from MY AMERICA: A POETRY ATLAS OF THE UNITED STATES selected by Lee Bennett Hopkins, illustrated by Stephen Alcom. Copyright © 2000. Used with permission of Simon & Schuster Books for Young Readers, an imprint of Simon & Schuster Children's Publishing.*

- AMBER WAS BRAVE, ESSIE WAS SMART: THE STORY OF AMBER AND ESSIE TOLD HERE IN POEMS AND PICTURES, by Vera B. Williams (Greenwillow); a story of two sisters facing life's ups and downs together. The sadly realistic, touching, funny, sobering, award-winning tale of two sisters told in free verse.

- FATHERS, MOTHERS, SISTERS, BROTHERS: A COLLECTION OF FAMILY POEMS, written by Mary Ann Hoberman and illustrated by Marylin Hafner (Penguin).

- AUTUMNBLINGS, by Douglas Florian (Greenwillow). Wonderful word play celebrates the season.

- SUMMERSAULTS, by Douglas Florian (Greenwillow); see description above.

- WINTER EYES, by Douglas Florian (Greenwillow); another of the seasonal collections.

- WINTER POEMS, selected by Barbara Rogasky and illustrated by Trina Schart Hyman (Scholastic). Twenty-five poems from Shakespeare and Sandburg to haiku celebrate the season.

- PIECES A YEAR IN POEMS & QUILTS, by Anna Grossnickle Hines (HarperCollins); poems illustrated with quilts; includes an afterword on the story behind the making of the quilts.

- IT'S VALENTINE'S DAY, poems by Jack Prelutsky and illustrated by Yossi Abolafia (HarperCollins); silly, laugh-out-loud fun; a nonfattening treat for this holiday.

- MY BOOK OF FUNNY VALENTINES, written by Margo Lundell and illustrated by Nate Evans (Scholastic); silly fun.

- EASTER BUDS ARE SPRINGING POEMS FOR EASTER, selected by Lee Bennett Hopkins and illustrated by Tomie dePaola (Boyds Mills Press).

- THE ICE CREAM STORE, written by Dennis Lee and illustrated by David McPhail (HarperCollins). Take a sweet trip with the kids to an ice cream store!

- ANNA'S GARDEN SONGS, poems by Mary Q. Steele and illustrated by Lena Anderson (HarperCollins).

- ANNA'S SUMMER SONGS, poems by Mary Q. Steele and illustrated by Lena Anderson (HarperCollins).

- IT'S HALLOWEEN, poems by Jack Prelutsky and illustrated by Marylin Hafner (HarperCollins); no horror, just humor.

- HIST WHIST, written by e. e. cummings and illustrated by Deborah Kogan Ray (Crown); exquisitely illustrated.

- LITTLE TREE, written by e. e. cummings and illustrated by Deborah Kogan Ray (Crown); a Christmas poem illustrated with dreamy paintings.

- IT'S CHRISTMAS, poems by Jack Prelutsky and illustrated by Marylin Hafner (Greenwillow); silly fun, re-readable.

- FESTIVALS, poems by Myra Cohn Livingston and illustrated by Leonard Everett Fisher (Holiday House); a collection of poems on an array of festivals celebrated by people of different faiths and cultures.

- WHEN I HEARD THE LEARN'D ASTRONOMER, written by Walt Whitman illustrated by Loren Long (Simon & Schuster). A boy's fascination with the stars goes beyond the hallowed walls of the lecture hall. Youthful, simple wonder is celebrated both in the words of this poem from LEAVES OF GRASS and in the lush illustrations that make it accessible to young children; a Parents' Choice Gold Award winner. See also the biography, WALT WHITMAN: WORDS FOR AMERICA, written by Barbara Kerley and illustrated by Brain Selznick (Scholastic).

*Cover from WHEN I HEARD THE LEARN'D ASTRONOMER by Walt Whitman, illustrated by Loren Long. Copyright © 2004. Used with permission of Simon & Schuster Books for Young Readers, an imprint of Simon & Schuster Children's Publishing.*

- PAUL REVERE'S RIDE, written by Henry Wadsworth Longfellow and illustrated by Ted Rand (Dutton). This picture book illustrates the moonlit journey that was immortalized by this epic poem, told in its entirety here.

- STOPPING BY WOODS ON A SNOWY EVENING, written by Robert Frost and illustrated by Susan Jeffers (Dutton); a picture book presentation of the well-loved poem.

- SCIENCE VERSE, written by Jon Scieszka and illustrated by Lane Smith (Penguin); wacky poems about topics in science that are take-offs on well-known poems; see the read-aloud plan elsewhere in this resource.

- HERE'S WHAT YOU DO WHEN YOU CAN'T FIND YOUR SHOE (INGENIOUS INVENTIONS FOR PESKY PROBLEMS), written by Andrea Perry and illustrated by Alan Snow (Atheneum); zany suggestions for useful inventions; see the read-aloud plan in *Children's Book Corner, Grades 1–2.*

- MARVELOUS MATH: A BOOK OF POEMS, selected by Lee Bennett Hopkins and illustrated by Karen Barbour (Aladdin).

- MATHEMATICKLES!, poems by Betsy Franco and illustrated by Steven Salerno (McElderry); lyrical language + simple math = fun!; visually and auditorally appealing.

*Cover from HERE'S WHAT YOU DO WHEN YOU CAN'T FIND YOUR SHOE (INGENIOUS INVENTIONS FOR PESKY PROBLEMS) by Andrea Perry, illustrated by Alan Snow. Copyright © 2003. Used with permission of Atheneum Books for Young Readers, an imprint of Simon & Schuster Children's Publishing.*

*Cover from MATHEMATICKLES! by Betsy Franco, illustrated by Steven Salerno.*
*Copyright © 2003. Used with permission of Margaret K. McElderry Books,*
*an imprint of Simon & Schuster Children's Publishing.*

See also the following how-to guides:

- HOW TO WRITE POETRY, by Paul Janeczko (Scholastic).

- POETRY FROM A TO Z: A GUIDE FOR YOUNG WRITERS, compiled by Paul Janeczko (Simon & Schuster).

- POETRY MATTERS: WRITING A POEM FROM THE INSIDE OUT, by Ralph Fletcher (HarperCollins).

- POEM-MAKING: WAYS TO BEGIN WRITING POETRY, by Myra Cohn Livingston (HarperCollins).

A useful reference for teachers and librarians:

- PASS THE POETRY, PLEASE! 3rd edition, by Lee Bennett Hopkins (HarperCollins).

# Chapter Books for Growing Readers

**NOURISH, ENCOURAGE, AND REINFORCE READING SKILLS WITH CHAPTER BOOKS: THE BUILDING BLOCKS OF THE MIDDLE GRADES**

Sad to say, not all kids love to read. Although this surely is not news, some of the titles listed below may be. Here is a collection of some of the best chapter books around. These gems not only will attract those kids who love print on paper, they will also snag uninterested readers. Show reluctant readers the wonders that lie between the covers, and they may just find they like it there. To capture student interest, consider reading aloud the first few paragraphs, a page, or the first chapter of the book. I guarantee young readers will take over from there. Be ready. You'll want to have this list handy when students come begging for more.

The books listed here vary in reading levels and reflect interests spanning the third and fourth grades. However, as individual needs and interests vary, it is imperative that teachers and librarians choose and recommend titles accordingly. Standards, programs, children, and personal needs are widely divergent, and there is a vast difference between and among third and fourth graders within classrooms and across the nation. Use professional judgment; know the books you recommend.

*Books are listed in descending order of reading difficulty for each category.*

## Single Titles

**DEAR MR. HENSHAW:** Written by Beverly Cleary and illustrated by Paul O. Zelinsky; (HarperCollins); Newbery Award winner about a boy navigating his parents' divorce through the letters he writes, real and imaginary, to an author. Upper fourth-grade reading level.

**STONE FOX:** Written by John Reynold Gardiner and illustrated by Greg Hargreaves; (HarperCollins); poignant story about a boy and his loyal sled dog. Fourth-grade reading level.

**CHARLOTTE'S WEB:** The classic written by E. B. White and illustrated by Garth Williams (HarperCollins). Fourth-grade reading level.

**SHILOH:** Written by Phyllis Reynolds Naylor (Atheneum), Newbery Medal winner about a boy who cares for an abused dog; life lessons and ethical issues abound. Fourth-grade reading level.

**BRIDGE TO TERABITHIA:** Written by Katherine Paterson and illustrated by Donna Diamond (HarperCollins), death of a friend; numerous awards including the Newbery Medal. Fourth-grade reading level.

**FLIP-FLOP GIRL:** Written by Katherine Paterson (Penguin), an ALA Notable book about a girl and her adjustment to a new life when she moves in with her Grandma after the death of her father. Fourth-grade reading level.

**STORIES FROM WAYSIDE SCHOOL:** By Louis Sachar (HarperCollins). Hilarious, interrelated short stories about one very weird and wacky school. See also related titles including SIDEWAYS ARITHMETIC FROM WAYSIDE SCHOOL (Scholastic). Fourth-grade reading level.

**TALES OF A FOURTH GRADE NOTHING:** By well-known author, Judy Blume (Dutton). See also DOUBLE FUDGE, FUDGE-A-MANIA, and OTHERWISE KNOWN AS SHEILA THE GREAT. Fourth-grade reading level.

**DEAR MRS. RYAN, YOU'RE RUINING MY LIFE:** Written by Jennifer B. Jones (Walker). Mom's a recently divorced writer; Dad's a pro at baseball and sometimes shows up for his son's games. Add a neighborhood bully and a spunky best friend, and you've got a funny and warmhearted story. Fourth-grade reading level.

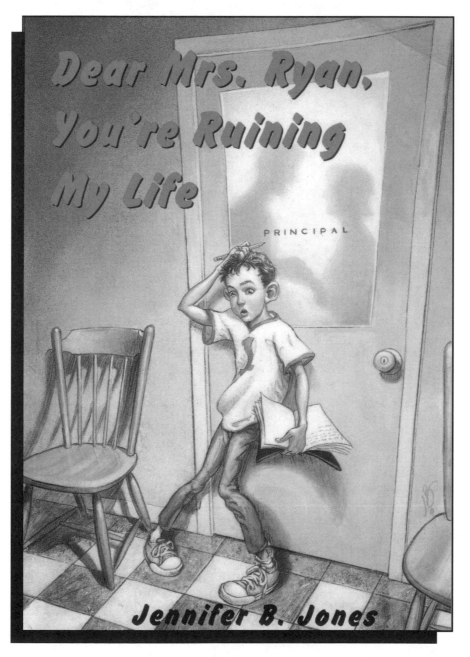

*Cover from DEAR MRS. RYAN, YOU'RE RUINING MY LIFE by Jennifer B. Jones.
Copyright © 2000. Cover published by arrangement with Walker & Co.*

*Cover of JACK ADRIFT: FOUTH GRADE WITHOUT A CLUE © 2004 by Jack Gantos. Cover art © 2004 by Beata Szpura. Used with the permission of Farrar Straus Giroux.*

**JACK ADRIFT: FOURTH GRADE WITHOUT A CLUE:** Written by the popular and oh-so-funny award-winning author Jack Gantos (Farrar, Straus &Giroux), who is known best for his Joey Pigza and Rotten Ralph books. Fourth-grade reading level.

**OPHIE OUT OF OZ:** Written by Kathleen O'Dell (Dial). The story of a 12-year-old who moves from glamorous California to plain old Oregon and must find her way among the TV Girls, the weird girls, and the principal, who understands just how important Dorothy shoes are, even if they don't fit anymore. Other titles by this author include AGNES PARKER, GIRL IN PROGRESS, and its sequel, AGNES PARKER . . . HAPPY CAMPER? Fourth-grade reading level.

**THE BRAVEST THING:** Laurel adopts a rabbit and learns life lessons in this touching story by Donna Jo Napoli (Penguin). Fourth-grade reading level.

**SARAH, PLAIN AND TALL:** Written by Patricia MacLachlan (HarperCollins); courage, pluck, and wisdom packed into a hugely entertaining slim novel about a mail-order bride who comes to live with a family on the prairie; Newbery Award. See also the sequel, SKYLARK. Fourth-grade reading level.

**SKINNYBONES:** Written by Barbara Park (Knopf). A small kid with a big mouth and lots of attitude is not so great at sports but oh-so-great at getting out of tough spots. Fourth-grade reading level.

**MR. MYSTERIOUS & COMPANY:** Written by Sid Fleischman and illustrated by Eric von Schmidt (Greenwillow). There's magic and wizardry on the ride out west. Look out! Fourth-grade reading level.

**THE KITE FIGHTERS:** Written by Linda Sue Park (Clarion). A boy in fifteenth-century Korea competes in the New Year kite competition. Fourth-grade reading level.

**CABIN ON TROUBLE CREEK:** Written by Jean Van Leeuwen (Dial). Two brothers face danger in the wilderness in 1803. Fourth-grade reading level.

**THE SIGN OF THE BEAVER:** Written by Elizabeth George Speare (Houghton Mifflin). Matt guards the home site in eighteenth-century Maine; Newbery Honor Medal. Fourth-grade reading level.

**THE COURAGE OF SARAH NOBLE:** Written by Alice Dalgliesh (Atheneum); set in the wilds of Connecticut; Sarah relies on pluck and her mother's advice in this true story. Fourth-grade reading level.

**THE MATCHLOCK GUN:** Written by Walter Edmonds (Putnam). It's 1756, in the midst of the French and Indian War, and Edward must protect his home; Newbery Medal. Fourth-grade reading level.

**RED DOG:** Written by Bill Wallace (Holiday House). Wyoming, wilderness, a boy, his dog, and three nasty gold prospectors make for adventure. Fourth-grade reading level.

**POCAHONTAS AND THE STRANGERS:** Written by Clyde Robert Bulla (HarperCollins); a Best Books for Children biography of the Indian princess who helped the settlers. Fourth-grade reading level.

**THE DOUBLE LIFE OF POCAHONTAS:** This book, written by Jean Fritz (Penguin), has won multiple awards. Fourth-grade reading level.

**PEDRO'S JOURNAL: A VOYAGE WITH CHRISTOPHER COLUMBUS:** Written by Pam Conrad and illustrated by Peter Koeppen (Boyds Mills Press); a fictional story in journal style about what the trip might have been like, told from a cabin boy's point of view. Fourth-grade reading level.

**POLLYANNA:** Written by Eleanor H. Porter (Bantam Doubleday Dell); classic novel about a young girl with spunk and spirit who makes a difference. Fourth-grade reading level.

**PIPPI LONGSTOCKING:** Written by Astrid Lindgren and illustrated by Nancy Seligsohn (Viking). This lively redhead has been making friends for generations. See also PIPPI GOES ON BOARD. Fourth-grade reading level.

**STUART LITTLE:** Written by E. B. White and illustrated by Garth Williams (HarperCollins); the classic mouse tale; better than the movie! Fourth-grade reading level.

**THE FOURTH GRADE WIZARDS:** Written by Barthe DeClements (Viking); recovering from the loss of a mom in the midst of life as a fourth grader. Fourth-grade reading level.

**THREE TERRIBLE TRINS:** One of Dick King-Smith's wonderful fantasies, illustrated by Mark Teague (Crown); about a family of mice. Fourth-grade reading level.

**NO DOGS ALLOWED!:** Written by Bill Wallace (Holiday House). A girl who loses her horse learns to love again. Fourth-grade reading level.

**THE DOUBLE-DIGIT CLUB:** Written by Marion Dane Bauer (Holiday House).Turning 10 years old means being invited to be part of Valerie's exclusive club. When Paige gets asked she joins, leaving the narrator, her controlling best friend, who won't be 10 for two months, out in the cold for the summer. How Sarah grows is the crux of this coming-of-age story for girls. Fourth-grade reading level.

**THE CONFE$$ION$ AND $ECRET$ OF HOWARD J. FINGERHUT:** Written by Esther Hershenhorn and illustrated by Ethan Long (Holiday House).This humorous and clever novel is a "how-to" written by the main character, who details his travails and eventual successes at running a business and winning the fourth-grade yearlong contest (sort of). It's that last part that will keep students reading the monthly installments through June. Upper third-, beginning fourth-grade reading level.

**THE BIRCHBARK HOUSE:** By Louise Erdrich (Hyperion); award-winning book about pioneer settlement, as seen through the eyes of a Native American girl. Contrast to LITTLE HOUSE ON THE PRAIRIE, by Laura Ingalls Wilder. Fourth-grade reading level.

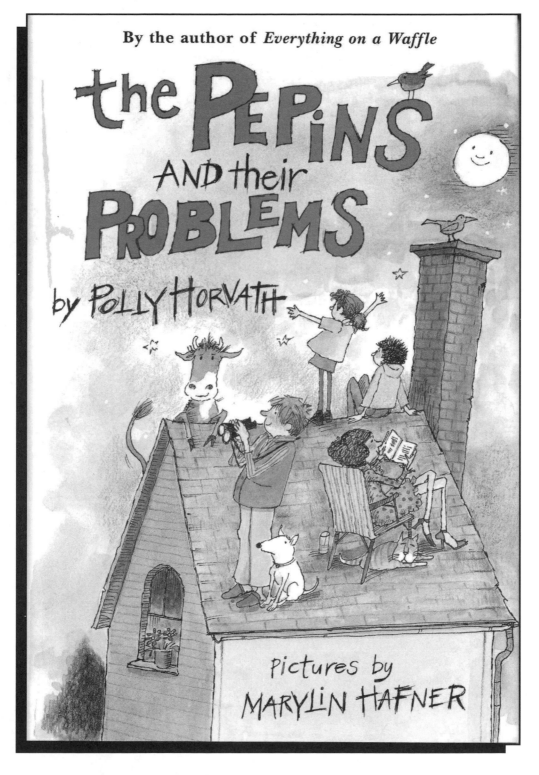

*Cover of THE PEPINS AND THEIR PROBLEMS © 2004 by Polly Horvath. Cover art © 2004 by Marylin Hafner. Used with the permission of Farrar Straus Giroux.*

*Cover from THE DOUBLE-DIGIT CLUB by Marion Dane Bauer. Copyright © 2004.*
*Reprinted with permission of Holiday House.*

*Cover from THE CONFE$$IONS AND $ECRET$ OF HOWARD J. FINGERHUT by Esther Hershenhorn. Illustrated by Ethan Long. Copyright © 2002. Reprinted with permission of Holiday House.*

**THE PEPINS AND THEIR PROBLEMS:** Written by Newbery Honor and National Book Award finalist, Polly Horvath, and illustrated by Marylin Hafner (Farrar, Straus & Giroux). In this fanciful story of the endearing Pepins, the author uses her "powers" to get suggestions from readers all over the country to help the hapless Pepins solve all sorts of problems, from toads in their shoes to finding eating utensils. Fourth-grade reading level.

**THE FISH IN ROOM 11:** Written by Heather Dyer (Scholastic). This delightful fantasy is reminiscent of those feel-good, kind triumphs over nasty stories we all loved to read as kids. Upper third-, beginning fourth-grade reading level.

**FOURTH-GRADE FUSS:** You can't beat Johanna Hurwitz for nailing kids' actions and their concerns at a variety of elementary school ages. This one is just right for middle graders. Illustrated by Andy Hammond (HarperCollins). Third- to fourth-grade reading level.

**THE SCHOOL MOUSE:** A fantasy by Dick King-Smith of BABE: THE GALLANT PIG fame about a school mouse who learns to read and uses it to save her family. Illustrated by Cynthia Fisher (Hyperion). Upper third-, fourth-grade reading level.

*THE TRANSMOGRIFICATION OF ROSCOE WIZZLE. Jacket Illustration Copyright ©
2001 Vladimir Radunsky. Text Copyright © 2001 David Elliot. Reproduced by permission of the publisher Candlewick Press, Inc., Cambridge, MA.*

**THE TRANSMOGRIFICATION OF ROSCOE WIZZLE:** By David Elliott (Candlewick); boy becomes bug in this light and funny mystery/fantasy. Upper third-, beginning fourth-grade reading level.

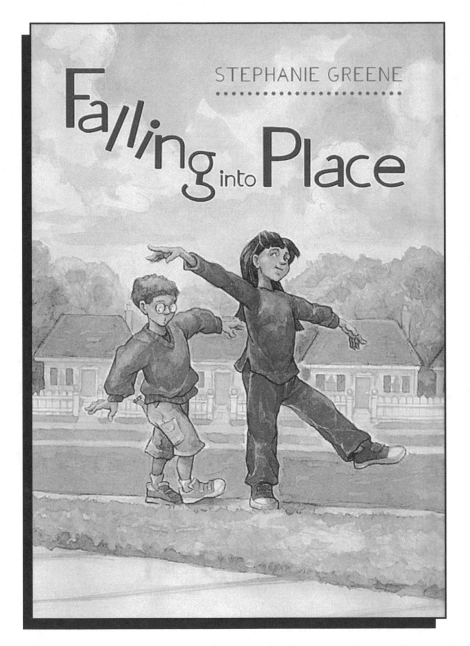

*Cover from FALLING INTO PLACE by Stephanie Greene. Jacket illustrations copyright © 2002 by Timothy Bush. Reprinted by permission of Clarion Books/Houghton Mifflin Company. All rights reserved.*

**FALLING INTO PLACE:** By Stephanie Greene (Clarion). This is the book for any reader who finds himself or herself part of a blended family. Not that this is the only problem the main character has. But Margaret is tough, just like her grandmother was, until, that is, her husband died. Then there's the nerdy cousin, Roy, and all the rules at Gram's new retirement community to cope with. How Margaret pulls it all together, despite Roy, is as unforgettable as the cast of characters who live behind the doors at Carol Woods: doors that can't be painted any color but black. Don't worry, Gram changes that by the end, right before the karaoke party. Upper third-grade reading level.

**THE BEST CHRISTMAS PAGEANT EVER:** Written by Barbara Robinson and illustrated by Judith Gwyn Brown (HarperCollins); the best Christmas novel ever for middle grades. Upper third-grade reading level.

**MATTHEW JACKSON MEETS THE WALL:** Written by Patricia Reilly Giff and illustrated by Blanche Sims (Dell). One of the Polk Street School series' most beloved kids moves from New York and the Polk Street School to a new neighborhood full of challenges. Upper third-grade reading level.

**MERMAID MARY MARGARET:** By Lynn E. Hazen (Bloomsbury). This delightful story about a fourth-grade girl who goes on a cruise with her grandmother in place of her grandfather, who passed away suddenly is written in a jaunty, light-hearted journal style. A real pleaser! Third-grade reading level.

**THE HERO OF THIRD GRADE:** Written by Alice DeLaCroix and illustrated by Cynthia Fisher (Holiday); see the read-aloud plan elsewhere in this resource. Third-grade reading level.

**THIRD GRADE STINKS!:** Contemporary story about classmates, written by Colleen O'Shaughnessy McKenna and illustrated by Stephanie Roth (Holiday House); see also DOGGONE . . . THIRD GRADE! and THIRD GRADE GHOULS. Third-grade reading level.

**SHOESHINE GIRL:** Written by Clyde Robert Bulla and illustrated by Leigh Grant (HarperCollins). This great story about a girl who spends the summer with her aunt and befriends the owner of a shoeshine stand when she wants to earn money is about so much more than that. Third-grade reading level.

**SEESAW GIRL:** Written by Linda Sue Park and illustrated by Jean and Mou-sien Tseng (Clarion); see the read-aloud plan elsewhere in this resource. Third-grade reading level.

**CHLOE IN THE KNOW:** By Judith Caseley (Greenwillow); the story of 10-year-old Chloe, the oldest child in the Kane family; humorous everyday life. See also other Kane family stories: HURRICANE HARRY and STARRING DOROTHY KANE. Third-grade reading level.

**7 X 9 = TROUBLE!:** Multiplication is the backdrop for this story written by Claudia Mills and illustrated by G. Brian Karas (Farrar, Straus & Giroux). Third-grade reading level.

**SPIDER STORCH'S FUMBLED FIELD TRIP:** Written by Gina Willner-Pardo and illustrated by Nick Sharratt (Whitman). Third-grade reading level.

*Cover from THIRD GRADE STINKS! By Colleen O'Shaughnessy McKenna. Illustrated by Stephanie Roth. Copyright © 2001. Reprinted with permission of Holiday House.*

*Cover from SAY WHAT? By Margaret Peterson Haddix, illustrated by James Bernardin. Copyright © 2004. Used with permission of Simon & Schuster Books for Young Readers, an imprint of Simon & Schuster Children's Publishing.*

**HOW TO EAT FRIED WORMS:** Written by Thomas Rockwell and illustrated by Emily Arnold McCully (Bantam Doubleday Dell). Ten-year-old Billy must eat 15 worms in 15 days to win a bet for $50, which he desperately needs to buy a minibike. Repulsive? You bet, unless you're 10 years old! Funny and warm-hearted; Third-grade reading level.

**THE MOUSE AND THE MOTORCYCLE:** Beloved and ever-popular classic tale, written by Beverly Cleary and illustrated by Louis Darling (Morrow. Third-grade reading level.

**A MOUSE CALLED WOLF:** Written by Dick King-Smith and illustrated by Jon Goodell (Knopf). Wolfgang Amadeus Mouse ("Wolf") wants to sing along with the lady of the house. When he does the fun and adventure begin! Third-grade reading level.

**SAY WHAT?:** Written by Margaret Peterson Haddix and illustrated by James Bernardin (Simon & Schuster). Although Haddix is best known for her gripping tales for middle school readers and beyond, this offering is just plain silly, and just enough off-center to keep the chapter book crowd grinning and turning the pages. In this story, the parents of a trio of siblings try a new method of discipline that involves saying something totally unrelated to the offense when their kids misbehave. When one of the children eats with her fingers instead of her fork, Mom scolds, "You'll put an eye out with that thing!" When they get caught smearing their fingerprints on the wall, Dad says, "Eat your vegetables." After some super-sleuthing, the children discover just what their parents are up to. Then the fun begins, as they turn the tables on their parents' plan. Third-grade reading level.

**GOONEY BIRD GREENE:** Written by Newbery winner Lois Lowry and illustrated by Middy Thomas (Houghton Mifflin). A most unusual free spirit joins a typical class, and nobody is the same from the moment she sets foot in the door. Third-grade reading level.

**AND THEN WHAT HAPPENED, PAUL REVERE?; SHHH! WE'RE WRITING THE CONSTITUTION; WHAT'S THE BIG IDEA, BEN FRANKLIN?: WHERE WAS PATRICK HENRY ON THE 29TH OF MAY?; WILL YOU SIGN HERE, JOHN HANCOCK?; WHY DON'T YOU GET A HORSE, SAM ADAMS?** and other titles that bring history alive; by Jean Fritz (Putnam); Third-grade reading level.

**ESIO TROT:** A Roald Dahl favorite illustrated by Quentin Blake (Penguin). Spell *tortoise* backwards and this is what you get; surefire favorite among middle graders. See also THE ENORMOUS CROCODILE, FANTASTIC MR. FOX, THE MAGIC FINGER, and THE TWITS for more irreverent humor. Third-grade reading level.

**PLEASING THE GHOST:** By Sharon Creech (HarperCollins). Uncle Arvie comes back to take care of some things left undone. How Dennis manages his uncle's ghost and grows in the process is fun and illuminating. Third-grade reading level.

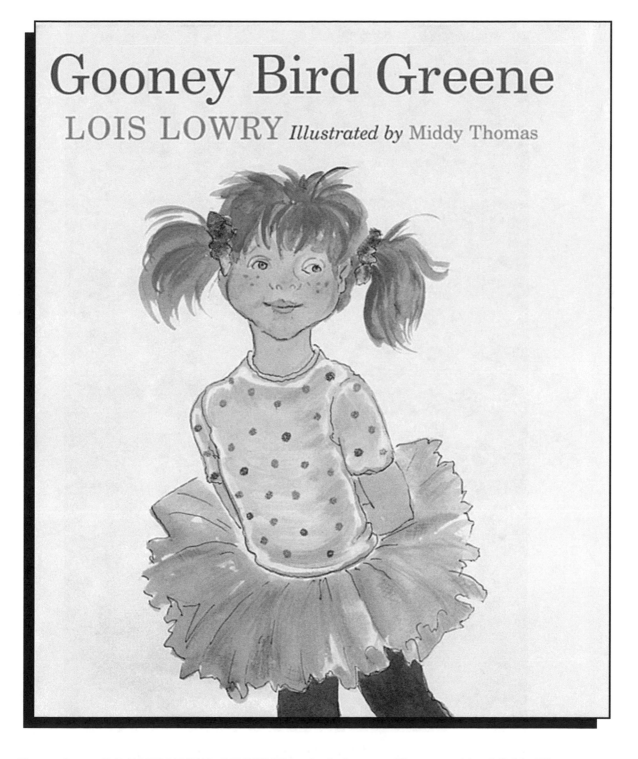

*Cover from GOONEY BIRD GREENE by Lois Lowry, illustrated by Middy Thomas.
Copyright © 2002. Reprinted by permission of Houghton Mifflin Company.
All rights reserved.*

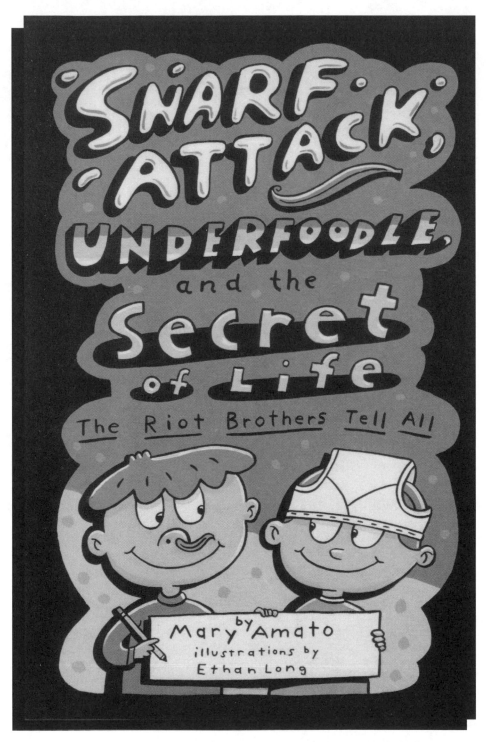

*Cover from SNARF ATTACK, UNDERFOODLE, AND THE SECRET OF LIFE: THE RIOT BROTHERS TELL ALL by Mary Amato. Illustrated by Ethan Long. Copyright © 2004. Reprinted with permission of Holiday House.*

**A NOSE FOR TROUBLE:** Written by Nancy Hope Wilson and illustrated by Doron Ben-Ami (Avon). Main character Maggie is in a wheelchair, but she shows the kids in her new school that she is "special" in other ways as well. See also the companion novel, A WHIFF OF DANGER, illustrated by Marie DeJohn (Avon). Upper second-, third-grade reading level.

**SNARF ATTACK, UNDERFOODLE, AND THE SECRET OF LIFE: THE RIOT BROTHERS TELL ALL:** Written by Mary Amato and illustrated by Ethan Long (Holiday House); silly, nonsensical, goofy humor that's sure to zap the funny bone of third-grade boys who will love that the main characters stick green beans up their nose to make the other one snarf his milk. Upper second-grade reading level.

**THE TWENTY-FOUR DAYS BEFORE CHRISTMAS:** Written by acclaimed author Madeleine L'Engle and illustrated by Carl Cassler (Dell). This is the story of a young girl waiting for the arrival of her new sibling with anxiety and eagerness. Upper second-grade reading level.

**THE KING'S EQUAL:** Written by Newbery Award winner Katherine Paterson and illustrated by Curtis Woodbridge (HarperCollins). This original fairy tale is a treasure.. Second-grade reading level.

**JACKSON JONES AND THE PUDDLE OF THORNS and JACKSON JONES AND MISSION GREENTOP:** By Mary Quattlebaum (Delacorte). The middle grade, inner-city main character is funny and wise in these companion early chapter books. Second-grade reading level.

**KEEP THE LIGHTS BURNING, ABBIE:** Written by Peter and Connie Roop and illustrated by Peter E. Hanson (Carolrhoda); based on the account of a brave girl who kept a lighthouse lit during a storm off the coast of Maine in 1856. A note from the authors prefaces this tale with more details about the girl who grew up to care for lighthouses throughout her life. Second-grade reading level.

**ANNA, GRANPA, AND THE BIG STORM:** Written by Carla Stevens and illustrated by Margot Thomas (Clarion). A girl and her grandfather get caught en route to a spelling bee in the legendary Great Blizzard of 1888. Second-grade reading level.

**BONY-LEGS:** A fairy tale in early chapter book form written by Joanna Cole and illustrated by Dirk Zimmer (Simon & Schuster); Scholastic Hello Reader. Second-grade reading level.

**SLEEPING UGLY:** A twist on the fairy tale written by award-winner Jane Yolen and illustrated by Diane Stanley (Putnam). Second-grade reading level.

## Series

**Chronicles of Narnia:** Classic fantasy by C. S. Lewis (HarperCollins); includes THE LION, THE WITCH AND THE WARDROBE. Upper fourth-, fifth-grade reading level.

**JULIE OF THE WOLVES:** Newbery Award winner and the first in a trilogy by Jean Craighead George (HarperCollins). See also MY SIDE OF THE MOUNTAIN, a Newbery Honor Award winner and the first in another trilogy by George. Upper fourth-grade reading level.

**Indian in the Cupboard Books:** This series of four novels by Lynne Reid Banks (Doubleday; Avon) has won the hearts of fourth graders everywhere, who love to role play with plastic figurines and have vivid imaginations to feed. Titles: THE INDIAN IN THE CUPBOARD, THE RETURN OF THE INDIAN, THE SECRET OF THE INDIAN, THE MYSTERY OF THE CUPBOARD, and THE KEY TO THE INDIAN. Upper fourth-grade reading level.

**Magic Shop Books:** By Bruce Coville (Harcourt). Middle grade fantasy chock-full of humor and timeless messages; includes THE MONSTER'S RING, THE SKULL OF TRUTH, JENNIFER MURDLEY'S TOAD, and JEREMY THATCHER, DRAGON HATCHER. Upper fourth-grade reading level.

**Anastasia Krupnik series:** By Lois Lowry (Bantam, Doubleday, Dell), this series chronicles the growth of a spunky, adorably independent and resourceful character anyone would want for a sister. Titles include ANASTASIA KRUPNIK, ANASTASIA AGAIN, ANASTASIA ON HER OWN, ANASTASIA'S CHOSEN CAREER, ANASTASIA HAS THE ANSWERS, ANASTASIA AT YOUR SERVICE, and ANASTASIA ABSOLUTELY. Fourth-grade reading level. See also the All About Sam series about Anastasia's little brother, written at a lower level.

**Joey Pigza Books:** From the National Book Award finalist, JOEY PIGZA SWALLOWED THE KEY, to the Newbery Honor Award winner, JOEY PIGZA LOSES CONTROL, to the final book in the trilogy, WHAT WOULD JOEY DO?, these fictional accounts of a boy plagued by ADD tug at the heart while managing to be hilarious, too. Jack Gantos (Farrar, Straus & Giroux) shines, and Joey is a boy who won't soon be forgotten. Fourth-grade reading level.

**Tales of Magic:** A series of books written by Edward Eager and illustrated by N. M. Bodecker (Harcourt; classic fantasy). Titles: HALF MAGIC, KNIGHT'S CASTLE, THE TIME GARDEN, and MAGIC BY THE LAKE. Fourth-grade reading level.

**A Series of Unfortunate Events:** Wildly popular fantasy written by Lemony Snicket and illustrated by Brett Helquist (HarperCollins). Titles include THE BAD BEGINNING, THE REPTILE ROOM, THE WIDE WINDOW, THE GRIM GROTTO, and THE SLIPPERY SLOPE. Fourth-grade reading level.

*Cover of JOEY PIGZA LOSES CONTROL © 2000 by Jack Gantos. Cover art © 2000 by Beata Szpura. Used with the permission of Farrar Straus Giroux.*

**Newfangled Fairy Tales: Classic Stories with a Twist:** Edited by Bruce Lansky and written by numerous well-known and well-loved authors (Meadowbrook). Fourth-grade reading level.

**Little House on the Prairie:** This classic historical fiction series written by Laura Ingalls Wilder and illustrated by Garth Williams (HarperCollins) has been loved and cherished since it was first published in the 1930s and 1940s. Generally fourth-grade reading level.

**Wild at Heart:** Created by award-winning author Laurie Halse Anderson (American Girl). Series of tales about kids who volunteer at an animal clinic. Fourth-grade reading level.

**Soup:** By Robert Newton Peck (Knopf). Series of autobiographical novels set in the 1920s in rural Vermont. Titles include SOUP, SOUP FOR PRESIDENT, SOUP ON WHEELS, and SOUP 1776. Fourth-grade reading level.

**RAMONA THE PEST and related titles:** By Beverly Cleary (Morrow). Classics not to be missed by middle graders. Upper third-grade reading level.

**The Boxcar Children:** The classic series created by Gertrude Chandler Warner (Whitman) about the four Alden children and their adventures in and around their boxcar home; newly redesigned covers; over 100 titles. Upper third-grade reading level.

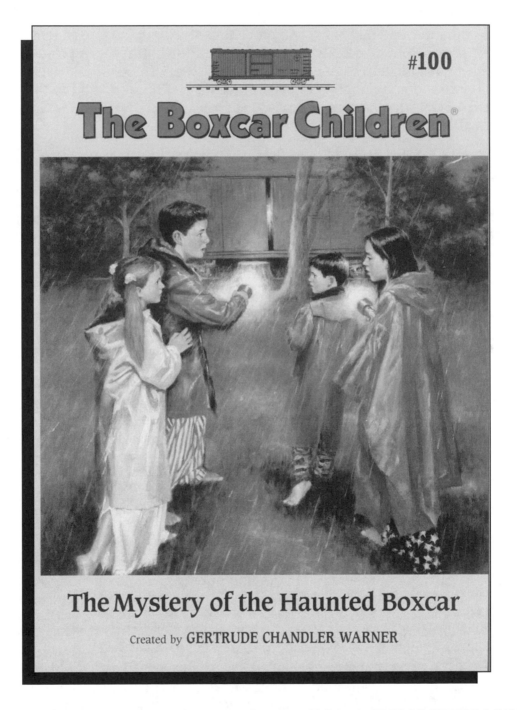

*Cover from The Boxcar Children (60th Anniversary Edition): THE MYSTERY OF THE HAUNTED BOXCAR by Gertrude Chandler Warner, illustrated by L. Kate Deal. Copyright © 2002. Reprinted with permission from A. Whitman & Co.*

**The Princess Tales:** Series by award-winning author Gail Carson Levine (HarperCollins). Titles include CINDERELLIS AND THE GLASS HILL, THE PRINCESS TEST, and THE FAIRY'S MISTAKE. Upper third-grade reading level.

**My Father's Dragon:** Three tales written by Ruth Stiles Gannett and illustrated in black and white by Ruth Chrisman Gannett (Random House). The first title is a Newbery Honor Award winner, a warmhearted fantasy adventure about a boy's trip to Wild Island to save a dragon. This set of books has been winning the hearts and imaginations of children since 1948. In addition to MY FATHER'S DRAGON, the trilogy includes ELMER AND THE DRAGON and THE DRAGONS OF BLUELAND. Third-grade reading level.

**The Freddy Collection:** Reissued classics written by Walter R. Brooks and illustrated by Kurt Wiese (Puffin); about the adventures of a pig and his friends from the farm (a horse, a cat, a rooster, a rat, a dog, and a cow). Titles include FREDDY THE DETECTIVE, FREDDY AND THE BEAN HOME NEWS, FREDDY GOES TO FLORIDA, and FREDDY PLAYS FOOTBALL. Third-grade reading level.

**The Spiderwick Chronicles:** By Tony DiTerlizzi and Holly Black (Simon & Schuster). Five books make up this fantasy series by an award-winning team that has garnered much interest as a solid choice for readers who can't quite tackle (or lift) the Harry Potter series. Titles: THE FIELD GUIDE, THE SEEING STONE, LUCINDA'S SECRET, THE IRONWOOD TREE, and THE WRATH OF MULGARATH. Third-grade reading level.

**Encyclopedia Brown: Boy Detective:** Written by Donald J. Sobol and illustrated by Leonard Shortall (Dutton). Numerous titles about this "Sherlock Holmes in sneakers," otherwise known as 10-year-old Leroy Brown, who got the name Encyclopedia because his mind is like one. He helps his dad, the police chief of Idaville, solve his toughest cases while sitting around the dinner table in their home on Rover Avenue. What's not to love about these surefire winners? Third-grade reading level.

**Dear America/My Name Is America:** Published by Scholastic and written by a variety of authors, these books are based on historical events and real people but feature fictional main characters; journal style. Titles include THE JOURNAL OF FINN REARDON: A NEWSIE, by Susan Campbell Bartoletti; DREAMS IN THE GOLDEN COUNTRY: THE DIARY OF ZIPPORAH FELDMAN, A JEWISH IMMIGRANT GIRL, by Kathryn Lasky; WHEN CHRISTMAS COMES AGAIN: THE WORLD WAR I DIARY OF SIMONE SPENCER, by Beth Seidel Levine; SO FAR FROM HOME: THE DIARY OF MARY DRISCOLL, AN IRISH MILL GIRL, by Barry Denenberg; and A COAL MINER'S BRIDE: THE DIARY OF ANETKA KAMINSKA, by Susan Campbell Bartoletti. Third- to fourth-grade reading level.

*Cover from The Spiderwick Chronicles, Book 4: THE IRONWOOD TREE by Holly Black and Tony DiTerlizzi, illustrated by Tony DiTerlizzi. Copyright © 2004. Used with permission of Simon & Schuster Books for Young Readers, an imprint of Simon & Schuster Children's Publishing.*

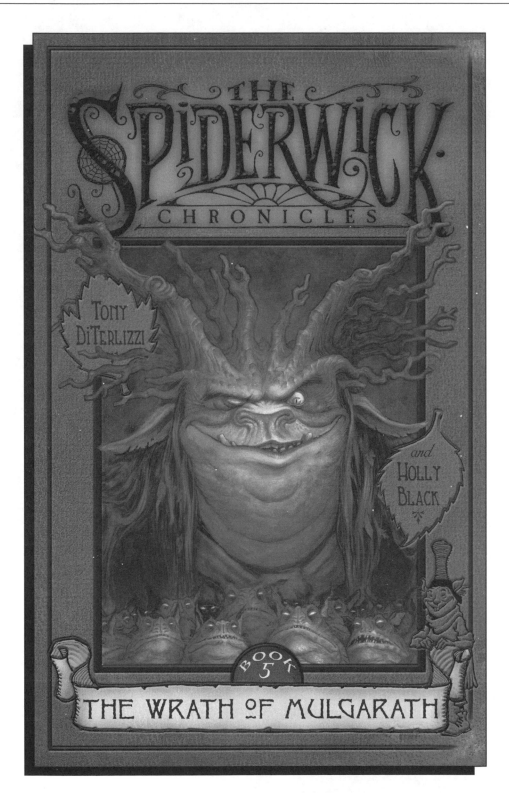

*Cover from The Spiderwick Chronicles, Book 5: THE WRATH OF MULGARATH by Holly Black and Tony DiTerlizzi, illustrated by Tony DiTerlizzi. Copyright © 2004. Used with permission of Simon & Schuster Books for Young Readers, an imprint of Simon & Schuster Children's Publishing.*

**The Matt Christopher Series:** The "#1 Sports series for kids" boasts the publisher, Little, Brown. Numerous titles by the late Christopher; recent titles are ghost-written. Titles include FAIRWAY PROBLEM, MASTER OF DISASTER, DIVE RIGHT IN, and AT THE PLATE WITH ICHIRO and ON THE BIKE WITH LANCE ARMSTRONG (sports biographies). Third- to fourth-grade reading level.

**The Robert Series:** By Barbara Seuling (Cricket); see the read-aloud plan for OH NO, IT'S ROBERT elsewhere in this resource. Third-grade reading level.

**Clue series:** Each of these books, created by Parker C. Hinter and based on the board game by Parker Brothers, offers simple cases for readers to solve. The clues are found in the stories as well as the illustrations. Solutions follow each short case. Published by Scholastic; copyright Waddingtons Games Ltd. A great group read, car game, or holiday pastime. Third-grade reading level.

**Third-Grade Detectives (Ready-for-Chapters):** Written by George E. Stanley and illustrated by Salvatore Murdocca (Aladdin). Interactive in style, these stories encourage the reader to help solve the cases that Mr. Merlin, beloved teacher and former spy, presents to his students. The first title, THE CLUE OF THE LEFT-HANDED ENVELOPE, involves secret codes and encourages working together to solve a problem. The tenth title, THE MYSTERY OF THE STOLEN STATUE, revolves around a stolen statue that's been smashed to pieces and deposited in a dumpster. Third-grade reading level.

**Doyle and Fossey Science Detectives:** Written by Michele Torrey and illustrated by Barbara Johansen Newman (Penguin). Science and mystery meet in these chapter books featuring likable characters and simple science experiments. Titles include THE CASE OF THE GASPING GARBAGE, THE CASE OF THE MOSSY LAKE MONSTER, THE CASE OF THE GRAVEYARD GHOST, and THE CASE OF THE BARFY BIRTHDAY. Third-grade reading level.

**The Cam Jansen Series:** By David A. Adler (Penguin); about a resourceful, inquisitive gal with a photographic memory. Simple black-and-white line drawings by Susanna Natti accompany the text. Third-grade reading level

**Smart About:** Fact and humor meet in this nonfiction series of books about artists, inventors, history, and even chocolate! Titles include CLAUDE MONET: SUNSHINE AND WATERLILIES; NEGRO LEAGUES: ALL-BLACK BASEBALL; SMART ABOUT THE FIRST LADIES; MONEY: A RICH HISTORY, and SMART ABOUT CHOCOLATE. Third-grade reading level.

**Amber Brown:** Written by the zany and much-loved late author, Paula Danziger, and illustrated by Tony Ross (cover art of some titles by Jacqueline Rogers), these books are published in hardcover by Penguin and in paperback by Apple Books/Scholastic. The main character is a contemporary third-grade gal with realistic problems and believable friends. Amber is funny, feisty, and vastly popular. Titles include AMBER BROWN IN NOT A CRAYON, AMBER BROWN WANTS EXTRA CREDIT, FOREVER AMBER BROWN, AMBER BROWN GOES FOURTH, and I, AMBER BROWN. Third-grade reading level.

**The Littles:** A treasury of tales written by John Peterson and illustrated by Roberta Carter Clark (Scholastic), about a family six inches tall with tails. Titles include THE LITTLES, THE LITTLES AND THE BIG STORM, THE LITTLES AND THE TRASH TINIES, THE LITTLES TO THE RESCUE, THE LITTLES GO TO SCHOOL, THE LITTLES GIVE A PARTY, THE LITTLES AND THE LOST CHILDREN, and TOM LITTLE'S GREAT HALLOWEEN SCARE. Third-grade reading level.

**Mrs. Piggle-Wiggle:** Written by Betty MacDonald and illustrated by Hilary Knight (with the exception of FARM, which was illustrated by Maurice Sendak) (HarperCollins). A character children will love who endears herself to the kids in her neighborhood because she smells like cookies, Mrs. Piggle-Wiggle lives in an upside-down house, and she was once married to a pirate! But best of all, she helps children overcome any problem from hating baths to eating too slowly. Pure delight, fine fun. Titles include MRS. PIGGLE-WIGGLE, MRS. PIGGLE-WIGGLE'S MAGIC, MRS. PIGGLE WIGGLE'S FARM, and HELLO, MRS. PIGGLE-WIGGLE. Third-grade reading level.

**The Hilarious Adventures of Paddington:** Written by Michael Bond with illustrations by Peggy Fortnum (Dell). Who doesn't recognize the adorable bear with the yellow hat and blue overcoat with a tag attached that says, "Please look after this BEAR thank you"? Sweet, humorous, gentle tales that are sure to please. Titles include A BEAR CALLED PADDINGTON, MORE ABOUT PADDINGTON, PADDINGTON HELPS OUT, PADDINGTON AT LARGE, PADDINGTON AT WORK, PADDINGTON ABROAD, and PADDINGTON MARCHES ON. Third-grade reading level.

**The Time Warp Trio:** Written by Jon Scieszka and illustrated by Lane Smith (Puffin); humorous high jinks, for which this team is legendary, meet history. Titles include TUT TUT; THE GOOD, THE BAD, AND THE GOOFY; KNIGHTS OF THE KITCHEN TABLE; THE NOT-SO-JOLLY ROGER; YOUR MOTHER WAS A NEANDERTHAL; and SAM SAMURAI. Third-grade reading level.

**Who Was? series:** Written and illustrated by various authors (Grosset & Dunlap); paperback pen-and-ink illustrated biographies; titles include WHO WAS MOZART?, WHO WAS MARK TWAIN?, WHO WAS ALBERT EINSTEIN?, and WHO WAS ELEANOR ROOSEVELT? Third-grade reading level.

**Beryl E. Bean:** Written by Ricki Stern and Heidi P. Worcester and illustrated by Amy June Bates (HarperCollins). A soccer star solves mysteries and finds adventures when sidelined by a broken arm in these contemporary stories. Third-grade reading level.

**Mostly Ghostly:** He's b-a-a-a-a-ck! R. L. Stine of GOOSEBUMPS fame has a new series of mild middle grade chillers. Titles include WHO LET THE GHOSTS OUT?, HAVE YOU MET MY GHOULFRIEND?, ONE NIGHT IN DOOM HOUSE, and LITTLE CAMP OF HORRORS; published by Delacorte. Third-grade reading level.

**Jake Drake:** Written by award-winning author Andrew Clements and illustrated by Dolores Avendano (Aladdin Ready-for Chapters Books); about Jake in various grades handling common problems such as bullies, competing against the know-it-alls in the science fair, and the downside of being the class clown. Titles include JAKE DRAKE, BULLY BUSTER; JAKE DRAKE, KNOW-IT-ALL and JAKE DRAKE, TEACHER'S PET. Upper second-grade reading level.

**Hello Reader!:** These single-title slim readers make up a library of their own. Published by Scholastic, there are four levels, the highest of which is designated for grade 3 and is suitable for reluctant readers. Over the years many authors and illustrators have contributed to this line, and a bounty of subjects is covered, from fairy tales and mysteries to nonfiction. A brief note to "family members" about encouraging young readers can be found at the front of each book. Favorite titles for grades 3 and 4 include BONY-LEGS (see listing above); WHEN THE GIANTS CAME TO TOWN, written by Marcia Leonard and illustrated by R. W. Alley; THREE SMART PALS, written by Joanne Rocklin and illustrated by Denise Brunkus; GREAT BLACK HEROES: FIVE BRAVE EXPLORERS, written by Wade Hudson and illustrated by Ron Garnett; INVISIBLE INC.#1: THE SCHOOLYARD MYSTERY, written by Elizabeth Levy and illustrated by Denise Brunkus; DANCING WITH MANATEES, written by Faith McNulty and illustrated by Lena Shiffman; ARMIES OF ANTS, written by Walter Retan and illustrated by Jean Cassels; and THE BRAVEST DOG EVER: THE TRUE STORY OF BALTO, written by Natalie Standiford and illustrated by Donald Cook. Note: Scholastic is no longer publishing new titles in this line.

**Step into Reading:** Published by Random House, there are four levels in this series, which, similar to other publishers' series, offers a variety of books on myriad subjects with a message to parents at the front of the book. Step 3 is suitable for reluctant readers in the middle grades.

**I Can Read Books:** This recently redesigned and repackaged series by HarperCollins boasts five levels. Advanced Reading 4 comprises simple chapter books for grades 3 and up. Authors, illustrators, and topics vary, and over 60 million copies of books from this series have been sold since 1957.

**Let's-Read-and-Find-Out Science:** Listed as one of the top 10 nonfiction series by Booklist (American Library Association), these leveled books published by HarperCollins present science concepts in a colorful, engaging manner. Level 2 is suitable for third-grade readers. Representative titles include GERMS MAKE ME SICK!, written by Melvin Berger and illustrated by Marylin Hafner; and EARTHQUAKES, written by Franklyn M. Branley and illustrated by Megan Lloyd.

**The Stories Julian Tells; More Stories Julian Tells:** Written by Ann Cameron and illustrated by Ann Strugnell (Knopf). The main character featured in these books likes to tell stories: tall, tall tales that get him into a heap of trouble. Mischievous humor, lots of imagination, and a cast of three-dimensional characters including Dad, little bro Huey, and best friend Gloria. For more books about these characters, see titles about Huey and Gloria as well as additional titles featuring Julian. Upper second-grade reading level.

**Magic Tree House:** Written by Mary Pope Osborne and illustrated by Sal Murdocca (Random House). These new and popular classics chronicle the fantastical adventures of Jack and his sister Annie when they climb into the tree house that has appeared mysteriously in the woods near their home. Titles include DINOSAURS BEFORE DARK, MIDNIGHT ON THE MOON, AFTERNOON ON THE AMAZON, PIRATES PAST NOON, and POLAR BEARS PAST BEDTIME. Upper second-grade reading level

**The Kids of the Polk Street School:** A library of titles written by teacher, reading consultant, and award-winning author Patricia Reilly Giff and illustrated by Blanche Sims (Dell), about the kids in Ms. Rooney's classroom. Heartwarming, reassuring, inviting chapter books. Other series by the same author include New Kids at the Polk Street School and Polka Dot Private Eye. Upper second-grade reading level.

**Judy Moody:** Written by Megan McDonald and illustrated by Peter Reynolds (Candlewick). Here's a character sure to be remembered and certain to be loved by many. Enjoy free spirit, Judy's escapades with little bro "Stink," best friend Rocky, and "pest" friend Frank. Get the picture? Titles include JUDY MOODY, JUDY MOODY PREDICTS THE FUTURE, JUDY MOODY SAVES THE WORLD!, JUDY MOODY GETS FAMOUS!, and JUDY MOODY, M.D. THE DOCTOR IS IN! Upper second-grade reading level.

**Riverside Kids:** Written by the prolific Johanna Hurwitz (HarperCollins), these books feature Nora, Teddy, Elisa, and Russell and are enjoyable, entertaining reads. Titles include BUSYBODY NORA, E IS FOR ELISA, RIP-ROARING RUSSELL, and SUPERDUPER TEDDY and RUSSELL SPROUTS. Mid-second-grade reading level

**Sly the Sleuth and the Pet Mysteries**: Written by award-winner Donna Jo Napoli with her son, Robert Furrow, and illustrated by Heather Maione (Dial). Three cases are solved by super-sleuth Sylvia, who has opened her very own detective agency; see also Sly the Sleuth and the Sports Mysteries. Second-grade reading level.

JUDY MOODY, M.D.: THE DOCTOR IS IN! Text Copyright © 2004 Megan McDonald. Illustration Copyright © 2004 Peter H. Reynolds. Judy Moody Font Copyright © 2004 Peter H. Reynolds. Reproduced by permission of the publisher, Candlewick Press, Inc., Cambridge, MA.

# Short Stories for In-Between Times

When time is short and you don't want to begin a new book, such as just before a school break or on the last day of the week, rather than skipping your daily read-aloud, reach for a short story instead. The collections listed here offer a variety of genres to choose from, from historical to humorous, from mystery to musings. These stories, penned by some of the best authors for children today, can be read in one sitting. They also are great for author studies. Encourage students who *love* the story to look for other work by the author.

- IT'S GREAT TO BE EIGHT, a collection of stories by such authors as Beverly Cleary, Paula Danziger, Ann M. Martin, and Louis Sachar (Scholastic).

- IT'S GREAT TO BE NINE, a collection of stories by such authors as Judy Blume, Patricia MacLachlan, Jerry Spinelli, and Johanna Hurwitz (Scholastic).

- IT'S GREAT TO BE TEN, a collection of stories by such authors as Barbara Park, Lois Lowry, Katherine Paterson, Christopher Paul Curtis, and Elizabeth Levy (Scholastic).

- SIDEWAYS STORIES FROM WAYSIDE SCHOOL, by Louis Sachar (HarperCollins). This school is one classroom wide and 30 stories high. And that's just the beginning. See also WAYSIDE SCHOOL IS FALLING DOWN, WAYSIDE SCHOOL GETS A LITTLE STRANGER, SIDEWAYS ARITHMETIC FROM WAYSIDE SCHOOL, and MORE SIDEWAYS ARITHMETIC FROM WAYSIDE SCHOOL (Scholastic).

- TRIPPING OVER THE LUNCH LADY AND OTHER SCHOOL STORIES, edited by Nancy E. Mercado (Dial); a collection of stories by such authors as Avi, Sarah Weeks, and Angela Johnson.

- RIBBITING TALES: ORIGINAL STORIES ABOUT FROGS, edited by Nancy Springer and illustrated by Tony DiTerlizzi (Philomel); a collection of stories by such authors as Brian Jacques, Jane Yolen, Bruce Coville, and Janet Taylor Lisle.

- GRAVEN IMAGES, by Paul Fleischman (HarperCollins); three stories: one about wooden boys, one about weathervanes, and one about statues; Newbery Honor.

- GREAT QUICKSOLVE WHODUNIT PUZZLES, written by Jim Sukach and illustrated by Lucy Corvino (Sterling); mini-mysteries to solve, with solutions.

# Reading-Related Resources for Busy Teachers

## RESOURCE BOOKS

These informative and user-friendly guides are great, and they ought to be handy and accessible to the professional staff. Strive to have them readily available on your school or public library's professional shelf and advertise that they're there. If you can manage to add them to the classroom resource shelf, that's even better.

- **Reconsidering Read-Aloud,** by Mary Lee Hahn (Stenhouse)

- **The New Read-aloud Handbook,** by Jim Trelease (Penguin Books)

- **Hey! Listen to This: Stories to Read-Aloud,** by Jim Trelease (Penguin Books)

- **Let's Read About . . . Finding Books They'll Love to Read,** by Bernice Cullinan (Scholastic)

- **Michele Landsberg's Guide to Children's Books,** by Michele Landsberg (Penguin Books)

- **Pass the Poetry, Please! 3rd edition,** by Lee Bennett Hopkins (HarperCollins)

- **The Art of Teaching Reading,** by Lucy McCormick Calkins (Longman)

The following are dual-purpose reference books, written for parents and great for use by teachers in working with parents:

- **How to Get Your Child to Love Reading: For Ravenous and Reluctant Readers Alike,** by Esme Raji Codell (Algonquin Books)

- **Reading Magic: Why Reading Aloud to Our Children Will Change Their Lives Forever**, by Mem Fox (Harcourt)

## PERIODICALS

The advantage of subscriptions to these magazines is that they provide timely information about recent publications, spotlight authors and illustrators, announce award winners, and explore other subjects of interest related to the field of children's literature.

**The Horn Book Magazine:** Published every other month, this magazine, founded in 1924, is chock-full of reviews, publisher ads, editorials, and features reflecting a deep passion for and commitment to enduring quality in books for children and young adults. Address: 56 Roland St., Suite 200, Boston, MA 02129; Telephone:

800-325-1170; Fax: 617-628-0882; Internet: magazine@hbook.com. Subscription: $45.00, individual; $55.00, institutional. Special introductory rates.

**Booklist:** Published twice monthly September through June and monthly in July and August by the American Library Association, this is a highly regarded source of reviews on all literature pertaining to children. Address: Kable Fulfillment Services, Agency Processing Team, 308 E. Hitt St., Mount Morris, IL 61054; Telephone: 888-350-0949; Fax: 815-734-1252; e-mail: blnk@kable.com. U.S. subscriptions: $79.95.

**Book Links:** Published six times per year by the American Library Association, this resource connects children's books, K–8, to curricula in science, social studies, and language arts. Included in each issue are suggestions for novels to teach, advice, author interviews, reviews, and thematic bibliographies. Address: PO Box 615, Mt. Morris, IL 61054-7566; Telephone: 888-350-0950; Fax: 815-734-1252; e-mail: blnk@kable.com. Subscription: $27.95.

**School Library Journal:** Founded in 1954, and now in both print and online formats, this resource serves librarians in school and public libraries. It boasts more book reviews than any other resource of its kind. Address: PO Box 16178, North Hollywood, CA 91615-6178; Telephone: 800-595-1066; Fax: 818-487-4566; e-mail: slj@reedbusiness.com. Subscription: $124.00.

**The Reading Teacher:** Published eight times a year for members of the International Reading Association, this magazine targets elementary school teachers. Address: 800 Barksdale Rd., PO Box 8139, Newark, DE 19714-8139; Telephone: 800-336-7323; e-mail: www.reading.org.

**Kirkus Review:** Founded in 1933, this resource is currently available in print and online editions. Specialists in the field review 5,000 titles per year, of which children's books is one category. Telephone: 646-654-5865; Fax: 646-654-5518; e-mail: mhazzard@vnubuspubs.com. Contact for rates and packages.

Also:

**The Children's Book Council:** This nonprofit organization is the official sponsor of National Children's Book Week and Young People's Poetry Week. It is "dedicated to encouraging literacy and the use and enjoyment of children's books." The CBC distributes a variety of useful materials about books and reading. Its catalog contains posters, friezes, streamers, bookmarks, postcards, and a variety of other products for sale. Address: 568 Broadway, New York, NY 10012; Telephone: 212-966-1990; Fax: 212-966-2073. Credit card orders for materials: 800-999-2160 or e-mail: catalogs@cbcbooks.org. (See Web site listing.)

## WEB SITES

Want to learn more about children's literature from the computer screen? Here is a list of professional Web sites that deliver a wealth of information on books for children. A list of publisher Web sites follows.

- **www.ala.org**—American Library Association Web site; Useful link: www.ala.org/booklist/—Lists notable children's titles published in the past year arranged by age.

- **www.slj.com/articles/articles/articlesindex.asp**: *School Library Journal* link; see "Best Books of the Year."

- **www.readingrainbow.org**—*Reading Rainbow* site; includes a listing of all the books covered on its episodes since the program's inception.

- **www.cbcbooks.org**—Web site of the Children's Book Council, a nonprofit trade association of children's book publishers, the purpose of which is to promote reading in children. For information, tips, and activities for Children's Book Week, celebrated annually in November, go to http://cbcbooks.org/html/book_week.html.

- **www.acs.ucalgary.ca/~dkbrown/**—Visit this site for an in-depth look at various aspects of children's books, developed by David K. Brown, Director of Doucette Library of Teaching Resources at the University of Calgary, Calgary, Alberta Canada.

- **www.reading.org**—International Reading Association Web site. Newly revamped in September 2004, the site is now easier to navigate. Products, services, and professional information are clearly available. Subscribers can also access IRA journals. Go to www.reading.org/choices for downloadable Children's Choices lists, those books favored among children; there is also a Teachers' Choices list of those books chosen by teachers that coordinate well with curriculum.

- **www.bookhive.org/books/**—On this Web site of the Public Library of Charlotte and Mecklenburg County, North Carolina, reviews are handily listed for books, grouped according to author, title, illustrator, age level, genre, and number of pages.

- **www.earlyreading.info**—This Web site, developed by the Regional Educational Laboratory at Pacific Resources for Education and Learning (PREL), helps teachers and others who work with children in pre-K to grade 3 meet the challenge set by the Reading First initiative of having all students in the United States read at grade level by the time they reach third grade.

- **www.readwritethink.org**—Focuses on reading and language arts; provided by the International Reading Association (IRA) and the National Council of Teachers of English (NCTE). The calendar feature located in the Highlights section of the homepage gives monthly listings of peer-reviewed lesson plans and classroom activities related to literacy and books.

- **www.trelease-on-reading.com**—Web site of Jim Trelease, author of *The Read-Aloud Handbook* (Penguin Books).

- **www.rifreadingplanet.org**—An interactive site for parents and children.

- **http://marcopolo.worldcom.com**—Its goal is to provide "the highest quality standards-based Internet content and professional development to K–12 teachers and students" in the United States and beyond.

- **www.ncrel.org/sdrs/areas/issues/content/cntareas/reading/li100.htm**—"Critical Issues Addressing the Literacy Needs of Emergent and Early Readers"; North Central Educational Laboratory.

- **www.icdlbooks.org International Children's Digital Library**—Web site

- **www.readingrockets.org**—A national service of public television station WETA in Washington, D.C., this site offers "information about teaching kids to read and helping those who struggle."

- **www.minnesotahumanities.org**—Provides support to those working to improve literacy of both children and their parents. Includes free reading guides for children's books, ways to involve dads, and bilingual initiatives.

- **www.kidsource.com/NICHCY/literature.html**—A bibliography of children's books on or about various disabilities.

## Online Bookstores

- **www.amazon.com**—The largest online bookstore

- **www.bn.com**—Barnes & Noble online

## Publishers

To order directly from publishers, you can visit their Web sites for ordering information. You will note that for the larger publishers, such as Simon & Schuster, the imprints have links from the main Web address. In some publishing companies, imprints act independently of one another; in other publishing houses, they share departments.

- **Harry N. Abrams, Inc.:** www.abramsbooks.com

- **American Girl:** www.americangirl.com

*Imprint:* American Girl Library

- **Boyds Mills Press:** www.boydsmillspress.com

*Imprint:* Wordsong (poetry)

- **Candlewick Press:** www.candlewick.com

- **Clarion:** www.houghtonmifflinbooks.com

- **Farrar, Straus & Giroux:** www.fsgkidsbooks.com

- **Harcourt Children's Book Division:** www.harcourtbooks.com

*Imprints:* Gulliver Books, Silverwhistle

- **HarperCollins Children's Books:** www.harperchildrens.com

*Imprints:* HarperFestival; Joanna Cotler Books, Greenwillow

- **Henry Holt and Company:** www.henryholt.com
- **Holiday House:** www.holidayhouse.com
- **Houghton Mifflin:** www.houghtonmifflinbooks.com
- **Hyperion Books for Children:** www.hyperionchildrensbooks.com
- **Kids Can Press:** www.kidscanpress.com
- **Lee & Low:** www.leeandlow.com
- **Little, Brown & Company:** www.littlebrown.com
- **Meadowbrook Press:** www.meadowbrookpress.com
- **Penguin Group USA:** www.us.penguingroup.com

*Imprints*: Dial Books for Young Readers, Dutton Children's Books, G. P. Putnam's Sons, Philomel, Putnam, Puffin, Penguin, Viking, Grosset & Dunlap

- **Random House:** www.randomhouse.com/kids/

*Imprints*: Knopf Delacorte Dell Young Readers Group, Random House Children's Books, Golden Books for Young Readers, Crown

- **Scholastic:** www.scholastic.com

*Imprints*: Scholastic Press, Cartwheel Books, Blue Sky Press, Orchard Books

- **Simon & Schuster Children's Publishing Division:** www.simonsayskids.com

*Imprints*: Aladdin, Atheneum, Margaret K. McElderry Books, Simon & Schuster Books for Young Readers, Paula Wiseman Books

- **Albert Whitman & Company:** www.albertwhitman.com

# Author-Illustrator Web Sites Welcome Readers

Listed below in alphabetical order are Web sites of authors and illustrators particularly of interest to third and fourth graders. These sites give information, provide activities, and offer the reader the chance to "virtually" meet favorite authors and illustrators.

Robert Byrd—www.penguinputnam.com/nf/Author/AuthorPage

Tomie dePaola—www.tomie.com

Marla Frazee—www.marlafrazee.com

Kathleen Krull—www.kathleenkrull.com

Ann Whitehead Nagda—www.AnnNagda.com

Linda Sue Park—www.lspark.com

Elizabeth Partridge—www.elizabethpartirdge.com

Patricia Polacco—www.patriciapolacco.com

Mary Quattlebaum—www.maryquattlebaum.com

Jon Scieszka—www.penguinputnam.com (Go to Young Readers and look for Scieszka's name in the Authors & Illustrators.)

Barbara Seuling—www.barbaraseuling.com

Peter Sís—www.petersis.com

# Roll Out the Red Carpet...
# Children's Book Awards

Numerous awards honor children's books, and through them, you have a reliable source for the best of the best in the field of children's literature. A handy reference is *The Horn Book,* which announces recent award winners in the back of each issue in a section entitled "The Hunt Breakfast." Web site: www.hbook.com. Other useful Web sites to visit for listings of prestigious national and international children's book awards are www.ala.org and www.childrenslit.com.

For picture books, look for news of the **Caldecott Award** winners in the spring of each year. For books intended for older readers, the **Newbery Award** is the benchmark. (See Parent Pull-Out Pages for more information on this prestigious award and a partial list of winners.) These awards are presented annually by the American Library Association, and listings can be found on its Web site, www.ala.org.

Below is a selected list of other notable awards presented in the United States that are of particular interest to those working with third and fourth graders.

**IRA Children's Choice Award:** Each year 10,000 students from across the country are asked to choose their favorite books from a list of recently published titles. Votes are tabulated and books are grouped according to reading levels. The lists are generated and distributed by the International Reading Association (IRA) in conjunction with the Children's Book Council. They appear in the October issue of the IRA journal, *The Reading Teacher.* (**Teachers' Choice Awards,** a list of 30 books rated by teams of teachers, librarians, and reading specialists, are announced in the November issue of *Reading Teacher.*) Copies can be obtained for $1.00, accompanied by a self-addressed, 9-by-12-inch envelope, from IRA, 800 Barksdale Rd., PO Box 8139, Newark, DE 19714-8139, or lists can be downloaded as PDF files from the IRA Web site: www.reading.org.

**The Golden Kite Award:** This annual award, established in 1973, is announced in late spring. It is presented to a member of the Society of Children's Book Writers and Illustrators for excellence in the field of children's books. Statuettes are awarded in four categories: fiction, nonfiction, picture book text, and picture illustration. Web site: www.scbwi.org.

**The Charlotte Zolotow Award:** Named for the well-known picture book author and awarded annually for outstanding text in a picture book. Go to www.soemadison.wisc.edu/ccbc/zolotow.htm for more information.

**Boston Globe-Horn Book Award:** Awarded annually in the fall for excellence in literature for children and young adults in the categories of fiction or poetry, nonfiction, and illustration. Winners are listed in *The Horn Book* in January. Web site: www.hbook.com.

**American Booksellers BookSense Book of the Year Award**: Formerly the ABBY award, it is presented each year to the children's book voted by members as the title they most enjoy recommending to customers. Web site: www.bookweb.org/news/awards/.

**Laura Ingalls Wilder Award:** Presented every two years by the Association for Library Services to Children (ALSC) to an author or illustrator whose books, published in the United States, have made a lasting contribution to the field over a period of years. Go to www.ala.org for more information.

**Robert F. Sibert Award Informational Book Award:** Awarded annually to the author of the best informational book for children, it is named in honor of the long-time president of Bound to Stay Bound Books. Go to www.ala.org for more information.

**Coretta Scott King Awards:** In honor of Martin Luther King Jr., awards are given annually to an African American author and an African American illustrator whose books provide inspiration and educate. Honors are also awarded. Go to www.ala.org for more information.

**Parents' Choice Awards:** These awards are given to books in a number of genres (as well as a variety of other media products) that "meet and exceed standards set by educators, scientists, performing artists, librarians, parents, and . . . kids." Award levels include Classic, Gold, Silver, Recommended, Approved, and Fun Stuff. Go to www.parents-choice.org for complete lists.

**Jane Addams Book Award:** Awarded by the Women's International League of Peace and Freedom to the children's book that promotes peace, social justice, and equality of the sexes and races. Go to www.janeaddamspeace.org for more information.

**Jefferson Cup:** Awarded annually since 1983 by the Virginia Library Association's Children's and Young Adult Round Table to a biography, historical fiction, or American history book written for children. For more information go to www.co.fairfax.va.us/library/reading/ya/jeffcup.htm.

**Notable Books for a Global Society (NBGS):** This committee of the International Reading Association's Reading and Children's Literature Special Interest Group annually selects 25 works written for children in grades K–12 notable for enhancing an understanding of cultural differences across the globe. Go to www.csulb.edu/org/childrens-lit or review the fall issue of *The Dragon Lode,* which includes teaching ideas and titles of related books.

**Scott O'Dell Award for Historical Fiction:** Awarded to a book for children or young adults published in English in the United States and set in the Americas, this honor was established by the author to encourage the writing of historical fiction for young readers. Web site: www.scottodell.com.

**Orbis Pictus Award for Outstanding Nonfiction for Children:** Awarded annually by the National Council of Teachers of English (NCTE) for excellence in this genre. The award is named in honor of the work of Johannes Amos Comenius, ORBIS PICTUS: THE WORLD IN PICTURES, published in 1657 and recognized as the first book written expressly for children. For more information visit www.ncte.org/elem/awards/orbispictus/.

**Outstanding Science Trade Books for Students K–12:** Originally known as Outstanding Science Trade Books for Children, these lists of books are selected by a review panel of the National Science Teachers Association (NSTA) in coordination with the Children's Book Council (CBC) and have been named yearly since 1973. The books are listed on the Web site: www.nsta.org/ostbc.

**Christopher Awards:** Founded in 1945 and committed to the Judeo-Christian tradition of service to God and humanity, the Christophers honor books, films, TV programs, and people who "affirm the highest values of the human spirit." Information and winners are listed on the Web site: www.christophers.org.

**Lee Bennett Hopkins Poetry Award:** Founded by Hopkins in 1993 to promote poetry, this award is presented annually to an American poet or anthologist for the most outstanding new book of children's poetry published in the previous calendar year. Web site: www.pabook.libraries.psu.edu/hopkinsaward.html.

Many states also give awards, such as the **Texas Bluebonnet Award** (www.txla.org/groups/tba), Minnesota's **Maud Hart Lovelace Book Award** (www. isd77. k12.mn.us/lovelace/lovelace.html), New York's **Charlotte Award** (www.nysreading. org/awards), and Wyoming's **Indian Paintbrush Book Award** (www.ccpls.org/html/ indianp.html). Go to www.carr.lib.md.us/read/stateawardsbks.htm for a general listing of state awards and their Web sites.

An international award worth noting is the **Hans Christian Andersen Award** (www.ibby.org/seiten/04_andersen.htm), considered to be the most prestigious award in children's literature in the world. Bestowed every two years by the International Board on Books for Young People (IBBY), it honors an author whose work has made a significant contribution internationally to children's literature.

Three English awards are the **Carnegie Medal,** which recognizes an outstanding children's book written in English and first published in the United Kingdom; the **Kate Greenaway Medal,** which parallels the Caldecott Award (go to www.carnegiegreenaway. org.uk); and the **Smarties Book Prize**, which is awarded annually to the best children's book published in the United Kingdom (www.booktrusted.com/nestle).

In Canada, the **Canadian Library Association Book of the Year for Children Award** honors a book of literary distinction, while the **Amelia Frances Howard-Gibbon Medal** is awarded to an outstanding illustrated book written by a Canadian and published in Canada. Web sites: www.cla.ca/awards/boyc.htm and www.cla.ca/awards/afhg.htm, respectively.

# Parent Pull-Out Pages

# Raising Readers

## Tips and Techniques for Parents

### by Judy Bradbury

## THE NUMBER 1 TIP FOR SUCCESS: READ ALOUD TO YOUR CHILD

Want a surefire way to help your child achieve in school? Read aloud to him or her. "Isn't my child too old?" you ask. *No way!!* **Reading aloud is the single most important thing you can do to improve your child's attitude toward reading.**

Incorporate these basic strategies, and you'll even find yourself looking forward to reading the next chapter of that book you've been sharing daily with your child. *What's going to happen next?* you wonder. A love of reading instilled in your child—that's what. Can you spell s-u-c-c-e-s-s?

### Surefire Techniques

1. Read aloud stories that appeal to you and that you know will interest your youngster. Every day. Choose books that will make you both giggle or shiver. If a book makes you want to keep reading even when supper is burning, it's a winner. If you love a book, you'll convey that to your child. If, on the other hand, you aren't enthused about the story, you'll probably give that away, too. Don't hesitate to re-read favorites, but be adventurous and choose new titles, too.

2. Skim a book before deciding on it. Consider content, length, and your child's interests. Review each chapter before reading it aloud. By becoming familiar with the plot, you'll be more apt to read with expression. When the character is frightened, shake! When the forest is creepy and spooky, whisper. Narrow your eyes, raise your eyebrows, lower your voice; show fear, happiness, surprise. And when something silly happens, enjoy those belly laughs! Draw your child into the story with the first sentence and make the last line memorable. You'll find your child begging you not to stop reading at a chapter's end and reaching for that book with eager anticipation the next day. Good, good, good. Because, remember, our mantra is *Read every day*.

3. Choose a cozy, distraction-free spot to enjoy your read-aloud time. Wrap yourself and your child around the book. Cuddle up, cover up, lie head-to-head beneath the reading lamp, make a reading cave with a blanket beneath the dining room table—do whatever will make your daily read-aloud time special. This is a time your child will cherish, savor, look forward to, and remember.

Reading aloud is one of the best gifts you can give to your child. It's free, it's easy, it expands your child's horizons, and it introduces one of life's most satisfying pleasures: the enjoyment that comes from the countless wonders found between the covers of a book.

*Children's Book Corner: A READ-ALOUD Resource with Tips, Techniques, and Plans for Teachers, Librarians, and Parents, by Judy Bradbury. Westport, CT: Libraries Unlimited, 2005.*

# Raising Readers

## Tips and Techniques for Parents

### by Judy Bradbury

## HOW TO SQUELCH AN INTEREST IN READING IN 10 EASY STEPS

1. Never buy your child a book as a present. Buy toys instead.

2. Don't get caught reading a book yourself. Or a magazine or newspaper.

3. Avoid the public library at all costs. Never mind that it's free.

4. Use newspapers only to wrap fish or potato peels.

5. Forget the book. Watch the movie.

6. Keep the TV on at all times. No exceptions.

7. Careful! Don't ever consider buying your child a book about anything he or she is interested in.

8. Don't put a reading light in his or her room. Banish flashlights from the bedroom, too. You don't want your child sneaking a peek at a book after "lights out."

9. When your child mentions a good book he or she is reading in school, change the subject.

10. Never, ever, ever read aloud to your child. *Ever.* If you do, you're doomed.

*Children's Book Corner: A READ-ALOUD Resource with Tips, Techniques, and Plans for Teachers, Librarians, and Parents*, by Judy Bradbury. Westport, CT: Libraries Unlimited, 2005.

# Raising Readers

## Tips and Techniques for Parents

### by Judy Bradbury

### GIRL TALK: BOOKS GUARANTEED
### TO GIVE YOUR DAUGHTER BOOK BURN*

Think carefully before you purchase or borrow the books listed here. If you have chores that need doing, if you were hoping to carry on a conversation, however brief, with your 8 to 10-year-old daughter, if you mind that the flashlight goes on under the covers once the overhead light is turned out, then please, please, please don't pick up these books.

If, however, you love the healthy look of book burn in spite of all of the potential drawbacks listed above, don't delay! Pick one up today.

- ANASTASIA KRUPNIK, by Lois Lowry. Feisty and smart, this gal is a timeless wonder; first in a series. See also the All About Sam series.

- OPHIE OUT OF OZ, by Kathleen O'Dell. A 12 year-old who moves from glamorous California to plain old Oregon adjusts to her new home. See also AGNES PARKER, GIRL IN PROGRESS and its sequel, AGNES PARKER . . . HAPPY CAMPER?, also by O'Dell.

- THE CARE AND KEEPING OF FRIENDS (American Girl Library). See also THE CARE AND KEEPING OF YOU: THE BODY BOOK FOR GIRLS and GOOD SPORTS: WINNING, LOSING, AND EVERYTHING IN BETWEEN, also American Girl Library books full of clear and helpful advice suitable for middle grade girls.

- SARAH, PLAIN AND TALL, by Patricia MacLachlan; courage, pluck and wisdom packed into a hugely entertaining slim novel; Newbery Award winner. Sequel: SKYLARK.

*A pink nose, reminding one of sunburn, that a reader gets as a result of keeping her nose in a book too long. No long-term effects, with the exception of higher test scores, have been associated with this condition. For more details, consult your local librarian, who can speak from personal experience.

*Children's Book Corner: A READ-ALOUD Resource with Tips, Techniques, and Plans for Teachers, Librarians, and Parents*, by Judy Bradbury. Westport, CT: Libraries Unlimited, 2005.

# Raising Readers

## Tips and Techniques for Parents
### by Judy Bradbury

## LOOK AT THOSE MUSCLES! BOOKS GUARANTEED TO GIVE YOUR SON BOOK BICEPS*

Think carefully before you purchase or borrow the books listed here. If you have chores that need doing, if you were hoping to carry on a conversation, however brief, with your 8- to 10-year-old son, if you mind that the flashlight goes on under the covers once the overhead light is turned out, then please, please, please don't pick up these books.

If, however, you love the healthy look of book biceps in spite of all of the potential drawbacks listed above, don't delay! Pick one up today.

- TIME WARP TRIO series, by Jon Scieszka; hilarious "history."

- INDIAN IN THE CUPBOARD books, by Lynne Reid Banks; plastic figurines come to life.

- THE TRANSMOGRIFICATION OF ROSCOE WIZZLE, by David Elliott; boy becomes bug.

- STONE FOX, by John Reynold Gardiner; boy and sled dog.

- DEAR MRS. RYAN, YOU'RE RUINING MY LIFE, by Jennifer B. Jones. Mom's a recently divorced writer; funny and warm.

- SNARF ATTACK, UNDERFOODLE, AND THE SECRET OF LIFE: THE RIOT BROTHERS TELL ALL, by Mary Amato.

- SIDEWAYS STORIES FROM WAYSIDE SCHOOL, by Louis Sachar, and related titles, all hilarious.

- JOEY PIGZA books, by Jack Gantos; popular and somehow funny award winners about a boy with learning difficulties and other problems.

*Those muscles in the forearms that a reader gets from holding up a book. Long-term effects associated with this condition include higher test scores, increased brain power, and the ability to carry heavy grocery bags into the house. For more details, consult your local librarian, who can speak from personal experience.*

*Children's Book Corner: A READ-ALOUD Resource with Tips, Techniques, and Plans for Teachers, Librarians, and Parents*, by Judy Bradbury. Westport, CT: Libraries Unlimited, 2005.

# Raising Readers

## Tips and Techniques for Parents

### by Judy Bradbury

## BOOKS MIDDLE GRADERS WILL REMEMBER
## WHEN THEY'RE MIDDLE-AGED

Think back to when you were 8, 9, and 10 years old. Besides bicycling, pick-up kickball games, popsicles, and endless summer days, which books do you remember? If you were a reader, betcha can't name just one. Even if you weren't a reader, betcha can name at least one. Here's an armful of too-good-to-be-missed books for your 8- to 10-year-old.

Go ahead, make a memory. Want two memories for the price of one? Read the book aloud to your middle grader.

CHARLOTTE'S WEB, by E. B. White

CHRONICLES OF NARNIA, by C. S. Lewis

LITTLE HOUSE ON THE PRAIRIE, by Laura Ingalls Wilder

TALES OF A FOURTH GRADE NOTHING, by Judy Blume

Anastasia Krupnik series, by Lois Lowry

Harry Potter series, by J. K. Rowling

A Series of Unfortunate Events, by Lemony Snicket

THE BEST CHRISTMAS PAGEANT EVER, by Barbara Robinson

Books by Roald Dahl and Beverly Cleary

Poetry by Jack Prelutsky and Shel Silverstein

*Children's Book Corner: A READ-ALOUD Resource with Tips, Techniques, and Plans for Teachers, Librarians, and Parents*, by Judy Bradbury. Westport, CT: Libraries Unlimited, 2005.

# Raising Readers

## Tips and Techniques for Parents

### by Judy Bradbury

## ALL-STAR AUTHORS FOR MIDDLE GRADE READERS

The next time you make a quick trip to the library in search of a wonderful read for your middle grader, take along this handy list of today's all-star authors. The next time you need a birthday gift for one of your middle grader's friends, look no further. Pull out this very same handy dandy list (arranged in alphabetical order) of masters at reaching the middle grader. Slap, dash, you're done, and what a good job it is! The only other thing you need is a bow!

Beverly Cleary—Meet RAMONA QUIMBY, HENRY HUGGINS, and other delightful, unforgettable characters!

Andrew Clements—See especially FRINDLE, THE LANDRY NEWS, THE REPORT CARD, THE JANITOR'S BOY, THE JACKET, A WEEK IN THE WOODS, and the Jake Drake Ready-for-Chapter series.

Lois Lowry—See especially the Anastasia Krupnik series, the All About Sam series, and GOONEY BIRD GREENE.

Louis Sachar—See especially SIDEWAYS STORIES FROM WAYSIDE SCHOOL and related titles, and THERE'S A BOY IN THE GIRL'S BATHROOM.

Jon Scieszka—See especially the Time Warp Trio series, THE STINKY CHEESE MAN AND OTHER FAIRLY STUPID TALES, MATH CURSE, and SCIENCE VERSE.

See also Jean Fritz and Johanna Hurwitz!

*Note: Authors often write books for a variety of age levels; choose accordingly.*

*Children's Book Corner: A READ-ALOUD Resource with Tips, Techniques, and Plans for Teachers, Librarians, and Parents*, by Judy Bradbury. Westport, CT: Libraries Unlimited, 2005.

# Raising Readers

## Tips and Techniques for Parents

by Judy Bradbury

### THAT COULD BE ME! CONTEMPORARY FICTION FOR THIRD-GRADE READERS

Here's a list of realistic fiction stories that feature everyday kids facing everyday situations. From figuring out who is scribbling in the classroom library books to memorizing multiplication tables, how these characters manage their woes and triumphs will be sure to grab your child's attention. Who needs TV?!

- The Robert Series, written by Barbara Seuling and illustrated by Paul Brewer (OH NO, IT'S ROBERT; ROBERT TAKES A STAND; ROBERT AND THE GREAT ESCAPE, and other titles).

- THE HERO OF THIRD GRADE, written by Alice DeLaCroix and illustrated by Cynthia Fisher.

- THIRD GRADE STINKS!, written by Colleen O'Shaughnessy McKenna and illustrated by Stephanie Roth (See also DOGGONE . . . THIRD GRADE!, and THIRD GRADE GHOULS).

- 7 X 9 = TROUBLE!, written by Claudia Mills and illustrated by G. Brian Karas.

- SPIDER STORCH'S FUMBLED FIELD TRIP, written by Gina Willner-Pardo and illustrated by Nick Sharratt.

- MATTHEW JACKSON MEETS THE WALL, written by Patricia Reilly Giff and illustrated by Blanche Sims.

- RAMONA THE PEST and related titles, by Beverly Cleary.

*Note: Authors often write books for a variety of age levels; choose accordingly.*

*Children's Book Corner: A READ-ALOUD Resource with Tips, Techniques, and Plans for Teachers, Librarians, and Parents*, by Judy Bradbury. Westport, CT: Libraries Unlimited, 2005.

# Raising Readers

## Tips and Techniques for Parents

### by Judy Bradbury

## THAT COULD BE ME! CONTEMPORARY FICTION FOR FOURTH-GRADE READERS

Here's a list of realistic fiction—books that feature fourth-grade kids facing everyday situations. From a pen pal who can't speak English to vacationing with a grieving grandmother, these characters' woes and triumphs are sure to grab your child's attention. Get real! (Read a book.)

- DEAR WHISKERS, written by Ann Whitehead Nagda and illustrated by Stephanie Roth. See also MEOW MEANS MISCHIEF. This is the one about the pen pal.

- Anastasia Krupnik series, written by the award-winning author Lois Lowry, that girls can't put down. See also the All About Sam series, about Anastasia's younger brother.

- THE CONFE$$ION$ AND $ECRET$ OF HOWARD J. FINGERHUT, written by Esther Hershenhorn and illustrated by Ethan Long; class project on business gets hairy.

- TALES OF A FOURTH GRADE NOTHING, by well-known author Judy Blume. See also DOUBLE FUDGE, FUDGE-A-MANIA, and OTHERWISE KNOWN AS SHEILA THE GREAT.

- JACK ADRIFT: FOURTH GRADE WITHOUT A CLUE, by popular and oh-so-funny award-winning author Jack Gantos, who is known best for his Joey Pigza books about a boy with learning difficulties.

- MERMAID MARY MARGARET, written by Lynn E. Hazen; a girl traveling with her grieving grandmother keeps a journal. A pleaser!

*Note: Authors often write books for a variety of age levels; choose accordingly.*

*Children's Book Corner: A READ-ALOUD Resource with Tips, Techniques, and Plans for Teachers, Librarians, and Parents*, by Judy Bradbury. Westport, CT: Libraries Unlimited, 2005.

# Raising Readers

## Tips and Techniques for Parents

### by Judy Bradbury

## FAR OUT! FANTASTIC FANTASY FOR THIRD- AND FOURTH-GRADE READERS

Here's a list of fantasy titles that transport third- and fourth-grade readers to other worlds, other times, and imaginary places featuring mythical, mystical characters. Yes, there is fantasy beyond Harry Potter. So while you're waiting for the next installment, don't despair. Choose one of these worthy reads.

- THE MOUSE AND THE MOTORCYCLE, beloved and ever-popular classic written by Beverly Cleary and illustrated by Louis Darling.

- MY FATHER'S DRAGON, three tales written by Ruth Stiles Gannett about a boy who saves a dragon that have been winning the hearts of children since 1948. In addition to MY FATHER'S DRAGON, the trilogy includes ELMER AND THE DRAGON and THE DRAGONS OF BLUELAND.

- The Spiderwick Chronicles, a solid choice for readers who can't quite tackle (or lift) the Harry Potter series; by Tony DiTerlizzi and Holly Black; Titles: THE FIELD GUIDE, THE SEEING STONE, LUCINDA'S SECRET, THE IRONWOOD TREE, and THE WRATH OF MULGARATH.

Other highly acclaimed fantasy for middle graders:

- DIAL-A-GHOST, THE GREAT GHOST RESCUE, and other titles by Eva Ibbotson.

- A Series of Unfortunate Events, by Lemony Snicket.

- Books by Roald Dahl, Edward Eager, and Dick King-Smith.

- See also the Magic Shop Books, by Bruce Coville, TIME CAT, by Lloyd Alexander, and THE PHANTOM TOLLBOOTH, a classic by Norton Juster, for more advanced readers.

*Note: Authors often write books for a variety of age levels; choose accordingly.*

*Children's Book Corner: A READ-ALOUD Resource with Tips, Techniques, and Plans for Teachers, Librarians, and Parents*, by Judy Bradbury. Westport, CT: Libraries Unlimited, 2005.

# Raising Readers

## Tips and Techniques for Parents

### by Judy Bradbury

### I'M SERIOUS! SERIES FICTION THAT'S WORTH YOUR MIDDLE GRADER'S TIME

Is your child one of those kids who loves to read EVERYTHING by one particular author or EVERY book in a series? Be honest: you went through that phase, too, didn't you? Remember Nancy Drew or the Hardy Boys? Here's a list of series that are worth any middle grader's time and sure bets to keep reticent readers reading. Most of these titles can be found at the library or in inexpensive paperback. WAY cheaper than an electronic game!

**Wild at Heart:** Kids volunteer at an animal clinic; series created by award-winning author Laurie Halse Anderson (American Girl Library).

**The Boxcar Children:** Classic series created by Gertrude Chandler Warner about four children and their adventures in and around their boxcar home; over 100 titles.

**The Time Warp Trio:** Written by Jon Scieszka and illustrated by Lane Smith; humorous nonsense, for which this team is legendary, with a bit of history thrown in. Titles include TUT TUT; THE GOOD, THE BAD, AND THE GOOFY; KNIGHTS OF THE KITCHEN TABLE; THE NOT-SO-JOLLY ROGER; and YOUR MOTHER WAS A NEANDERTHAL.

**The Littles:** A treasury of tales written by John Peterson and illustrated by Roberta Carter Clark about a family six inches tall with tails. Titles include THE LITTLES, THE LITTLES AND THE BIG STORM, THE LITTLES AND THE TRASH TINIES, and THE LITTLES TO THE RESCUE.

**Mrs. Piggle-Wiggle:** A character who smells like cookies, lives in an upside-down house, and was once married to a pirate helps children overcome problems, from hating baths to eating too slowly; written by Betty MacDonald and illustrated by Hilary Knight or Maurice Sendak. Titles: MRS. PIGGLE-WIGGLE, MRS. PIGGLE-WIGGLE'S MAGIC, MRS. PIGGLE- WIGGLE'S FARM, and HELLO, MRS. PIGGLE-WIGGLE.

*Children's Book Corner: A READ-ALOUD Resource with Tips, Techniques, and Plans for Teachers, Librarians, and Parents*, by Judy Bradbury. Westport, CT: Libraries Unlimited, 2005.

# Raising Readers

## Tips and Techniques for Parents

### by Judy Bradbury

## "SURVIVOR" STORIES: TALES THAT PIT THE CHARACTER AGAINST NATURE—WITH NO CAMERA CREWS OR COMMERCIALS

Does your child crave adventure? Given a choice between a movie and popcorn or building a snow fort with a spoon, would your child ask for the flatware? Would she rather scale a rock wall than meet a rock star? Does he prefer Boy Scouts to boy-crazy girls? Then choose one of these survival stories that pack action, adventure, and obstacles onto every page. Will the character make it? Can he beat the odds? Will she find her way? Read and find out!

- JULIE OF THE WOLVES, Newbery Award winner and the first in a trilogy by Jean Craighead George. See also MY SIDE OF THE MOUNTAIN, a Newbery Honor Award winner and the first in another trilogy by George.

- CABIN ON TROUBLE CREEK, by Jean Van Leeuwen; two brothers face danger in the wilderness in 1803.

- STONE FOX, by John Reynolds Gardiner; about a boy and his sled dog.

- THE SIGN OF THE BEAVER, by Elizabeth George Speare; Matt guards the home site in eighteenth-century Maine; Newbery Honor Medal.

- THE COURAGE OF SARAH NOBLE, by Alice Dalgliesh; set in the wilds of Connecticut, Sarah relies on pluck and her mother's advice in this true story.

- THE MATCHLOCK GUN, by Walter Edmonds. It's 1756 in the midst of the French and Indian War, and Edward must protect his home; Newbery Medal.

- For advanced readers, check out DOGSONG and WOODSONG, by Gary Paulsen, and ISLAND OF THE BLUE DOLPHINS, by Scott O'Dell.

- Finally, don't forget fantasy. Although set in imaginary worlds, these stories are often tales of survival.

*Note: Authors often write books for a variety of age levels; choose accordingly.*

*Children's Book Corner: A READ-ALOUD Resource with Tips, Techniques, and Plans for Teachers, Librarians, and Parents*, by Judy Bradbury. Westport, CT: Libraries Unlimited, 2005.

# Raising Readers

## Tips and Techniques for Parents

by Judy Bradbury

### HA HA HA! BOOKS GUARANTEED TO CAUSE MIDDLE-GRADER GIGGLES

You have to admit a middle grader's laugh is pretty infectious. It's spontaneous and without guile. Put two or three middle graders together, and they'll laugh at the gross, the corny, and the slapstick with such abandon that it's hard not to follow down their riotous path. You can't fight 'em, so you might as well join 'em. Here are a few titles to get them going.

- Poetry by Jack Prelutsky—Try SOMETHING BIG HAS BEEN HERE, THE FROGS WORE RED SUSPENDERS, SCRANIMALS, IT'S HALLOWEEN, IT'S CHRISTMAS, and IT'S VALENTINES' DAY.

- Books by Roald Dahl—Look for THE TWITS, THE ENORMOUS CROCODILE, and ESIO TROT.

- SIDEWAYS STORIES FROM WAYSIDE SCHOOL and related titles by Louis Sachar.

- Poetry selected by Bruce Lansky—NO MORE HOMEWORK! NO MORE TESTS! KIDS' FAVORITE FUNNY SCHOOL POEMS, and KIDS PICK THE FUNNIEST POEMS: POEMS THAT MAKE KIDS LAUGH.

- PARTS, MORE PARTS, and EVEN MORE PARTS, by Tedd Arnold.

- THE TRUE STORY OF THE 3 LITTLE PIGS!, by Jon Scieszka.

- THE BEST CHRISTMAS PAGEANT EVER, by Barbara Robinson.

- JOKES FOR CHILDREN and MORE JOKES FOR CHILDREN, by Marguerite Kohl and Frederica Young.

- COLOSSAL FOSSILS: DINOSAUR JOKES and numerous other collections of jokes, riddles, and rhymes by Charles Keller.

- FUNNY YOU SHOULD ASK: HOW TO MAKE UP JOKES AND RIDDLES WITH WORDPLAY, by Marvin Terban.

*Children's Book Corner: A READ-ALOUD Resource with Tips, Techniques, and Plans for Teachers, Librarians, and Parents*, by Judy Bradbury. Westport, CT: Libraries Unlimited, 2005.

# Raising Readers

## Tips and Techniques for Parents

### by Judy Bradbury

## HISTORICAL FICTION: TIME TRAVEL FOR MIDDLE GRADERS

Middle graders love to escape to other times. Whether it's the American Revolution or medieval England, there's an allure to travel beyond the corner store. If your child learns a little history along the way, it makes the journey all the more worthwhile.

- THE BIRCHBARK HOUSE, by Louise Erdrich; Award-winning book about pioneer settlement as seen through the eyes of a Native American girl. Contrast to LITTLE HOUSE ON THE PRAIRIE, by Laura Ingalls Wilder.

- THE KITE FIGHTERS, by Linda Sue Park. A boy in fifteenth-century Korea competes in the New Year kite competition.

- My Name Is America/Dear America series, based on historical events and real people, but whose main characters are fictional. Titles include

  THE JOURNAL OF FINN REARDON: A NEWSIE and A COAL MINER'S BRIDE: THE DIARY OF ANETKA KAMINSKA, both by Susan Campbell Bartoletti;

  DREAMS IN THE GOLDEN COUNTRY: THE DIARY OF ZIPPORAH FELDMAN, A JEWISH IMMIGRANT GIRL, by Kathryn Lasky; and

  WHEN CHRISTMAS COMES AGAIN: THE WORLD WAR I DIARY OF SIMONE SPENCER, by Beth Seidel Levine.

- The Time Warp Trio series, by Jon Scieszka. These books are hilarious take-offs on events in history. Titles include

  SEE YOU LATER, GLADIATOR;

  KNIGHTS OF THE KITCHEN TABLE; and

  YOUR MOTHER WAS A NEANDERTHAL.

- The Magic Tree House series, by Mary Pope Osborne; easy to read, enjoyable paperback series. Titles include

  HOUR OF THE OLYMPICS and

  PIRATES PAST NOON.

*Children's Book Corner: A READ-ALOUD Resource with Tips, Techniques, and Plans for Teachers, Librarians, and Parents*, by Judy Bradbury. Westport, CT: Libraries Unlimited, 2005.

# Raising Readers

## Tips and Techniques for Parents

### by Judy Bradbury

## HISTORICAL NONFICTION AND BIOGRAPHY: TIME TRAVEL FOR MIDDLE GRADERS, PART II

Informative yet inviting! Fact blended with action makes for memorable reading. Who says history has to be a snoozer? Fasten your seat belts!

- You won't be disappointed with books by Jean Fritz. Titles include

    AND THEN WHAT HAPPENED, PAUL REVERE?;

    SHHH! WE'RE WRITING THE CONSTITUTION;

    WHAT'S THE BIG IDEA, BEN FRANKLIN?;

    WHERE WAS PATRICK HENRY ON THE 29TH OF MAY?;

    WILL YOU SIGN HERE, JOHN HANCOCK?; and

    THE DOUBLE LIFE OF POCAHONTAS.

- Award-winner Russell Freedman has several books for inquiring middle grade minds. Try

    IMMIGRANT KIDS and

    INDIAN CHIEFS.

- Ditto for Jim Murphy. His titles include

    THE BOYS' WAR: CONFEDERATE AND UNION SOLDIERS TALK ABOUT THE CIVIL WAR; and

    AN AMERICAN PLAGUE: THE TRUE AND TERRIFYING STORY OF THE YELLOW FEVER OF 1793.

- WALT WHITMAN: WORDS FOR AMERICA, by Barbara Kerley.

- The Who Was series introduces middle graders to important people in history with simple illustrations and snippets of intriguing facts strategically placed alongside the text. See also the Smart About series. They are both published by Grosset & Dunlap. Titles include

    WHO WAS SACAGAWEA?;

    WHO WAS ALBERT EINSTEIN?; and

    SUNFLOWERS AND SWIRLY STARS: PABLO PICASSO.

- One more title! THE INCREDIBLE JOURNEY OF LEWIS & CLARK, by Rhoda Blumberg.

*Children's Book Corner: A READ-ALOUD Resource with Tips, Techniques, and Plans for Teachers, Librarians, and Parents*, by Judy Bradbury. Westport, CT: Libraries Unlimited, 2005.

# Raising Readers

## Tips and Techniques for Parents

### by Judy Bradbury

## TOO-GOOD-TO-BE-MISSED: BOOKS FOR MIDDLE GRADERS THAT HAVE WITHSTOOD THE TEST OF TIME

I'm betting you remember one or two or maybe all of the books listed here. These classics have been around for a while, and generations of middle graders have loved reading them. So pass along a tradition.

- POLLYANNA, by Eleanor H. Porter; a young girl with spunk and spirit makes a difference.

- PIPPI LONGSTOCKING, by Astrid Lindgren; this lively redhead has been making friends for generations. See also PIPPI GOES ON BOARD.

- CHARLOTTE'S WEB, written by E. B. White and illustrated by Garth Williams; a farm, a spider, and Some Pig!

- STUART LITTLE, written by E. B. White and illustrated by Garth Williams; even better than the movie!

- Chronicles of Narnia, by C. S. Lewis; multiple book fantasy includes THE LION, THE WITCH, AND THE WARDROBE.

- Boxcar Children, by Gertrude Chandler Warner; adventures of the four Alden children in their boxcar home.

- Edward Eager's Tales of Magic series: HALF MAGIC, KNIGHT'S CASTLE, THE TIME GARDEN, and MAGIC BY THE LAKE; fantasy at its best.

- MY FATHER'S DRAGON, by Ruth Stiles Gannett; first of three tales about a boy, a dragon, and an island.

*Children's Book Corner: A READ-ALOUD Resource with Tips, Techniques, and Plans for Teachers, Librarians, and Parents*, by Judy Bradbury. Westport, CT: Libraries Unlimited, 2005.

# Raising Readers

## Tips and Techniques for Parents

### by Judy Bradbury

## WHAT IS THE NEWBERY MEDAL?

Awarded annually by the Association for Library Service to Children (ALSC), a division of the American Library Association, the Newbery Medal is given to the author of the most distinguished contribution to American literature for children. It is named for eighteenth-century British bookseller John Newbery and has been awarded since 1922.

While not the only worthwhile choices, Newbery Medal and Honor books are considered hallmarks of quality in books written for middle grade children. Listed below are Newbery winners especially appropriate for third- and fourth-grade readers.

### Selected Newbery Medal Winners

- TALE OF DESPEREAUX: BEING THE STORY OF A MOUSE, A PRINCESS, SOME SOUP, AND A SPOOL OF THREAD, by Kate DiCamillo (Candlewick)
- SHILOH, by Phyllis Reynolds Naylor (Atheneum)
- NUMBER THE STARS, by Lois Lowry (Houghton Mifflin)
- JOYFUL NOISE: POEMS FOR TWO VOICES, by Paul Fleischman (HarperCollins)
- LINCOLN: A PHOTOBIOGRAPHY, by Russell Freedman (Clarion)
- THE WHIPPING BOY, by Sid Fleischman (Greenwillow)
- SARAH, PLAIN AND TALL, by Particia MacLachlan (HarperCollins)
- DEAR MR. HENSHAW, by Beverly Cleary (Morrow)
- MRS. FRISBY AND THE RATS OF NIMH, by Robert C. O'Brien (Atheneum)
- MIRACLES ON MAPLE HILL, by Virginia Sorenson (Harcourt)
- GINGER PYE, by Eleanor Estes (Harcourt)
- DOOR IN THE WALL, by Marguerite de Angeli (Doubleday)
- KING OF THE WIND, by Marguerite O'Henry (Rand McNally)
- TWENTY-ONE BALLOONS, by William Pene du Bois (Viking)
- STRAWBERRY GIRL, by Lois Lenski; Lippincott
- RABBIT HILL, by Robert Lawson (Viking)
- ROLLER SKATES, by Ruth Sawyer (Viking)
- CADDIE WOODLAWN, by Carol Ryrie Brink (Macmillan)
- VOYAGES OF DOCTOR DOLITTLE, by Hugh Lofting (Lippincott)

*Children's Book Corner: A READ-ALOUD Resource with Tips, Techniques, and Plans for Teachers, Librarians, and Parents*, by Judy Bradbury. Westport, CT: Libraries Unlimited, 2005.

# Raising Readers

## Tips and Techniques for Parents

### by Judy Bradbury

## WHAT YOU CAN DO . . . WHEN YOUR CHILD WON'T READ

As our world becomes more technological and edu-tainment more sophisticated, it seems our children become less interested in books and reading. Should we, as parents, worry? Is reading old-fashioned? Can we learn all we need to know from machines?

Although the computer has become a household tool, we still have to read the manual to figure out how to hook it up. And don't forget about

- the instructions for installing those amazing computer games;

- the directions on the bag of microwave popcorn;

- the instructions on a speeding ticket;

- grocery ads, used car guarantees, leasing agreements;

- medical insurance riders;

- income tax forms;

- college financial aid applications; and

- Internet sites.

So the next time your child tells you he doesn't need to read, sit down and make a list together of the things he does that require reading.

Here are simple suggestions to encourage reading and reinforce its importance:

- Foster reading for information every day. When it's time to check the TV listing for what's on the box, have your child look it up. Then ask him to read the instructions on how to make that yummy popcorn.

- When your child is ready to play the new board game you bought, have her read the directions. Help with difficult words, but don't make it a skills lesson. Rather than interrupt the flow, just tell your child the word so she can keep on reading for meaning.

- Have your child read the garment care instructions for that new microfiber top. When choosing items from a mail-order catalog or online, suggest that your child read the descriptions and the instructions on how to place an order.

*Children's Book Corner: A READ-ALOUD Resource with Tips, Techniques, and Plans for Teachers, Librarians, and Parents*, by Judy Bradbury. Westport, CT: Libraries Unlimited, 2005.

- When a letter or card arrives in the mail, ask your child to read it to you while you deliver him or her to a soccer game.

- Write thank-you notes. Recommend that your child create personal greeting cards or read and choose cards at the store.

- Write notes and slip them in his lunch box, under her pillow, in his baseball mitt, or in her sneaker. Your note could praise her for a job well done, serve as a reminder, offer a riddle, or just to let him know what a great kid he is.

- Make words out of bread or cookie dough. While they bake, heat up some alphabet soup and then eat your words!

- Turn your refrigerator into a bulletin board: post notes, reminders, a calendar, the school newsletter, family news, cartoons, and jokes. Encourage your child to contribute.

- As you travel along in the car, ask your child what the road signs, building names, and billboards say.

- Visit the library. Make it a reward for helping with the grocery shopping, cleaning up toys, or treating a younger sibling nicely. Once there, let your child browse and roam. An added bonus: you get to choose a few books for yourself!

- Buy books as presents. For under $5.00 you can purchase a paperback or two. These make terrific gifts not only for holidays and birthdays but also to celebrate a football win, a lost tooth, a move to a new home, the first day of school, the first day of spring, a camping trip, Earth Day, or the start of summer vacation.

- Capitalize on your child's interests, hobbies, and current fads. Provide reading material related to *anything* in which your child shows an interest.

- Subscribe to children's magazines. Some of the best are *Click, Cobblestone, American Girl, Cricket, Spider,* and *Ranger Rick.* Check for age appropriateness and request a sample copy to be sure it is of interest to your child before purchasing a subscription.

- Subscribe to magazines for yourself and read them when your child is around. Modeling behavior is extremely effective (see library above).

- Read poetry. Every day. Take turns reading alternate verses, read seasonal poetry, and read silly as well as serious collections. In the morning as she brushes her teeth, in the evening as he sets the table, and before bed are perfect opportunities for "poetry pauses." Kid-friendly poets include Judith Viorst, Shel Silverstein, Doug Florian, Jack Prelutsky, John Ciardi, Lee Bennett Hopkins, Bruce Lansky, and Paul Fleischman, whose book of poetry, *Joyful Noise,* won the Newbery Award. This delightful collection features poetry designed for two people to read together—simultaneously!

- Read throughout the summer. Every day. On the hammock, under a tree, on the porch steps. If you're taking a vacation, ask your child to help plan your itinerary by reading about the area you will visit. And then pack lots of books.

*Children's Book Corner: A READ-ALOUD Resource with Tips, Techniques, and Plans for Teachers, Librarians, and Parents*, by Judy Bradbury. Westport, CT: Libraries Unlimited, 2005.

- When your child shows an interest in a particular movie, suggest reading the book first, if there is one. Or better yet, read it together. Then view the film and discuss the differences. Which did your child like better, book or film? What was different, omitted, added? Did the actors resemble the characters as your child pictured them? If your child enjoyed the book/movie, read other books on related topics or by the same author. Your librarian will be happy to suggest titles.

- Read aloud to your child. Every day. Since you'll be doing the reading, you don't have to consider your child's reading level. Just look for a book sure to spark his or her interest, and then make read-alouds part of your daily routine. Start when your child is in the crib, and keep it up until the day you drive your darling off to college. Ten to twenty minutes a day is all the time you need. You can adjust the length of the read-aloud sessions to the pacing of the book and your child's attention span. If there's one tip you take away from this article, this should be it. *Reading aloud is the single most important strategy for raising a child who loves to read.*

    *Note:* This is not the time to ask your child to read aloud to you. Reading orally involves figuring out the words and the phrasing, noting punctuation, and being expressive—all at the same time. That's a tall order for a reluctant reader, and consider this: How often do we read aloud in our everyday adult life? (Not counting reading aloud to our kids. Every day.)

- Keep abreast of your child's progress in school and request additional help should a reading problem become evident. Short-circuiting a reading problem early on helps to prevent a dislike for and avoidance of reading. After all, who eagerly chooses to do something he or she isn't good at?

As a parent you *can* interest your child in reading. With a little forethought, encouragement, and consistent reinforcement on your part—every day—your child's reluctance to read could be just a blip on the video screen of his or her life.

*Children's Book Corner: A READ-ALOUD Resource with Tips, Techniques, and Plans for Teachers, Librarians, and Parents*, by Judy Bradbury. Westport, CT: Libraries Unlimited, 2005.

# Raising Readers

## Tips and Techniques for Parents

### by Judy Bradbury

## RESOURCES ABOUT READING FOR PARENTS

Want to learn more about the benefits of books? Check out these readable references and welcoming Web sites.

### Books

These are not research-dense, sleep-inducing texts; they're interesting reading!

- **The New Read-Aloud Handbook, 5th Edition,** by Jim Trelease (Penguin)

- **Reading Magic: Why Reading Aloud to Our Children Will Change Their Lives Forever,** by Mem Fox (Harcourt)

- **How to Get Your Child to Love Reading: For Ravenous and Reluctant Readers Alike,** by Esmé Raji Codell (Algonquin Books)

- **Read to Me: Raising Kids Who Love to Read,** by Bernice Cullinan (Scholastic)

- **Parents Are Teachers, Too,** by Claudia Jones (Williamson)

- **Hey! Listen to This: Stories to Read-Aloud,** by Jim Trelease (Penguin)

- **Let's Read About . . . Finding Books They'll Love to Read,** by Bernice Cullinan (Scholastic)

- **A Parent's Guide to Children's Reading,** by Nancy Larrick (Bantam)

- **The Hurried Child: Growing Up Too Fast Too Soon, Third Edition,** by David Elkind (Perseus Publishing)

### Web Sites

- **www.trelease-on-reading.com**—Web site of Jim Trelease, author of The New Read-Aloud Handbook (Penguin)

- **www.ala.org/booklist**—Lists of notable children's books arranged by age

- **gpn.unl.edu/rainbow**—The *Reading Rainbow* site; includes a listing of all the books covered on its episodes since the program's inception

*Children's Book Corner: A READ-ALOUD Resource with Tips, Techniques, and Plans for Teachers, Librarians, and Parents*, by Judy Bradbury. Westport, CT: Libraries Unlimited, 2005.

- **www.pbs.org/launchingreaders**—A wonderful resource for parents and teachers

- **www.readingrockets.org**—A friendly site with all sorts of information for parents as well as teachers and librarians

## And Last But Not Least . . .

Public and school librarians and teachers, of course!

*Children's Book Corner: A READ-ALOUD Resource with Tips, Techniques, and Plans for Teachers, Librarians, and Parents*, by Judy Bradbury. Westport, CT: Libraries Unlimited, 2005.

Book Notes

# An Annotated Listing of Recommended Read-Aloud Titles Suitable for Grades 3 and 4 Organized According to Content Area Themes

Listed here are hundreds of books suitable for reading aloud to children in grades 3 and 4. Books are categorized and cross-referenced by subject(s) and briefly described to aid teachers, librarians, and parents in finding just the right book to connect with curriculum, address a concern, or celebrate a special occasion or holiday. Bibliographic information is included for each title. You may also consult the subject, title, and author indexes found at the back of this resource.

## WRITING/LANGUAGE ARTS

- THANK YOU, SARAH! THE WOMAN WHO SAVED THANKSGIVING, written by Laurie Halse Anderson and illustrated by Matt Faulkner (Simon & Schuster); a most incredible picture book written by an inspired award-winning author, with art by an illustrator who knows what makes a picture book stand out; biography, history, power-of-the-pen message.

*Cover from THANK YOU, SARAH! THE WOMAN WHO SAVED THANKSGIVING by Laurie Halse Anderson, illustrated by Matt Faulkner. Copyright © 2002. Used with permission of Simon & Schuster Books for Young Readers, an imprint of Simon & Schuster Children's Publishing.*

- HOW I SPENT MY SUMMER VACATION, by Mark Teague (Crown); a humorous tale in verse about how one lucky boy whose imagination needed a rest spent his summer. I dare you to read this before assigning the September sure-fire groan-getter. Nifty notes to parents and teachers suggesting extension activities are provided.

- MY NAME IS YOON, written by Helen Recorvits and illustrated by Gabi Swiatkowska (Farrar, Straus & Giroux). Yoon means Shining Wisdom in Korean, and young Yoon prefers to write her name in the Korean symbols that "dance together" rather than the English letters that stand alone. Yoon longs to return to the land she knows and loves. Readers witness Yoon gradually making the transition to her new home in America and finding some comfort in it. A wise and gentle teacher, a "ponytail friend," a firm father, and a supportive mother round out the cast in this fully engaging, simply told tale.

*Cover of MY NAME IS YOON © 2003 by Helen Recorvits. Art © 2003 by Gabi Swiatkowska. Used with the permission of Farrar Straus Giroux.*

- PUNCTUATION TAKES A VACATION, written by Robin Pulver and illustrated by Lynn Rowe Reed (Holiday House). The punctuation marks are mad and they're not taking it anymore. Tired of being ignored, off they go, leaving behind a befuddled class that can make no sense of their sentences now that the punctuation has taken a hike. Delightful and hilarious with a definite but lighthearted lesson. See the read-aloud plan for this book in *Children's Book Corner, Grades 1–2.*

- THE AMAZING POP-UP GRAMMAR BOOK, by Jennie Maizels and Kate Petty (Dutton); a book that lives up to its name by making learning about parts of speech fun!

- IN A PICKLE AND OTHER FUNNY IDIOMS, written by Marvin Terban and illustrated by Giulio Maestro (Clarion). Idioms are explained simply and illustrated with comical drawings.

- MAD AS A WET HEN AND OTHER FUNNY IDIOMS, written by Marvin Terban and illustrated by Giulio Maestro (Clarion). Idioms are explained simply and illustrated with comical drawings.

- IT FIGURES! FUN FIGURES OF SPEECH, written by Marvin Terban and illustrated by Giulio Maestro (Clarion). Figures of speech are defined and explained with lots of examples and illustrated with comical drawings.

- FUNNY YOU SHOULD ASK: HOW TO MAKE UP JOKES AND RIDDLES WITH WORDPLAY, written by Marvin Terban and illustrated by John O'Brien (Clarion); advice and examples illustrated with comical drawings.

- KITES SAIL HIGH: A BOOK ABOUT VERBS, by Ruth Heller (Grosset & Dunlap). Brightly illustrated verse makes parts of speech palatable. See the read-aloud plan elsewhere in this resource. See also:
    - A CACHE OF JEWELS AND OTHER COLLECTIVE NOUNS
    - MERRY-GO-ROUND A BOOK ABOUT NOUNS
    - MANY LUSCIOUS LOLLIPOPS: A BOOK ABOUT ADJECTIVES
    - UP, UP AND AWAY: A BOOK ABOUT ADVERBS
    - ALL MINE: A BOOK ABOUT PRONOUNS
    - FANTASTIC! WOW! AND UNREAL!: A BOOK ABOUT INTERJECTIONS AND CONJUNCTIONS
    - BEHIND THE MASK: A BOOK ABOUT PREPOSITIONS

- WRITE UP A STORM WITH THE POLK STREET SCHOOL, written by Patricia Reilly Giff and illustrated by Blanche Sims (Dell); an outstanding how-to. The author uses examples from her popular Kids of the Polk Street School series to illustrate writing concepts and techniques.

- WALT WHITMAN: WORDS FOR AMERICA, written by Barbara Kerley and illustrated by Brain Selznick (Scholastic). This magnificent picture book is a masterpiece, with impressive back material, including the complete text of many of the poems from which lines are excerpted throughout the book. It is most memorable for its exploration of how the Civil War shaped Whitman's life and his writing.

- HELLO MUDDAH, HELLO FADDAH! (A LETTER FROM CAMP), written by Allan Sherman and Lou Busch and illustrated by Jack E. Davis (Dutton). The catchy camp song is illustrated here in comic style befitting the lyrics; a great introduction to letter writing.

- THE BOY ON FAIRFIELD STREET: HOW TED GEISEL GREW UP TO BECOME DR. SEUSS, written by Kathleen Krull and illustrated by Steve Johnson and Lou Fancher (Random House); details the childhood of this legendary children's author and illustrator. See the read-aloud plan elsewhere in this resource.

- LOUISA MAY & MR. THOREAU'S FLUTE, written by Julie Dunlap and Marybeth Lorbiecki and illustrated by Mary Azarian (Dial); the story of the friendship between Louisa May Alcott and Henry David Thoreau, and how it inspired Alcott's writing.

- DEAR MR. HENSHAW, written by Beverly Cleary and illustrated by Paul O. Zelinsky (HarperCollins); novel about a boy navigating his parents' divorce with the help of the letters, real and imaginary, that he writes to an author; Newbery Medal.

- BEETHOVEN LIVES UPSTAIRS, written by Barbara Nichol and illustrated by Scott Cameron (Orchard Books); correspondence between a boy and his uncle about the "madman" who lives upstairs.

- SIDEWALK CIRCUS, presented by Paul Fleischman and illustrated by Kevin Hawkes (Candlewick); a wordless book about imagination and observation.

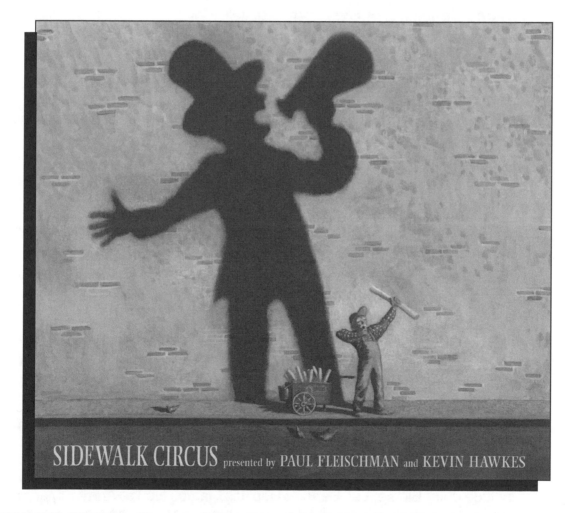

SIDEWALK CIRCUS presented by PAUL FLEISCHMAN and KEVIN HAWKES

- TIME FLIES, by Eric Rohmann (Crown); wordless wonder; Caldecott Honor; great to jumpstart a writing activity.

- THE MYSTERIES OF HARRIS BURDICK, by Chris Van Allsburg (Houghton Mifflin). Use your imagination to piece together the mysteries of these paintings; nearly wordless.

- TUESDAY, by David Wiesner (Clarion); Caldecott Medal; another wordless wonder; see suggestion above.

- LANGSTON'S TRAIN RIDE, written by Robert Burleigh and illustrated by Leonard Jenkins (Orchard); about the inspiration for Hughes's famous poem, "The Negro Speaks of Rivers" and how it led to Hughes's life as a writer.

- FRANK AND ERNEST, by Alexandra Day (Scholastic); the language of small diners explained humorously with the customers' orders on the left and their translation by the short order staff on the right. Yummy fun.

- STRINGBEAN'S TRIP TO THE SHINING SEA, by Vera B. Williams and Jennifer Williams (Greenwillow); chronicles a trip told through postcards sent home.

- THE JOLLY POSTMAN OR OTHER PEOPLE'S LETTERS; THE JOLLY POCKET POSTMAN; THE JOLLY CHRISTMAS POSTMAN, by Janet Ahlberg and Allan Ahlberg (Little, Brown); delightful interactive books that celebrate snail mail; with pocket envelopes holding letters.

- DEAR ANNIE, by Judith Caseley (Greenwillow). Letters between a girl and her grandfather chronicle events in her childhood.

- THE GARDENER, written by Sarah Stewart and illustrated by David Small (Farrar, Straus & Giroux); Caldecott Honor; correspondence between a girl and her parents during the Depression.

- THANK YOU, SANTA, written by Margaret Wild and illustrated by Kerry Argent (Omnibus Books); letters sent throughout the year between a girl and Santa; not a Christmas story.

- DEAR MRS. LARUE: LETTERS FROM OBEDIENCE SCHOOL, by Mark Teague (Scholastic); a delightfully perfect award-winning picture book; a read-aloud plan for this book can be found in *Children's Book Corner, Grades 1–2.*

- AUTHOR TALK, compiled and edited by Leonard S. Marcus (Simon & Schuster); 15 interviews with some of the best-loved children's book authors, who answer many of those often-asked questions; includes childhood and workspace photos, and a bibliography of each author's selected works. Authors include Judy Blume, Lee Bennett Hopkins, James Howe, Ann M. Martin, Gary Paulsen, Jon Scieszka, and Johanna Hurwitz. See the index for books written by these authors that are featured in this resource.

*Cover of THE GARDENER © 1997 by Sarah Stewart. Art © 1997 by David Small.
Used with the permission of Farrar Straus Giroux.*

## DRAMA

• THE WORLD OF THEATER, by Editions Gallimard Jeunesse (Scholastic).
Lift-the-flaps, gatefolds, detachable sections, and more give this book dra-
matic appeal.

• SMALL PLAYS FOR SPECIAL DAYS, written by Sue Alexander and illustrated by Tom Huffman (Clarion); an introduction to directed play-acting involving just two characters in skits focusing on various holidays. Suggestions
for easy props and costumes, and simple stage directions make for uncompli-
cated, snappy productions.

*Cover from SMALL PLAYS FOR SPECIAL DAYS by Sue Alexander. Jacket illustrations copyright © 2003 by Michelle Gengaro-Kokmen. Reprinted by permission of Clarion Books/Houghton Mifflin Company. All rights reserved.*

## SONG-RELATED BOOKS

- THERE WAS AN OLD LADY WHO SWALLOWED A FLY, by Simms Taback (Viking); Caldecott Honor Award.

- THE ERIE CANAL, by Peter Spier (Doubleday).

- THE STAR-SPANGLED BANNER, by Peter Spier (Doubleday); a Reading Rainbow Book.

- THE STORY OF THE STAR-SPANGLED BANNER, written by Steven Kroll and illustrated by Dan Andreasen (Scholastic).

- AMERICA THE BEAUTIFUL: A POP-UP BOOK, by Robert Sabuda (Simon & Schuster); a pop-up of the popular patriotic tune in which landmarks and geographical features characterizing our nation are cleverly depicted.

- AMERICA THE BEAUTIFUL, written by Katharine Lee Bates and illustrated by Wendell Minor (Putnam).

- AMERICA THE BEAUTIFUL, written by Katharine Lee Bates and illustrated by Neil Waldman (Atheneum).

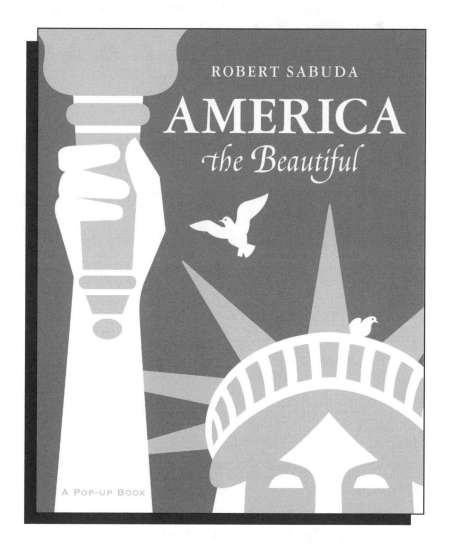

*Cover from AMERICA THE BEAUTIFUL: A POP-UP BOOK illustrated by Robert Sabuda. Copyright © 2004. Used with permission of Little Simon, an imprint of Simon & Schuster Children's Publishing.*

- YANKEE DOODLE: A SONG FROM THE AMERICAN REVOLUTION, illustrated by Todd Ouren (Picture Window Books).

- THIS LAND IS YOUR LAND, written by Woody Guthrie and illustrated by Kathy Jakobsen (Little, Brown); book and CD.

- GETTING TO KNOW YOU!: ROGERS AND HAMMERSTEIN FAVORITES, illustrated by Rosemary Wells (HarperCollins); 17 songs, signature illustrations; includes songbook.

- HAPPY ADOPTION DAY!, lyrics by John McCutcheon, illustrated by Julie Paschkis; Little, Brown.

- HELLO MUDDAH, HELLO FADDAH! (A LETTER FROM CAMP), written by Allan Sherman and Lou Busch and illustrated by Jack E. Davis (Dutton). The catchy camp song is illustrated here in comic style befitting the lyrics; a great introduction to letter writing.

- HUSH, LITTLE BABY: A FOLK SONG, with pictures by Marla Frazee; (Harcourt); great for demonstrating circular storytelling.

- THE FRIENDLY BEASTS, illustrated by Tomie dePaola (G. P. Putnam's Sons); old English Christmas carol.

- WE WISH YOU A MERRY CHRISTMAS, illustrated by Tracey Campbell Pearson (Dial).

- THE LITTLE DRUMMER BOY, words and music by Katherine Davis, Henry Onorati, and Harry Simeone; illustrated by Ezra Jack Keats (Macmillan).

- HANUKKAH LIGHTS, HANUKKAH NIGHTS, written by Leslie Kimmelman and illustrated by John Himmelman (HarperCollins); interactive press-the-button book includes "My Little Dreidel."

## THE ARTS

- CAN YOU FIND IT, TOO?, by Judith Cressy (Abrams). Twenty paintings by well-known artists, along with lists of details to look for in each, make this art appreciation and detail-detective book interactive fun.

- MATH-TERPIECES, written by Greg Tang and illustrated by Greg Paprocki (Scholastic); math functions + art masterpieces = fun while learning; see the read-aloud plan for this book in *Children's Book Corner, Grades 1–2*.

- SEURAT AND LA GRANDE JATTE, by Robert Burleigh (Abrams); an in-depth look at a famous painting; see the read-aloud plan elsewhere in this resource.

- Smart About series (Grosset & Dunlap); titles by various authors include VINCENT VAN GOGH: SUNFLOWERS AND SWIRLY STARS, PABLO PICASSO: BREAKING ALL THE RULES, CLAUDE MONET: SUNSHINE AND WATERLILIES, EDGAR DEGAS: PAINTINGS THAT DANCE, FRIDA KAHLO: THE ARTIST WHO PAINTED HERSELF, and HENRI MATISSE: DRAWING WITH SCISSORS.

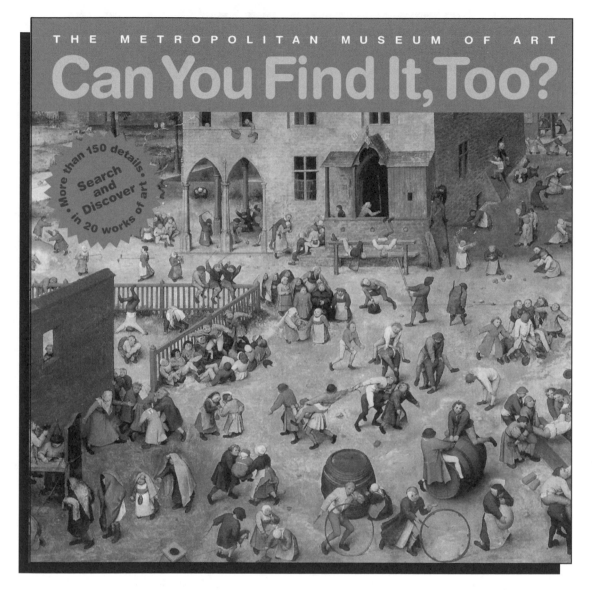

*Cover from CAN YOU FIND IT, TOO? SEARCH AND DISCOVER MORE THAN 150 DETAILS IN 20 WORKS OF ART by Judith Cressy. Copyright © 2004. Reprinted with permission of Abrams Books for Young Readers/Amulet Books.*

## EVENTS IN AMERICA'S HISTORY

- SARAH MORTON'S DAY: A DAY IN THE LIFE OF A PILGRIM GIRL, written by Kate Winters with photographs by Russ Kendall (Scholastic); takes place in 1627. Photographed at Plimoth Plantation on Cape Cod, Massachusetts. See the read-aloud plan for this book in *Children's Book Corner, Grades 1–2.*

- SAMUEL EATON'S DAY: A DAY IN THE LIFE OF A PILGRIM BOY, written by Kate Winters with photographs by Russ Kendall (Scholastic); companion to the book listed above.

*Cover from AMERICAN MOMENTS: SCENES FROM AMERICAN HISTORY by Robert Burleigh, illustrated by Bruce Strachan. Copyright © 2004. Reprinted with permission of Henry Holt Books for Young Readers.*

- ON THE MAYFLOWER: VOYAGE OF THE SHIP'S APPRENTICE & A PASSENGER GIRL, written by Kate Winters with photographs by Russ Kendall (Scholastic); companion to the books listed above.

- POCAHONTAS AND THE STRANGERS, by Clyde Robert Bulla (HarperCollins); a Best Books for Children biography of the Indian princess who helped the settlers.

- THE DOUBLE LIFE OF POCAHONTAS, by Jean Fritz (Penguin); winner of the Laura Ingalls Wilder Medal, the Boston Globe-Horn Book Award, and an ALA Notable Book.

- AMERICAN MOMENTS: SCENES FROM AMERICAN HISTORY, written by Robert Burleigh and illustrated by Bruce Strachan (Holt); a wonderful compendium of 18 single-page, present tense accounts of key events in American history that offer perfect introductions to various periods and events in American history; includes the Declaration of Independence, Lewis and Clark's expedition, Susan B. Anthony and Rosa Parks demanding their rights, Neil Armstrong on the moon, and remembering 9/11. Brief endnotes give further information on each event. Illustrated boldly with sculpted clay figures painted in oils.

• THE SALEM WITCH TRIALS: AN UNSOLVED MYSTERY FROM HISTORY, written by Jane Yolen and Heidi Elisabet Yolen Stemple and illustrated by Roger Roth (Simon & Schuster); one in a series of illustrated fact-based story books that explore popular theories on intriguing moments in history.

*Cover from THE SALEM WITCH TRIALS: AN UNSOLVED MYSTERY FROM HISTORY by Jane Yolen and Heidi Elisabet Yolen Stemple, illustrated by Roger Roth. Copyright © 2004. Used with permission of Simon & Schuster Books for Young Readers, an imprint of Simon & Schuster Children's Publishing.*

- ROANOKE: THE LOST COLONY: AN UNSOLVED MYSTERY FROM HISTORY, written by Jane Yolen and Heidi Elisabet Yolen Stemple and illustrated by Roger Roth (Simon & Schuster); another title in the series of illustrated fact-based story books that explore popular theories on intriguing moments in history.

- OX-CART MAN, written by Donald Hall and illustrated by Barbara Cooney (Viking); the life in seasons of a pioneer farmer and his family; Caldecott Medal.

- PAUL REVERE'S RIDE, written by Henry Wadsworth Longfellow and illustrated by Ted Rand (Dutton). This picture book illustrates the moonlit journey that was immortalized by Longfellow's epic poem, told in its entirety here.

- FIGHT FOR FREEDOM: THE AMERICAN REVOLUTIONARY WAR, by Benson Bobrick (Atheneum). One-page summaries with boxed "Quick Facts" opposite full-page illustrations in black and white, sepia tones, and color chronicle key events of the American Revolution.

- WHO'S THAT STEPPING ON PLYMOUTH ROCK?, by Jean Fritz (Putnam & Grosset)

- CAN'T YOU MAKE THEM BEHAVE, KING GEORGE?, by Jean Fritz (Putnam).

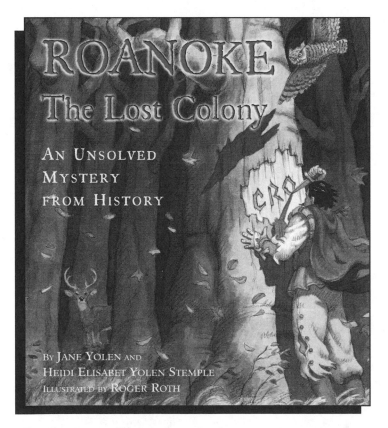

*Cover from ROANOKE: THE LOST COLONY: AN UNSOLVED MYSTERY FROM HISTORY by Jane Yolen and Heidi Elisabet Yolen Stemple, illustrated by Roger Roth. Copyright © 2003. Used with permission of Simon & Schuster Books for Young Readers, an imprint of Simon & Schuster Children's Publishing.*

- AND THEN WHAT HAPPENED, PAUL REVERE?, by Jean Fritz (Putnam).

- SHHH! WE'RE WRITING THE CONSTITUTION, by Jean Fritz (Putnam).

- WHAT'S THE BIG IDEA, BEN FRANKLIN?, by Jean Fritz (Putnam).

- WHERE WAS PATRICK HENRY ON THE 29TH OF MAY?, by Jean Fritz (Putnam).

- WILL YOU SIGN HERE, JOHN HANCOCK?, by Jean Fritz (Putnam).

- WHY DON'T YOU GET A HORSE, SAM ADAMS?, by Jean Fritz (Putnam).

- THE STORY OF THE STAR-SPANGLED BANNER, written by Steven Kroll and illustrated by Dan Andreasen (Scholastic).

- THE STAR-SPANGLED BANNER, by Peter Spier (Doubleday); a Reading Rainbow Book.

- AMERICA THE BEAUTIFUL, written by Katharine Lee Bates and illustrated by Wendell Minor (Putnam).

- AMERICA THE BEAUTIFUL: A POP-UP BOOK, by Robert Sabuda (Simon & Schuster); a pop-up of the popular patriotic tune in which landmarks and geographical features characterizing our nation are cleverly depicted.

- AMERICA THE BEAUTIFUL, written by Katharine Lee Bates and illustrated by Neil Waldman (Atheneum).

- THANK YOU, SARAH! THE WOMAN WHO SAVED THANKSGIVING, written by Laurie Halse Anderson and illustrated by Matt Faulkner (Simon & Schuster); a most incredible picture book by an inspired award-winning author, with art by an illustrator who knows what makes a picture book stand out; biography, history, power-of-the-pen message.

- SARAH, PLAIN AND TALL, by Patricia MacLachlan (HarperCollins); courage, pluck, and wisdom packed into a hugely entertaining slim novel about a mail-order bride who comes to live with a family on the prairie; Newbery Award. See also the sequel, SKYLARK.

- THE INCREDIBLE JOURNEY OF LEWIS & CLARK, by Rhoda Blumberg (Lothrop, Lee & Shepard); winner of the Golden Kite Award.

- THE LEWIS & CLARK EXPEDITION: JOIN THE CORPS OF DISCOVERY TO EXPLORE UNCHARTED TERRITORY, written by Carol A. Johmann and illustrated by Michael Kline (Ideals); includes myriad hands-on activities such as building a model keelboat and learning to dead reckon; 2003 Parents' Choice Silver Honor Award.

- Little House on the Prairie, written by Laura Ingalls Wilder and illustrated by Garth Williams (HarperCollins); classic series that has been loved and cherished by girls since it was first published in the 1930s and 1940s.

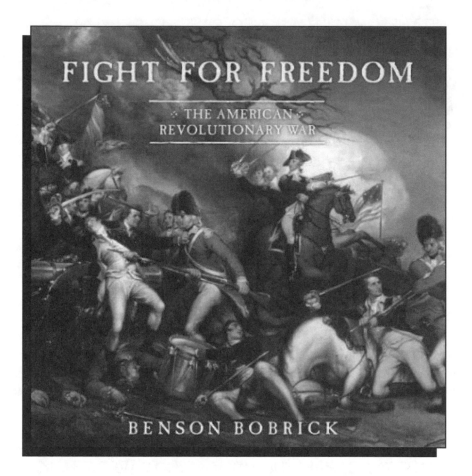

*Cover from FIGHT FOR FREEDOM: THE AMERICAN REVOLUTIONARY WAR by Benson Bobrick. Copyright © 2004. Used with permission of Atheneum Books for Young Readers, an imprint of Simon & Schuster Children's Publishing.*

- THE BIRCHBARK HOUSE, by Louise Erdrich (Hyperion); award-winning book about pioneer settlement, as seen through the eyes of a Native American girl. Contrast to LITTLE HOUSE ON THE PRAIRIE by Laura Ingalls Wilder.

- ARAMINTA'S PAINT BOX, written by Karen Ackerman and illustrated by Betsy Lewin (Atheneum). Young Araminta and her paint box travel across the country to California in the 1800s.

- INDIAN CHIEFS, by Russell Freedman (Holiday House); chronicles the "decline of the American Indian" as exploration in America in the 1800s expanded into areas already settled by Native Americans. Six Indian leaders tell their stories, including Sitting Bull and Red Cloud.

- MISS BRIDIE CHOSE A SHOVEL, written by Leslie Connor and illustrated by Mary Azarian (Houghton Mifflin); fictional account of the immigrant experience and farm life in America in the 1850s; see the read-aloud plan elsewhere in this resource.

- THE GOOD, THE BAD, AND THE GOOFY, written by Jon Scieszka and illustrated by Lane Smith (Viking); part of the Time Warp Trio series; a spin on Custer's Last Stand.

- A WOMAN FOR PRESIDENT: THE STORY OF VICTORIA WOODHULL, written by Kathleen Krull and illustrated by Jane Dyer (Walker); details the life of the woman who, in 1872, when women did not yet have the right to vote, ran against Ulysses S. Grant for president of the United States.

- SWEET CLARA AND THE FREEDOM QUILT, written by Deborah Hopkinson and illustrated by James E. Ransome (Knopf); about the Underground Railroad; the recipient of the1994 International Reading Association's Children's Book Award. See also the companion book, UNDER THE QUILT OF NIGHT, by the same author/illustrator team, published by Atheneum.

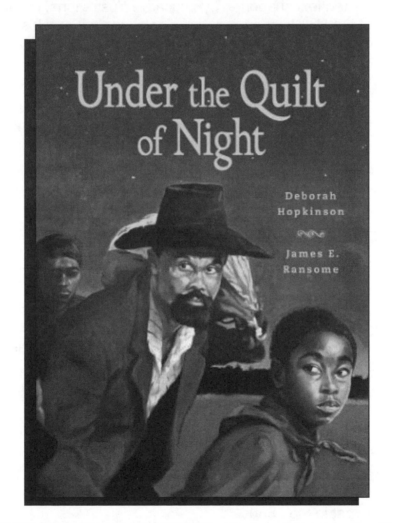

*Cover from UNDER THE QUILT OF NIGHT by Deborah Hopkinson, illustrated by James E. Ransome. Copyright © 2002. Used with permission of Anne Schwartz Books/Atheneum Books for Young Readers, an imprint of Simon & Schuster Children's Publishing.*

- PINK AND SAY, by Patricia Polacco (Philomel); based on the true story of Pinkus Aylee, a Union soldier who fought in the colored army during the Civil War, and his friendship with Sheldon Russell Curtis, a white Union soldier who deserted and then rejoined the army to fight for the cause; see the read-aloud plan elsewhere in this resource.

- RED LEGS: A DRUMMER BOY OF THE CIVIL WAR, by Ted Lewin (HarperCollins). Spare text and rich illustrations tell the story of a Civil War battle; based on true accounts of the life of Stephen Benjamin Bartow, who fought in the 14th Regiment, Company E, otherwise known as the Red-Legged Devils "because of the color of their uniform and their tough fighting spirit."

- WALT WHITMAN: WORDS FOR AMERICA, written by Barbara Kerley and illustrated by Brain Selznick (Scholastic). This magnificent picture book, through finely crafted text supported by evocative illustrations, illuminates the sobering effect of the Civil War on America's beloved poet and his work; a masterpiece with impressive back material, including the complete text of many of the poems from which lines are cited throughout the book.

- THE BOYS' WAR: CONFEDERATE AND UNION SOLDIERS TALK ABOUT THE CIVIL WAR, by Jim Murphy (Houghton Mifflin). Based on actual diaries and letters, this book explores why boys joined the war, how they lived as soldiers, and what they wore in battle.

- THE AMAZING IMPOSSIBLE ERIE CANAL, by Cheryl Harness (Simon & Schuster); detailed, explanatory illustrations accompany the text; see the read-aloud plan elsewhere in this resource.

- THE ERIE CANAL, by Peter Spier (Doubleday).

- ICE-CREAM CONES FOR SALE!, by Elaine Greenstein (Scholastic); a fanciful, factual account with historical perspective on the man who invented the beloved ice-cream cone and myriad others who claimed they did.

- GOING WEST! JOURNEY ON A WAGON TRAIN TO SETTLE A FRONTIER. written by Carol A. Johmann and illustrated by Michael Kline (Williamson); history, story, and craft activities; Ben Franklin Silver Award.

- A CHRISTMAS LIKE HELEN'S, written by Natalie Kinsey-Warnock and illustrated by Mary Azarian (Houghton Mifflin); nostalgic tale of yesteryear Christmases in snowy, rural Vermont; beautiful art; a Parents' Choice Silver Honor Award winner.

- ORANGES ON GOLD MOUNTAIN, written by Elizabeth Partridge and illustrated by Aki Sogabe (Penguin). A Chinese boy makes his home on the California coast in the 1850s.

- IMMIGRANT KIDS, by Russell Freedman (Dutton); tells the story of European immigrants who came through Ellis Island to settle in America in the late 1800s and early 1900s.

- PEPPE THE LAMPLIGHTER, written by Elisa Bartone and illustrated by Ted Lewin (Lothrop, Lee & Shepard); A Caldecott Honor Book about a boy in Little Italy at the turn of the century who lights the street lamps by hand in a time when there was no electricity.

- SOUP, written by Robert Newton Peck (Knopf); one of a series of autobiographical novels set in the 1920s in rural Vermont;. Other titles include SOUP FOR PRESIDENT, SOUP ON WHEELS, and SOUP 1776.

- THE GARDENER, written by Sarah Stewart and illustrated by David Small (Farrar, Straus & Giroux); Caldecott Honor; letters between a girl and her folks during the Depression.

- THE STORY OF VALENTINE'S DAY, written by Clyde Robert Bulla and illustrated by Susan Estelle Kwas (HarperCollins); straightforward history of one of our oldest holidays; includes craft ideas and a recipe at the back of the book.

- GOIN' SOMEPLACE SPECIAL, written by Patricia C. McKissack and illustrated by Jerry Pinkney (Atheneum); finding acceptance at the public library in pre-Civil Rights era.

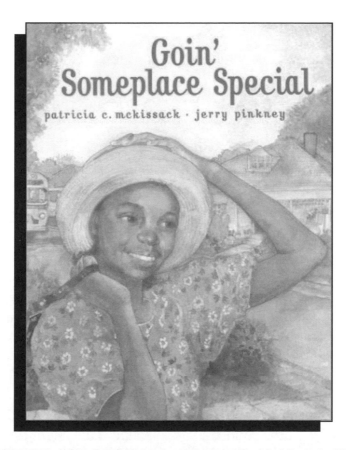

*Cover from GOIN' SOMEPLACE SPECIAL by Patricia C. McKissak, illustrated by Jerry Pinkney. Copyright © 2001. Used with permission of Anne Schwartz Books/Atheneum Books for Young Readers, an imprint of Simon & Schuster Children's Publishing.*

- WHEN I WAS YOUNG IN THE MOUNTAINS, written by Cynthia Rylant and illustrated by Diane Goode (Dutton); a memoir of growing up in Appalachia; Caldecott Honor Award and Reading Rainbow Book.

- ALL THE PLACES TO LOVE, written by Patricia MacLachlan and illustrated by Mike Wimmer (HarperCollins); lush illustrations. The places that touch our hearts make us who we are and connect us to those we love.

- My Name Is America/Dear America series, written by a variety of authors (Scholastic); about real events in American history as seen through the eyes of fictional characters; told in journal style.

- Who Was? series, written by various authors (Grosset & Dunlap); includes WHO WAS HELEN KELLER? WHO WAS MARK TWAIN? WHO WAS SACAGAWEA? WHO WAS THOMAS JEFFERSON? WHO WAS ALBERT EINSTEIN? WHO WAS ELEANOR ROOSEVELT? WHO WAS HARRIET TUBMAN? and WHO WAS BEN FRANKLIN?

## Biography

### Figures in History

- LEONARDO: BEAUTIFUL DREAMER, by Robert Byrd (Dutton); award-winning biography of Leonardo da Vinci; see the read-aloud plan elsewhere in this resource.

- STARRY MESSENGER: GALILEO GALILEI, by Peter Sis (Farrar, Straus & Giroux); biography with absorbing illustrations; see the read-aloud plan elsewhere in this resource.

- THE TREE OF LIFE, by Peter Sis (Farrar, Straus & Giroux); biography of naturalist and geologist Charles Darwin.

- THE FAIRY TALE LIFE OF HANS CHRISTIAN ANDERSEN, written by Eva Moore and illustrated by Trina Schart Hyman (Scholastic).

- AMERICAN MOMENTS: SCENES FROM AMERICAN HISTORY, written by Robert Burleigh and illustrated by Bruce Strachan (Holt); a wonderful compendium of 18 single-page, present tense accounts of key events in American history that offer perfect introductions to various periods and events in American history; includes the Declaration of Independence, Lewis and Clark's expedition, Susan B. Anthony and Rosa Parks demanding their rights, Neil Armstrong on the moon, and remembering 9/11. Brief endnotes give further information on each event. Illustrated boldly with sculpted clay figures painted in oils.

- ABRAHAM LINCOLN, written by Amy L. Cohn and Suzy Schmidt and illustrated by David A. Johnson (Scholastic); a tall, slim, engaging biography. See the read-aloud plan for this book in *Children's Book Corner, Grades 1–2*.

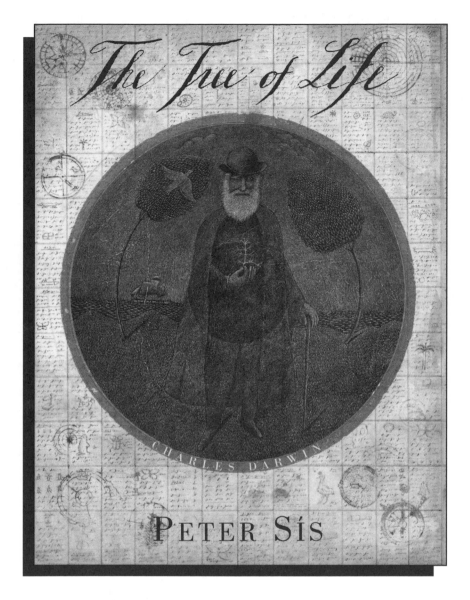

*Cover of THE TREE OF LIFE © 2003 by Peter Sís. Used with the permission of Farrar Straus Giroux*

- THANK YOU, SARAH! THE WOMAN WHO SAVED THANKSGIVING, written by Laurie Halse Anderson and illustrated by Matt Faulkner (Simon & Schuster); a most incredible picture book by an inspired award-winning author, with art by an illustrator who knows what makes a picture book stand out; biography, history, power-of-the-pen message.

- A WOMAN FOR PRESIDENT: THE STORY OF VICTORIA WOODHULL, written by Kathleen Krull and illustrated by Jane Dyer (Walker); details the life of the woman who, in 1872, when women did not yet have the right to vote, ran against Ulysses S. Grant for president of the United States.

- SO YOU WANT TO BE PRESIDENT?, written by Judith St. George and illustrated by David Small (Philomel). Short, humorous anecdotes profile American presidents through Bill Clinton; winner of the Caldecott Medal.

- SO YOU WANT TO BE AN INVENTOR?, written by Judith St. George and illustrated by David Small (Philomel); in the style of the book listed above.

- TO FLY: THE STORY OF THE WRIGHT BROTHERS, written by Wendie C. Old and illustrated by Robert Andrew Parker (Clarion).

- FLY HIGH! THE STORY OF BESSIE COLEMAN, written by Louise Borden and Mary Kay Kroeger and illustrated by Teresa Flavin (McElderry Books).

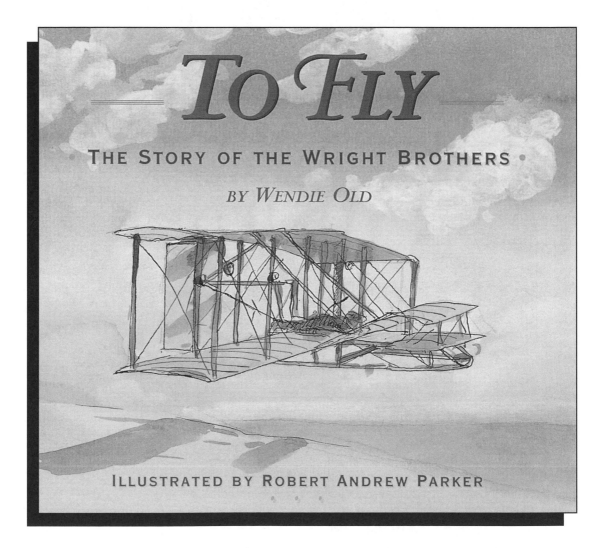

*Cover from TO FLY: THE STORY OF THE WRIGHT BROTHERS by Wendie Old. Jacket illustrations copyright © 2002 by Robert Andrew Parker. Reprinted by permission of Clarion Books/Houghton Mifflin Company. All rights reserved.*

*Cover from FLY HIGH! THE STORY OF BESSIE COLEMAN by Louise Borden and Mary Kay Kroeger, illustrated by Teresa Flavin. Copyright © 2001. Used with permission of Margaret K. McElderry Books, an imprint of Simon & Schuster Children's Publishing.*

- LISTENING TO CRICKETS: A STORY ABOUT RACHEL CARSON, written by Candice F. Ransom and illustrated by Shelly O. Haas (Carolrhoda); easy reader biography.

- MARTIN'S BIG WORDS: THE LIFE OF DR. MARTIN LUTHER KING, JR., written by Doreen Rappaport and illustrated by Bryan Collier (Hyperion); an outstanding, multiple award-winning book. See the read-aloud plan for this book in *Children's Book Corner, Grades 1–2*.

- MARY SMITH, by A. U'Ren (Farrar, Straus & Giroux); the story of knocker-up Mary Smith who, in the 1920s before alarm clocks were widely used, shot dried peas from a rubber tube at the windows of her clients to wake them for work.

- PLAYERS IN PIGTAILS, written by Shana Corey and illustrated by Rebecca Gibbon (Scholastic); a fictional tale based on fact about a young woman who plays in the All-American Girls Professional Baseball League during World War II.

- STEVEN SPIELBERG: CRAZY FOR MOVIES, by Susan Goldman Rubin (Abrams); includes photos and family interviews that recall Spielberg's boyhood as well as his accomplishments.

*Cover from MARTIN'S BIG WORDS: THE LIFE OF DR. MARTIN LUTHER KING, JR. written by Doreen Rappaport, © 2001. Reprinted with permission of Hyperion Books for Children.*

*Cover of MARY SMITH © 2003 by Andrea U'Ren.*
*Used with the permission of Farrar Straus Giroux.*

## Figures in the Arts

- DEGAS AND THE DANCE, by Susan Goldman Rubin (Abrams); biography of the "painter of dancing girls" illustrated with more than 30 original works of art by Degas.

- LEONARDO: BEAUTIFUL DREAMER, by Robert Byrd (Dutton); award-winning biography of Leonardo da Vinci; see the read-aloud plan elsewhere in this resource.

- FRIDA KAHLO: THE ARTIST WHO PAINTED HERSELF, written by Margaret Frith and illustrated by Tomie dePaola (Grosset & Dunlap); part of the Smart About Art series; about Mexico's "most celebrated female artist," with reproductions of Kahlo's paintings as well as illustrations by dePaola.

- UNCLE ANDY'S, by James Warhola (Penguin); an amusing peek at Andy Warhol's world, written by his nephew. See the read-aloud plan for this book in *Children's Book Corner, Grades 1–2*.

- ACTION JACKSON , written by Jan Greenberg and Sandra Jordan and illustrated by Robert Andrew Parker (Roaring Brook Press); a Robert F. Sibert Honor Book; about Jackson Pollock.

- THE POT THAT JUAN BUILT, written by Nancy Andrews-Goebel and illustrated by David Diaz (Lee & Low Books); about Juan Quezada, "premier potter in Mexico."

- THE DINOSAURS OF WATERHOUSE HAWKINS, written by Barbara Kerley and illustrated by Brain Selznick (Scholastic); a Caldecott Honor book highlighting the life of the artist and sculptor who, in the mid-1800s, showed the world what a dinosaur looked like. See the read-aloud plan for this book in *Children's Book Corner, Grades 1–2.*

- BILL PEET: AN AUTOBIOGRAPHY, by Bill Peet (Houghton Mifflin); Caldecott Honor Book about this author/illustrator's life, filled with his classic illustrations that extend the text; amusing, absorbing, informative.

- HATTIE AND THE WILD WAVES, by Barbara Cooney (Penguin); about a girl who loves to paint, written and illustrated by the Caldecott Medal winner.

- TALKING WITH ARTISTS, compiled and edited by Pat Cummings (Bradbury); a reference book for children in which children's book illustrators answer questions about where they get ideas, what their work day is like, and how they make their pictures. Artists highlighted include Chris Van Allsburg, Tom Feelings, David Wiesner, Lane Smith, Leo Dillon and Diane Dillon, and Lisa Campbell Ernst. See the index for books illustrated by these artists featured in *Children's Book Corner.*

- AUTHOR TALK, compiled and edited by Leonard S. Marcus (Simon & Schuster); 15 interviews with some of the best-loved children's book authors that answer many of those often-asked questions; includes childhood photos and home-office photos, and a bibliography of each author's selected works. Authors include Judy Blume, Lee Bennett Hopkins, James Howe, Ann M. Martin, Gary Paulsen, Jon Scieszka, and Johanna Hurwitz. See the index for books written by these authors featured in *Children's Book Corner.*

- THE FAIRY TALE LIFE OF HANS CHRISTIAN ANDERSEN, written by Eva Moore and illustrated by Trina Schart Hyman (Scholastic).

- WALT WHITMAN: WORDS FOR AMERICA, written by Barbara Kerley and illustrated by Brain Selznick (Scholastic); This magnificent picture book, through finely crafted text supported by evocative illustrations, illuminates the sobering effect of the Civil War on America's beloved poet and his work; a masterpiece with impressive back material, including the complete text of many of the poems from which lines are cited throughout the book.

- LOUISA MAY & MR. THOREAU'S FLUTE, written by Julie Dunlap and Marybeth Lorbiecki and illustrated by Mary Azarian (Dial); the story of the friendship between Louisa May Alcott and Henry David Thoreau and how it inspired Alcott's writing.

- AMERICAN BOY: THE ADVENTURES OF MARK TWAIN, by Don Brown (Houghton Mifflin); Samuel Clemens's boyhood.

- THE BOY ON FAIRFIELD STREET: HOW TED GEISEL GREW UP TO BECOME DR. SEUSS, written by Kathleen Krull and illustrated by Steve Johnson and Lou Fancher (Random House); biography of the childhood of this legendary children's author and illustrator. See the read-aloud plan elsewhere in this resource.

- HENRY HIKES TO FITCHBURG, HENRY BUILDS A CABIN, and HENRY CLIMBS A MOUNTAIN, by D. B. Johnson (Houghton Mifflin); intriguing facets of Henry David Thoreau's life.

- LANGSTON'S TRAIN RIDE, written by Robert Burleigh and illustrated by Leonard Jenkins (Orchard); about the inspiration for Hughes's famous poem, "The Negro Speaks of Rivers" and how it led to Hughes's life as a writer.

- TALLCHIEF: AMERICA'S PRIMA BALLERINA, written by Maria Tallchief with Rosemary Wells and illustrated by Gary Kelley (Penguin); autobiography.

- HANDEL, WHO KNEW WHAT HE LIKED, written by M. T. Anderson and illustrated by Kevin Hawkes (Candlewick); recipient of the Boston Globe–Horn Book Honor Award for Nonfiction.

*HANDEL, WHO KNEW WHAT HE LIKED. Text Copyright © 2001 M.T. Anderson. Illustrations Copyright © 2001 Kevin Hawkes. Reproduced by permission of the publisher Candlewick Press, Inc., Cambridge, MA.*

- WHEN MARIAN SANG, written by Pam Munoz Ryan and illustrated by Brian Selznick (Scholastic); Robert F. Sibert Honor Award; about American singer Marian Anderson's rise to fame in the 1930s.

- Smart About series (Grosset & Dunlap); titles by various authors include VINCENT VAN GOGH: SUNFLOWERS AND SWIRLY STARS; PABLO PICASSO: BREAKING ALL THE RULES; CLAUDE MONET: SUNSHINE AND WATERLILIES; EDGAR DEGAS: PAINTINGS THAT DANCE; and HENRI MATISSE: DRAWING WITH SCISSORS.

## WORLD CULTURES

- THE FIREKEEPER'S SON, written by Linda Sue Park and illustrated by Julie Downing (Clarion). The setting is the 1800s in Korea, but the theme is universal: choosing between the needs of others and one's own wishes; by the Newbery Award-winning author, with glowing watercolor illustrations that are true to the text.

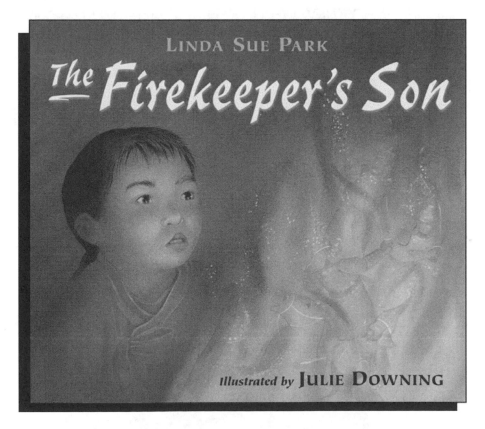

*Cover from THE FIREKEEPER'S SON by Linda Sue Park. Jacket illustrations copyright © 2004 by Julie Downing. Reprinted by permission of Clarion Books/Houghton Mifflin Company. All rights reserved.*

- TALKING DRUMS: A SELECTION OF POEMS FROM AFRICA SOUTH OF THE SAHARA, edited by Veronique Tadjo (Bloomsbury); traces African history in stories in verse, arranged in chapters from the Animal Kingdom and People to Pride and Defiance. Some of the poems, such as "Friendship," transcend cultures to speak universally on common themes.

- THE DAY OF AHMED'S SECRET, written by Florence Parry Heide and Judith Heide Gilliland and illustrated by Ted Lewin (Lothrop, Lee & Shepard); a day in the life of a boy in Cairo who has a secret—he has learned to write his name.

- TUT, TUT, written by Jon Scieszka and illustrated by Lane Smith (Viking); part of the Time Warp Trio series; this take on ancient Egypt will not leave kids yawning.

- SEE YOU LATER, GLADIATOR, written by Jon Scieszka and illustrated by Lane Smith (Viking); the Time Warp Trio is at it again.

- SAM SAMURAI, written by Jon Scieszka and illustrated by Lane Smith (Viking); the Time Warp Trio are really in trouble this time!

- CHILDREN OF THE WIND AND WATER: FIVE STORIES ABOUT NATIVE AMERICAN CHILDREN, written by Stephen Krensky and illustrated by James Watling (Scholastic); stories of various tribes of North America from the southeastern United States to the Pacific Northwest.

- FIESTA USA, written and photographed by George Ancona (Penguin). Four Hispanic holidays, as celebrated in the United States, are explored: Las Posadas, El Dia de los Muertos, Los Matachines, and La Fiesta de los Reyes Magos.

- PYRAMIDS, by Anne Millard (Scholastic); short passages and detailed illustrations help readers distinguish among Egyptian, Nubian, Mayan, Aztec, and modern pyramids and explain their histories.

- PYRAMIDS!, written by Avery Hart and Paul Mantel and illustrated by Michael Kline (Williamson); includes experiments and hand-on activities.

- MISS RUMPHIUS, by Barbara Cooney (Viking); classic story of an aunt who travels the world and leaves something behind everywhere she goes.

- MY GREAT-AUNT ARIZONA, written by Gloria Houston and illustrated by Susan Condie Lamb (HarperCollins). A great-aunt who was also a great teacher introduces her students to the world.

## GEOGRAPHY

- AMERICA THE BEAUTIFUL: A POP-UP BOOK, by Robert Sabuda (Simon & Schuster); a pop-up of the popular patriotic tune in which landmarks and geographical features characterizing our nation are cleverly depicted.

- MY AMERICA: A POETRY ATLAS OF THE UNITED STATES, selected by Lee Bennett Hopkins and illustrated by Stephen Alcorn (Simon & Schuster); outstanding illustrations accompany the work of well-known poets as well as newcomers.

- A WORLD OF WONDERS: GEOGRAPHIC TRAVELS IN VERSE AND RHYME, written by J. Patrick Lewis and illustrated by Alison Jay (Dial). Travel around the world and learn intriguing facts by way of witty, jaunty verse.

- GEOGRA-FLEAS! RIDDLES ALL OVER THE MAP, written by Joan Holub and illustrated by Regan Dunnick (Whitman). Dogs riddled with fleas put geography on the map.

*Cover from GEOGRA-FLEAS! RIDDLES ALL OVER THE MAP by Joan Holub, illustrated by Regan Dunnick. Copyright © 2004. Reprinted with permission from A. Whitman & Co.*

- ALL THE PLACES TO LOVE, written by Patricia MacLachlan and illustrated by Mike Wimmer (HarperCollins); lush illustrations depicting aspects of American life; about how the places that touch our hearts make us who we are and connect us to those we love.

## SCIENCE

- HOW DO YOU LIFT A LION?, by Robert E. Wells (Whitman); introduction to levers, pulleys, and wheels, and how they help us move things.

- YIKES—LICE!, written by Donna Caffey and illustrated by Patrick Girouard (Whitman); a gentle approach to facts about the parasite and sensible treatment.

*Cover from HOW DO YOU LIFT A LION? by Robert E. Wells. Copyright © 1996. Reprinted with permission from A. Whitman & Co.*

- The Magic School Bus series, written by Joanna Cole and illustrated by Bruce Degen (Scholastic). These books transformed science from a boring, obscure subject to a vibrant and loved one among the seven- to nine-year-old crowd. Chock-full of information presented in a funny, appealing format, each book finds the kids in Ms. Frizzle's class taking a field trip aboard their magic yellow bus. They discover the how and why of everything from the ocean floor to the planets before they return to their classroom, where any kid would be happy to have a desk.

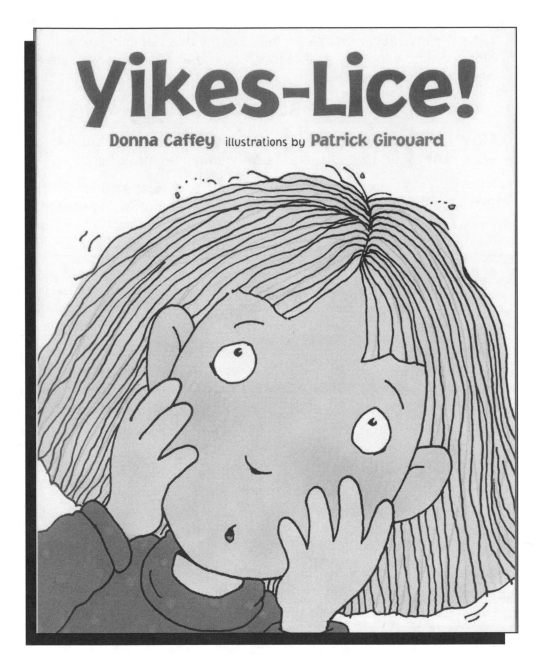

*Cover from YIKES—LICE! by Donna Caffey, illustrated by Patrick Girouard.
Copyright © 1998. Reprinted with permission from A. Whitman & Co.*

- SCIENCE VERSE, written by Jon Scieszka and illustrated by Lane Smith (Penguin); see the read-aloud plan elsewhere in this resource.

- WESTLANDIA, written by Paul Fleischman and illustrated by Kevin Hawkes (Candlewick); Parents' Choice Honor; a boy starts his own civilization in his backyard.

- THE GREAT BRIDGE-BUILDING CONTEST, written by Bo Zaunders and illustrated by Roxie Munro (Abrams); the true story of a woodworker with a third-grade education who, in the mid-1800s, built one of the country's sturdiest covered bridges. It still stands today in West Virginia.

- BRIDGES! AMAZING STRUCTURES TO DESIGN, BUILD & TEST, written by Carol A. Johmann and Elizabeth J. Rieth (Williamson). Science and history blend with how-to instructions and experiments; 2000 Parents' Choice Recommended.

- JAKE DRAKE, KNOW-IT-ALL, written by Andrew Clements and illustrated by Dolores Avendaño (Aladdin Ready-for Chapters Book); fiction about a third-grade boy who competes in a science fair; readers learn details about science fairs and the scientific process throughout this story.

- HERE'S WHAT YOU DO WHEN YOU CAN'T FIND YOUR SHOE (INGENIOUS INVENTIONS FOR PESKY PROBLEMS), written by Andrea Perry and illustrated by Alan Snow (Atheneum); zany suggestions for useful inventions; see the read-aloud plan in *Children's Book Corner Grades 1–2*.

- CHIMP MATH: LEARNING ABOUT TIME FROM A BABY CHIMPANZEE, by Ann Whitehead Nagda and Cindy Bickel (Holt); see the read-aloud plan elsewhere in this resource.

- POLAR BEAR MATH: LEARNING ABOUT FRACTIONS FROM KLONDIKE AND SNOW, by Ann Whitehead Nagda and Cindy Bickel (Holt).

- TIGER MATH: LEARNING TO GRAPH FROM A BABY TIGER, by Ann Whitehead Nagda and Cindy Bickel (Holt).

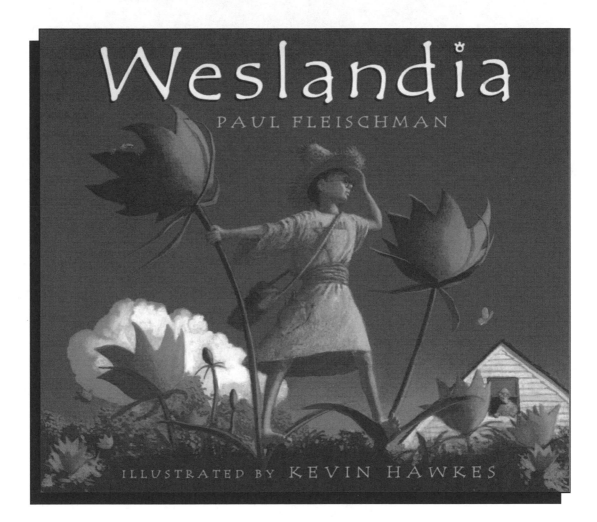

*WESLANDIA. Text Copyright © 1999 Paul Fleischman. Illustrations Copyright © 1999 Kevin Hawkes. Reproduced by permission of the publisher Candlewick Press, Inc., Cambridge, MA.*

- KOKO'S KITTEN, written by Dr. Francine Patterson with photographs by Ronald H. Cohn (Scholastic); the amazing true story of a gorilla and her kitten.

- ANIMALS BORN ALIVE AND WELL, by Ruth Heller (Grosset & Dunlap); see the read-aloud plan for this book in *Children's Book Corner, Grades 1–2.*

- CHICKENS AREN'T THE ONLY ONES, by Ruth Heller (Grosset & Dunlap); in the style of the book listed above.

- GOING ON A WHALE WATCH, by Bruce McMillan (Scholastic); simple text with drawings and photographs.

*Cover from JAKE DRAKE, KNOW-IT-ALL by Andrew Clements, illustrated by Dolores Avendaño. Copyright © 2001. Used with permission of Simon & Schuster Books for Young Readers, an imprint of Simon & Schuster Children's Publishing.*

- BUGS FOR LUNCH, written by Margery Facklam and illustrated by Sylvia Long (Charlesbridge). Simple rhymes, accompanied by illustrations done in pen and ink and watercolors, teach about creatures that munch bugs for lunch.

- THE REASON FOR A FLOWER, by Ruth Heller (Grosset & Dunlap). Bright and colorful illustrations accompany rhyming, factual text.

- PLANTS THAT NEVER EVER BLOOM, by Ruth Heller (Putnam); in the style of the book listed above.

- THE POPCORN BOOK, by Tomie dePaola (Holiday House); facts, recipes, and darn cute illustrations.

- GERMS MAKE ME SICK!, written by Melvin Berger and illustrated by Marylin Hafner (HarperCollins); a classic Let's-Read-and-Find-Out Science title.

- ROCKS HARD, SOFT, SMOOTH, AND ROUGH, written by Natalie M. Rosinsky and illustrated by Matthew John (Picture Window Books); includes ample back material.

- THE SUN, THE WIND AND THE RAIN, written by Lisa Westberg Peters and illustrated by Ted Rand (Holt). Basic geology parallels a story about a day at the beach building a sandcastle.

*Cover from THE SUN, THE WIND AND THE RAIN by Lisa Westberg Peters, illustrated by Ted Rand. Copyright © 1990. Reprinted with permission of Henry Holt Books for Young Readers.*

- STARRY MESSENGER: GALILEO GALILEI, by Peter Sís (Farrar, Straus & Giroux); biography with absorbing illustrations; see the read-aloud plan elsewhere in this resource.

- THE GLOW-IN-THE-DARK NIGHT SKY BOOK, written by Clint Hatchett and illustrated by Stephen Marchesi (Random House); star maps that glow in the dark.

- THE CLOUD BOOK, by Tomie dePaola (Holiday House); common types of clouds and what they tell us.

- THE MOST AMAZING SCIENCE POP-UP BOOK, written and engineered by Jay Young (HarperCollins); includes a working record player, compass, microscope, sundial, and more.

- 53½ THINGS THAT CHANGED THE WORLD AND SOME THAT DIDN'T, written by Steve Parker and designed and illustrated by David West (Millbrook). From the toilet to fusion power, inventions are explained with the help of detailed illustrations.

- ACCIDENTS MAY HAPPEN: FIFTY INVENTIONS DISCOVERED BY MISTAKE, written by Charlotte Foltz Jones and illustrated by John O'Brien (Delacorte). Short passages and bulleted "Flabbergasting Facts" make for enjoyable and fascinating quick reads.

- FROM RAGS TO RICHES: PEOPLE WHO STARTED BUSINESSES FROM SCRATCH, by Nathan Aaseng (Lerner); with photographs.

- WIND AND WEATHER, by Editions Gallimard Jeunesse (Scholastic). Overlays, gatefolds, and more make weather study accessible.

- PYRAMIDS, by Anne Millard (Scholastic). Short passages and detailed illustrations help readers distinguish among Egyptian, Nubian, Mayan, Aztec, and modern pyramids and explain their histories.

- PYRAMIDS!, written by Avery Hart and Paul Mantel and illustrated by Michael Kline (Williamson); includes experiments and hand-on activities.

- LEONARDO: BEAUTIFUL DREAMER, by Robert Byrd (Dutton); award-winning biography of Leonardo da Vinci; see the read-aloud plan elsewhere in this resource.

- LISTENING TO CRICKETS: A STORY ABOUT RACHEL CARSON, written by Candice F. Ransom and illustrated by Shelly O. Haas (Carolrhoda); easy reader biography.

## MATH

- MATH CURSE, written by Jon Scieszka and illustrated by Lane Smith (Penguin); indescribably delicious fun you can enjoy in little chunks or the whole enchilada; guaranteed to make math mirthful!

- MINNIE'S DINER: A MULTIPLYING MENU, written by Dayle Ann Dodds and illustrated by John Manders (Candlewick). "Make it a double" is no trouble, or is it?

- SIDEWAYS ARITHMETIC FROM WAYSIDE SCHOOL, by Louis Sachar (Scholastic). In this wacky school, they do math in memorable ways! See also MORE SIDEWAYS ARITHMETIC FROM WAYSIDE SCHOOL.

- 7 X 9 = TROUBLE!, written by Claudia Mills and illustrated by G. Brian Karas (Farrar, Straus & Giroux). Multiplication is the backdrop for this story.

- CAN YOU COUNT TO A GOOGOL?, by Robert E. Wells (Whitman); helps readers grasp the size of this number with concrete examples.

*MINNIE'S DINER: A MULTIPLYING MENU. Text Copyright © 2004 Dayle Ann Dodds. Illustrations Copyright © John Manders. Reproduced by permission of the publisher, Candlewick Press, Inc., Cambridge, MA.*

*Cover from CAN YOU COUNT TO A GOOGOL? by Robert E. Wells.
Copyright © 2000. Reprinted with permission from A. Whitman & Co.*

- HOW MUCH IS A MILLION?, written by David M. Schwartz and illustrated by Steven Kellogg (HarperCollins); counting, comparing, quantifying to explain the enormity of a million, a billion, and a trillion.

- CHIMP MATH: LEARNING ABOUT TIME FROM A BABY CHIMPANZEE, by Ann Whitehead Nagda and Cindy Bickel (Holt); see the read-aloud plan elsewhere in this resource.

- POLAR BEAR MATH: LEARNING ABOUT FRACTIONS FROM KLONDIKE AND SNOW, by Ann Whitehead Nagda and Cindy Bickel (Holt).

- TIGER MATH: LEARNING TO GRAPH FROM A BABY TIGER, by Ann Whitehead Nagda and Cindy Bickel (Holt).

- RIDDLE-ICULOUS MATH, written by Joan Holub and illustrated by Regan Dunnick (Whitman); math riddles.

- MATH-TERPIECES, written by Greg Tang and illustrated by Greg Paprocki (Scholastic); see the read-aloud plan for this book in *Children's Book Corner, Grades 1–2*.

- MATH FOR ALL SEASONS, written by Greg Tang and illustrated by Harry Briggs (Scholastic); math riddle poems involving addition, subtracting to add, and patterns.

- MARVELOUS MATH: A BOOK OF POEMS, selected by Lee Bennett Hopkins and illustrated by Karen Barbour (Aladdin).

*Cover from POLAR BEAR MATH: LEARNING ABOUT FRACTIONS FROM KLONDIKE AND SNOW by Ann Whitehead Nagda and Cindy Bickel. Copyright © 2004. Reprinted with permission of Henry Holt Books for Young Readers.*

*Cover from TIGER MATH: LEARNING TO GRAPH FROM A BABY TIGER by Ann Whitehead Nagda and Cindy Bickel. Copyright © 2000. Reprinted with permission of Henry Holt Books for Young Readers.*

- MATHEMATICKLES!, poems by Betsy Franco and illustrated by Steven Salerno (McElderry); visually and auditorially appealing; lyrical language + simple math = fun!

- THE FLY ON THE CEILING: A MATH MYTH, written by Dr. Julie Glass and illustrated by Richard Walz (Random House); Scholastic Step into Reading and Math Step 3; graphing and coordinates.

- THE CASE OF THE MISSING BIRTHDAY PARTY, written by Joanne Rocklin and illustrated by John Speirs (Scholastic); Scholastic Hello Math Reader Level 4; digits and place value.

- HOW MUCH IS THAT GUINEA PIG IN THE WINDOW?, written by Joanne Rocklin and illustrated by Meredith Johnson (Scholastic); Scholastic Hello Math Reader Level 4; money, addition, multiplication, calculation.

- EATING FRACTIONS, by Bruce McMillan (Scholastic). A meal is shared by two children and a dog; introduces the concept of fractions with photographs.

- DOGGONE LEMONADE STAND!, written by Judy Bradbury and illustrated by Cathy Trachok (McGraw-Hill). Christopher sets up a lemonade stand on the hottest day of the year; simple fractions.

*Cover from RIDDLE-ICULOUS MATH by Joan Holub, illustrated by Regan Dunnick. Copyright © 2003. Reprinted with permission from A. Whitman & Co.*

## GENERAL NONFICTION

- BETTER THAN A LEMONADE $TAND! SMALL BUSINESS IDEAS FOR KIDS, written by Daryl Bernstein and illustrated by Rob Husberg (Beyond Words). Authored by a 15-year-old, this book is filled with useful tips, hints, ideas, and lists of supplies for all sorts of businesses kids might venture into.

- MONEYMAKERS: GOOD CENTS FOR GIRLS, written by Ingrid Roper and illustrated by Susan Synarski (Pleasant Company); practical advice for making money, from watching tots to making bracelets out of buttons!

- MONEY: A RICH HISTORY, written by Jon Anderson and illustrated by Thor Wickstrom (Grosset & Dunlap); a title in the Smart About series.

- GROWING UP: IT'S A GIRL THING, written by Mavis Jukes and illustrated by Debbie Tilley (Knopf); handbook explains puberty to those who are curious about normal physiological changes. Subtitle: *Straight Talk About First Bras, First Periods, And Your Changing Body.*

- THE CARE AND KEEPING OF FRIENDS, illustrated by Nadine Bernard Westcott (Pleasant Company); an American Girl Library book about friendship.

- THE CARE AND KEEPING OF YOU: THE BODY BOOK FOR GIRLS, written by Valerie Lee Schaefer and illustrated by Norm Bendell (Pleasant Company). Just right for middle grade girls, this book answers questions on everything from bad breath to pimples.

- GOOD SPORTS: WINNING, LOSING, AND EVERYTHING IN BETWEEN, written by Therese Kauchak and illustrated by Norm Bendell (Pleasant Company); an American Girl Library book full of clear and helpful advice on sportsmanship and physical fitness.

## VALUES; CHARACTER EDUCATION

- SAM JOHNSON AND THE BLUE RIBBON QUILT, by Lisa Campbell Ernst (Lothrop, Lee & Shepard). When the women refuse to allow them to join the Women's Quilting Club, the men decide to form their own group. The rivalry that develops as each group prepares for the state fair will leave you in stitches.

- THE SCHOOL MOUSE, by Dick King-Smith of BABE: THE GALLANT PIG fame, about a school mouse who learns to read and uses it to save her family. Illustrated by Cynthia Fisher (Hyperion).

- THE ARABOOLIES OF LIBERTY STREET, written by Sam Swope and illustrated by Barry Root (Farrar, Straus & Giroux). The Pinches like everything the same—clean and quiet, dull and humorless. And then the Araboolies sweep into the neighborhood and the fun begins. Noise and joy prevail, as does the lesson that different isn't necessarily bad.

- OLD TURTLE, written by Douglas Wood and illustrated by Cheng-Khee Chee; Pfeifer-Hamilton (Scholastic); fable about man's relationship with nature, with themes of God and peace; ABA Book of the Year, 1993; IRA Children's Book Award, 1993.

- THE A+ CUSTODIAN, written by Louise Borden and illustrated by Adam Gustavson (McElderry). This affirming book gives a face and a nod of recognition to the often invisible person who shines up the school and keeps it humming. See also the read-aloud plan for THE JANITOR'S BOY by Andrew Clements (Simon & Schuster), elsewhere in this resource.

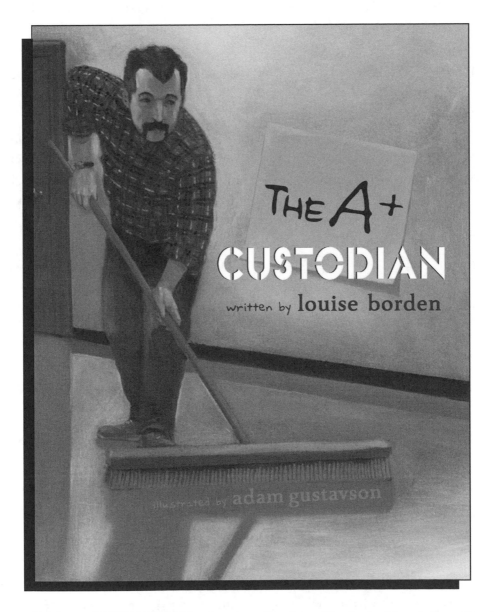

*Cover from THE A+ CUSTODIAN by Louise Borden, illustrated by Adam Gustavson. Copyright © 2004. Used with permission of Margaret K. McElderry Books, an imprint of Simon & Schuster Children's Publishing.*

- THE OTHER SIDE, written by Jacqueline Woodson and illustrated by E. B. Lewis (G. P. Putnam's Sons); see the read-aloud plan for this book in *Children's Book Corner, Grades 1–2*.

- LOUD-MOUTHED GEORGE AND THE SIXTH-GRADE BULLY, by Nancy Carlson (Carolrhoda); classic bully-gets-his-comeuppance story that doesn't disappoint.

- BULLY TROUBLE, written by Joanna Cole and illustrated by Marylin Hafner (Random House); Random House Step into Reading, Step 2.

- COCK-A-DOODLE DUDLEY, by Bill Peet (Houghton Mifflin). "I'm just a plain, ordinary rooster," claims Dudley. But about this he's wrong. Sol the sun and his barnyard buddies show Dudley—and readers—just how special he is. With spunky language and expressive, comical illustrations, this story about friendship triumphing over jealousy and bullyhood is sure to please. See the read-aloud plan for this book in *Children's Book Corner, Grades 1–2*.

- THE BEST CHRISTMAS PAGEANT EVER, written by Barbara Robinson and illustrated by Judith Gwyn Brown (HarperCollins); the best Christmas novel ever for middle grades, with life lessons being learned on every single page.

- POLLYANNA, by Eleanor H. Porter (Bantam Doubleday Dell); classic novel about a young girl with spunk and spirit who makes a difference.

- PIPPI LONGSTOCKING, written by Astrid Lindgren and illustrated by Nancy Seligsohn (Viking). This spunky redhead has been making friends for generations. See also PIPPI GOES ON BOARD.

- THE DOUBLE-DIGIT CLUB, by Marion Dane Bauer (Holiday House). Turning 10 years old means being invited to be part of Valerie's exclusive club. When Paige gets asked she joins, leaving the narrator, her controlling best friend, who won't be 10 for two months, out in the cold for the summer. How Sarah grows is the crux of this coming-of-age story for girls.

- THE EMPTY POT, by Demi (Holt). This Chinese tale exemplifies the value of truth and the wisdom in being proud when you've tried your hardest and done your best. See the read-aloud plan for this book, elsewhere in this resource.

- THE FIREKEEPER'S SON, written by Linda Sue Park and illustrated by Julie Downing (Clarion). The setting is the 1800s in Korea, but the theme is universal: choosing between the needs of others and one's own wishes; by the Newbery Award-winning author.

- WE LIVE HERE TOO! KIDS TALK ABOUT GOOD CITIZENSHIP, written by Nancy Loewen and illustrated by Omarr Wesley (Picture Window Books).

- AMAZING GRACE, written by Mary Hoffman and illustrated by Caroline Binch (Dial). Self-esteem blossoms in a warm, supportive extended family; see the read-aloud plan for this book in *Children's Book Corner, Grades 1–2*.

- THANK YOU, MR. FALKER, by Patricia Polacco (Philomel). A teacher helps a third grader learn to read; based on Polacco's personal experience.

- SHOESHINE GIRL, written by Clyde Robert Bulla and illustrated by Leigh Grant (HarperCollins); This great story about a girl who spends the summer with her aunt and befriends the owner of a shoeshine stand when she wants to earn money is about so much more than that.

- THE ANT AND THE ELEPHANT, by Bill Peet (Houghton Mifflin). Through expressive illustrations and zippy text, we meet a medley of irascible, ungrateful slugs of the wilderness that don't know how to be a friend or thank a stranger for acts of kindness. Playful word wit and humorous depictions of animals with human qualities and attitudes make learning about good deeds and manners painless and memorable. See the read-aloud plan for this book in *Children's Book Corner, Grades 1–2*.

- CHICKEN SUNDAY, by Patricia Polacco (Philomel); Children's Choice and ALA Notable Book about differences, friendship, and character.

- IT'S A SPOON, NOT A SHOVEL, written by Caralyn Buehner and illustrated by Mark Buehner (Puffin); see also I DID IT, I'M SORRY by the same author and illustrator.

- MANNERS, by Aliki (HarperCollins); see also COMMUNICATION by the same author/illustrator.

- SEVEN SPOOLS OF THREAD: A KWANZAA STORY, written by Angela Shelf Medearis and illustrated by Daniel Minter (Whitman); about teamwork, family, and the principles of Kwanzaa; see the read-aloud plan elsewhere in this resource.

- THE CHRISTMAS MENORAHS: HOW A TOWN FOUGHT HATE ,written by Janice Cohn and illustrated by Bill Farnsworth (Whitman); about a town that united against hatred; based on a true story.

- WHOA JEALOUSY!, by Woodleigh Marx Hubbard with Madeleine Houston (Penguin); an off-beat, quirky look at common feelings.

- STONE FOX, written by John Reynold Gardiner and illustrated by Greg Hargreaves (HarperCollins); poignant story about a boy and his loyal sled dog.

- THE KITE FIGHTERS, by Linda Sue Park (Clarion). A boy in fifteenth-century Korea competes in the New Year kite competition.

*Cover from THE CHRISTMAS MENORAHS: HOW A TOWN FOUGHT HATE by Janice Cohn, illustrated by Bill Farnsworth. Copyright © 1995. Reprinted with permission from A. Whitman & Co.*

## HANDICAPS

- A SHOW OF HANDS: SAY IT IN SIGN LANGUAGE, written by Mary Beth Sullivan and Linda Bourke with Susan Regan; illustrated by Linda Bourke (Lippincott); a Reading Rainbow Book.

- HANDSIGNS A SIGN LANGUAGE ALPHABET, by Kathleen Fain (Chronicle). Beautiful illustrations clearly depict hand signs.

- LOOKING OUT FOR SARAH, by Glenna Lang (Charlesbridge); fact-based story of a guide dog.

- KNOTS ON A COUNTING ROPE, written by Bill Martin Jr. and John Archambault and illustrated by Ted Rand (Holt). Witness a blind Navajo boy's growing confidence at the hand of his grandfather, his teacher, his support, by way of splendid spreads and lyrical language. At the end learn the meaning of the title and the strength to be found in abiding love. A treasure of a book, a book to treasure. See the read-aloud plan for this book in *Children's Book Corner, Grades 1–2*.

- NAOMI KNOWS IT'S SPRINGTIME, written by Virginia L. Kroll and illustrated by Jill Kastner (Boyds Mills Press). Although she is blind, Naomi knows spring has arrived.

- JEREMY'S DREIDEL, written by Ellie Gellman and illustrated by Judith Friedman (Kar-Ben Copies). Jeremy makes a Braille dreidel for his father, who is blind.

- A NOSE FOR TROUBLE, written by Nancy Hope Wilson and illustrated by Doron Ben-Ami (Avon). The main character Maggie is in a wheelchair, but she shows the kids in her new school that she is "special" in other ways as well. See also the companion novel, A WHIFF OF DANGER, illustrated by Marie DeJohn (Avon).

- THANK YOU, MR. FALKER, by Patricia Polacco (Philomel). A teacher helps a third grader learn to read; based on Polacco's personal experience.

- Joey Pigza Books, award-winning trilogy by Jack Gantos (Farrar, Straus & Giroux). Joey has trouble paying attention in school, and at times this is the least of his problems; humorous and thoughtful. Titles: JOEY PIGZA SWALLOWED THE KEY, JOEY PIGZA LOSES CONTROL, and WHAT WOULD JOEY DO?.

- Hank Zipzer: The World's Greatest Underachiever series, by Henry Winkler and Lin Oliver (Grosset & Dunlap). Titles include NIAGARA FALLS OR DOES IT?; I GOT A "D" IN SALAMI; DAY OF THE IGUANA; THE ZIPPITY ZINGER; THE NIGHT I FLUNKED MY FIELD TRIP, and HOLY ENCHILADA!

## FAMILY RELATIONSHIPS AND ISSUES

- SEVEN SPOOLS OF THREAD: A KWANZAA STORY, written by Angela Shelf Medearis and illustrated by Daniel Minter (Whitman); about teamwork, family, and the principles of Kwanzaa; see the read-aloud plan elsewhere in this resource.

- MERMAID MARY MARGARET, by Lynn E. Hazen (Bloomsbury); delightful story about a fourth-grade girl who goes on a cruise with her grandmother in place of her grandfather, who passed away suddenly; written in a jaunty, lighthearted; journal style. A real pleaser!

- Little House on the Prairie, written by Laura Ingalls Wilder and illustrated by Garth Williams (HarperCollins); classic series that has been loved and cherished since it was first published in the 1930s and 1940s.

- SARAH, PLAIN AND TALL, by Patricia MacLachlan (HarperCollins); courage, pluck, and wisdom packed into a hugely entertaining, slim novel about a mail-order bride who comes to live with a family on the prairie; Newbery Award. See also the sequel, SKYLARK.

- A CHRISTMAS LIKE HELEN'S, written by Natalie Kinsey-Warnock and illustrated by Mary Azarian (Houghton Mifflin); nostalgic tale of yesteryear Christmases in snowy, rural Vermont; beautiful art; a Parents' Choice Silver Honor Award.

- THE WEDNESDAY SURPRISE, written by Eve Bunting and illustrated by Donald Carrick (Clarion). Seven year-old Anna teaches her Grandma to read.

- THE MEMORY CUPBOARD A THANKSGIVING STORY, written by Charlotte Herman and illustrated by Ben F. Stahl (Whitman). Katie learns that it is people, not things, that make memories.

*Cover from THE MEMORY CUPBOARD: A THANKSGIVING STORY by Charlotte Herman, illustrated by Ben F. Stahl. Copyright © 2003. Reprinted with permission from A. Whitman & Co.*

- AMAZING GRACE, written by Mary Hoffman and illustrated by Caroline Binch (Dial). Self-esteem blossoms in a warm, supportive extended family; see the read-aloud plan for this book in *Children's Book Corner, Grades 1–2*.

- MISS RUMPHIUS, by Barbara Cooney (Viking); classic story of an aunt who travels the world and leaves something behind everywhere she goes.

- MY GREAT-AUNT ARIZONA, written by Gloria Houston and illustrated by Susan Condie Lamb (HarperCollins). A great-aunt who was also a great teacher introduces her students to the world.

- UNCLE MAGIC, written by Patricia Lee Gauch and illustrated by Deborah Kogan Ray (Holiday House); about an uncle and magic and the power of opening your heart and believing.

- SHOESHINE GIRL, written by Clyde Robert Bulla and illustrated by Leigh Grant (HarperCollins). This great story about a girl who spends the summer with her aunt and befriends the owner of a shoeshine stand when she wants to earn money is about so much more than that.

- WHEN LIGHTNING COMES IN A JAR, by Patricia Polacco (Philomel). You're invited to a Polacco-style family reunion, filled with traditions, memories, and something new.

- HOME AT LAST, written by Susan Middleton Elya and illustrated by Felipe Davalos (Lee & Low). An Hispanic family assimilates into the United States; see the read-aloud plan for this book in *Children's Book Corner, Grades 1–2*.

- THE MEMORY BOX, written by Mary Bahr and illustrated by David Cunningham (Whitman); sensitive and tender story about Alzheimer's disease.

- A BEAUTIFUL PEARL, written by Nancy Whitelaw and illustrated by Judith Friedman (Albert Whitman). A grandmother with Alzheimer's remembers her granddaughter's birthday.

- FLIP-FLOP GIRL, by Katherine Paterson (Penguin); an ALA Notable book about a girl and her adjustment to a new life when she moves in with her Grandma after the death of her father.

- AMBER WAS BRAVE, ESSIE WAS SMART: THE STORY OF AMBER AND ESSIE TOLD HERE IN POEMS AND PICTURES, by Vera B. Williams (Greenwillow); the sadly realistic, touching, funny, sobering, award-winning tale of two sisters facing life's ups and downs together; told in free verse.

- DEAR MR. HENSHAW, written by Beverly Cleary and illustrated by Paul O. Zelinsky (HarperCollins); novel about a boy navigating his parents' divorce with the help of the letters, real and imaginary, that he writes to an author; Newbery Medal.

*Cover from THE MEMORY BOX by Mary Bahr, illustrated by David Cunningham. Copyright © 1992. Reprinted with permission from A. Whitman & Co.*

- THE WAY A DOOR CLOSES, written by Hope Anita Smith and illustrated by Shane W. Evans (Holt). Told in verse, this story chronicles a father's leaving and eventual return, and the effect this experience has on the narrator, C.J., and his family.

- FALLING INTO PLACE, by Stephanie Greene (Clarion). This is the book for any reader who finds herself part of a blended family. Not that this is the only problem the main character has. But Margaret is tough, just like her grandmother was, until, that is, her husband died. Then there's the nerdy cousin, Roy, and all the rules at Gram's new retirement community to cope with. How Margaret pulls it all together, despite Roy, is as unforgettable as the cast of characters who live behind the doors at Carol Woods—doors that can't be painted any color but black. Don't worry, Gram changes that by the end, right before the karaoke party.

• FATHERS, MOTHERS, SISTERS, BROTHERS: A COLLECTION OF FAMILY POEMS, written by Mary Ann Hoberman and illustrated by Marylin Hafner (Penguin).

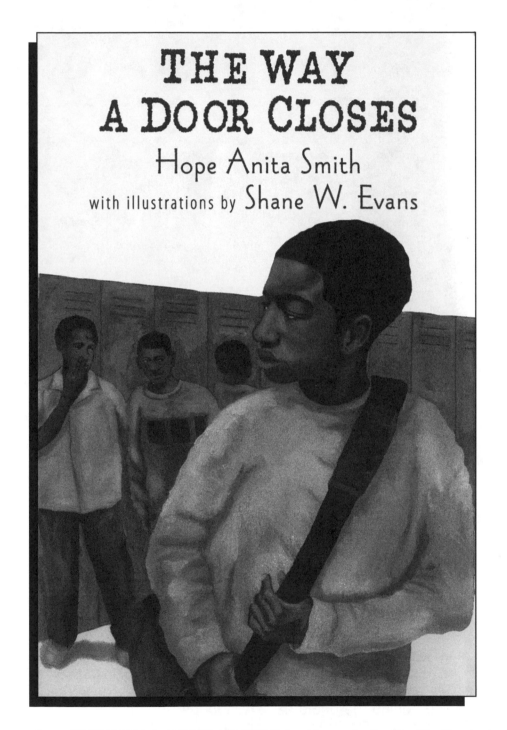

*Cover from THE WAY A DOOR CLOSES by Hope Anita Smith, illustrated by Shane W. Evans. Copyright © 2003. Reprinted with permission of Henry Holt Books for Young Readers.*

# DEATH

- A TASTE OF BLACKBERRIES, written by Doris Buchanan Smith and illustrated by Charles Robinson (Crowell); sudden death of a friend from bee stings.

- BRIDGE TO TERABITHIA, written by Katherine Paterson and illustrated by Donna Diamond (HarperCollins); death of a friend; numerous awards including the Newbery Medal.

- EVERYWHERE, by Bruce Brooks (HarperCollins); dealing with the death of a grandparent.

- FALLING INTO PLACE, by Stephanie Greene (Clarion). Margaret is tough, just like her grandmother was, until, that is, the man they both loved dies.

- MERMAID MARY MARGARET, by Lynn E. Hazen (Bloomsbury). A fourth grade girl goes on a cruise with her grandmother in place of her grandfather, who passed away suddenly; journal style.

- THE FOURTH GRADE WIZARDS, by Barthe DeClements (Viking); recovering from the loss of a mom in the midst of fourth-grade life.

- FLIP-FLOP GIRL, by Katherine Paterson (Penguin); an ALA Notable book about a girl and her adjustment to a new life when she moves in with her grandma after the death of her father.

- PLEASING THE GHOST, by Sharon Creech (HarperCollins). Uncle Arvie comes back to take care of some things left undone.

- NO DOGS ALLOWED!, by Bill Wallace (Holiday House). A girl who loses her horse learns to love again.

*See also listings in Children's Book Corner, Grades 1–2.*

# LEGENDS, FABLES, MYTHS, FAIRY TALES, FRACTURED FAIRY TALES, FOLK TALES, AND TALL TALES

- ELFWYN'S SAGA, by David Wisniewski (Lothrop, Lee & Shepard). Based on an Icelandic legend, this tale, illustrated with amazingly dimensional cut-paper art, tells the story of Elfwyn, born blind because of a curse, who sees more than her sighted clan and saves them from ruin.

- THE PAPER DRAGON, written by Marguerite W. Davol and illustrated by Robert Sabuda (Atheneum). Gatefold illustrations cut from painted tissue paper and adhered to handmade Japanese paper accompany this Chinese tale of a humble, loving scrollmaker and what he teaches a malevolent dragon; Golden Kite Award.

*Cover from THE PAPER DRAGON by Marguerite W. Davol, illustrated by Robert Sabuda. Copyright © 1997. Used with permission of Atheneum Books for Young Readers, an imprint of Simon & Schuster Children's Publishing.*

- HOW MANY SPOTS DOES A LEOPARD HAVE? AND OTHER TALES, written by Julius Lester and illustrated by David Shannon (Scholastic). Vanity, courage, trickery, and more are the subjects of this collection of a dozen tales beautifully told by an award-winning author and vividly illustrated by the award-winning illustrator of NO, DAVID.

- OLD TURTLE, written by Douglas Wood and illustrated by Cheng-Khee Chee; Pfeifer-Hamilton (Scholastic); fable about man's relationship with nature, with themes of God and peace; ABA Book of the Year, 1993; IRA Children's Book Award, 1993.

- THE LEGEND OF BLUEBONNET, retold and illustrated by Tomie dePaola (Putnam); a tale of the flower of Texas.

- THE SEA CHEST, written by Toni Buzzeo and illustrated by Mary GrandPre (Dial). Lush oil paintings by the woman who illustrated Harry Potter accompany a lyrical legend of coastal Maine.

- KOGI'S MYSTERIOUS JOURNEY, adapted by Elizabeth Partridge and illustrated by Aki Sogabe (Dutton); a tale about an artist's desire to bring life to his work and what he discovers as a result; cut-paper illustrations.

- THE KING'S CHESSBOARD, written by David Birch and illustrated by Devis Grebu (Dial); see the read-aloud plan elsewhere in this resource.

- THE EMPTY POT, by Demi (Holt). This Chinese tale exemplifies the value of truth and the wisdom in being proud when you've tried your hardest and done your best; see the read-aloud plan elsewhere in this resource.

- THE NIGHTINGALE, retold by Stephen Mitchell and illustrated by Bagram Ibatoulline (Candlewick). Breathtaking illustrations accompany well-crafted text in this retelling of the popular Andersen tale.

- THE TALE OF THE MANDARIN DUCKS, written by Katherine Paterson and illustrated by Leo and Diane Dillon (Penguin). Kindness and love win out over troubles borne.

- THE KING'S EQUAL, written by Newbery Award winner Katherine Paterson and illustrated by Curtis Woodbridge (HarperCollins). This original easy reader fairy tale is a treasure.

- CLEVER TOM AND THE LEPRECHAUN, retold and illustrated by Linda Shute (HarperCollins); lively illustrations of a spry character.

- FREDERICK, by Leo Lionni (Random House). A mouse's poetic words lighten and brighten dreary winter for his field mice friends.

- FABLES, by Arnold Lobel (HarperCollins); Caldecott Medal.

- AESOP'S FABLES, retold and illustrated by Brad Sneed (Dial). Fiftee tales (plus a sixteenth one told between the covers), illustrated from an up close, in-your-face perspective, are sure to please contemporary listeners.

- FAVORITE GREEK MYTHS, retold by Mary Pope Osborne and illustrated by Troy Howell (Scholastic). Twelve favorite Greek myths introduce young readers to mythology.

- IT'S ALL GREEK TO ME, written by Jon Scieszka and illustrated by Lane Smith (Viking). A Greek tragedy this is not; a hoot complete with cardboard thunderbolts meant to scare Cerberus off Mount Olympus; part of the Time Warp Trio series.

- KNIGHTS OF THE KITCHEN TABLE, written by Jon Scieszka and illustrated by Lane Smith (Viking); a take-off on KNIGHTS OF THE ROUND TABLE; the first in the Time Warp Trio series.

- CHICKEN LITTLE, retold and illustrated by Steven Kellogg (HarperCollins). you'll find it hard to resist this version, in which the foxy lady sports shades and a serious set of chops, and the turkey pumps iron at Big Bozo's Barnyard Gym.

- TURTLE'S RACE WITH BEAVER, told by Joseph Bruchac and James Bruchac and illustrated by Jose Aruego and Ariane Dewey (Dial); a tortoise and the hare tale adapted from Seneca oral tradition.

- RAVEN: A TRICKSTER TALE FROM THE PACIFIC NORTHWEST, told and illustrated by Gerald McDermott (Harcourt); Caldecott Honor; tale of a figure that is central to tribal arts of the Pacific Northwest.

- ABIYOYO, written by Pete Seeger and illustrated by Michael Hays (Macmillan); an adaptation of a South African folk tale; see the read-aloud plan elsewhere in this resource.

- ABIYOYO RETURNS, written by Pete Seeger and Paul DuBois Jacobs and illustrated by Michael Hays (Simon & Schuster); the sequel to ABIYOYO; see the read-aloud plan elsewhere in this resource.

- THE STORY OF FROG BELLY RAT BONE, by Timothy Basil Ering (Candlewick); a modern fable about the care and nurturing of our environment; see the read-aloud plan for this book in *Children's Book Corner, Grades 1–2*.

- STONE SOUP, written by Ann McGovern and illustrated by Winslow Pinney Pels (Scholastic); engaging illustrations.

- Newfangled Fairy Tales: Classic Stories with a Twist series, edited by Bruce Lansky and written by numerous well-known and well-loved authors (Meadowbrook).

- LON PO PO: A RED-RIDING HOOD STORY FROM CHINA, translated and illustrated by Ed Young (Putnam); Caldecott Medal.

- THE ROUGH-FACE GIRL, written by Rafe Martin and illustrated by David Shannon (G. P. Putnam's Sons); see the read-aloud plan for this book in *Children's Book Corner, Grades 1–2*.

- PRINCESS FURBALL, retold by Charlotte Huck and illustrated by Anita Lobel (HarperCollins); a variant of the Cinderella story in which the princess is smart and resourceful.

- MUFARO'S BEAUTIFUL DAUGHTERS AN AFRICAN TALE, retold and illustrated by John Steptoe (HarperCollins); Caldecott Honor; kindness triumphs.

- THE TALKING EGGS, written by Robert D. San Souci and illustrated by Jerry Pinkney (Dial); Caldecott Honor. Adapted from a Creole folktale, this story is a blend of Cinderella and other European fairy tales in which the honest, kind sister prevails over the evil sister and mother; Caldecott Honor Book.

- BONY-LEGS, written by Joanna Cole and illustrated by Dirk Zimmer (Simon & Schuster); Scholastic Hello Reader; a fairy tale in early chapter book form.

- BIGFOOT CINDERRRRRELLA, written by Tony Johnston and illustrated by James Warhola (G. P. Putnam's Sons). Cinderella is a member of a "band of Bigfoots" and a grizzly is her "beary godfather"; grrrrrreat!

- RUMPLESTILTSKIN'S DAUGHTER, by Diane Stanley; Morrow; no weepy maiden in a tower here! Her name is Hope, and she's strong and smart. See the read-aloud plan elsewhere in this resource.

- SLEEPING UGLY, written by Jane Yolen and illustrated by Diane Stanley (Putnam); a twist on the classic.

- HANSEL AND GRETEL, retold and illustrated by James Marshall (Dial).

- RED RIDING HOOD, retold and illustrated by James Marshall (Dial); a reassuring ending.

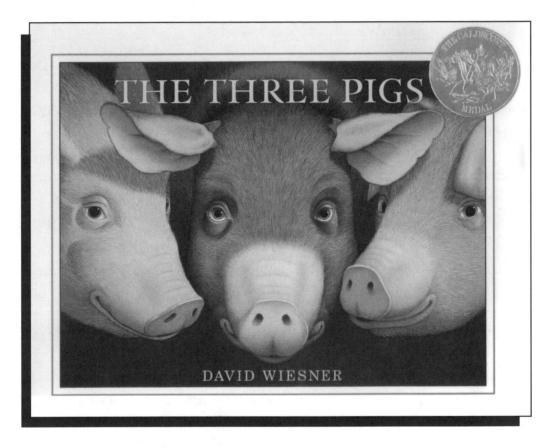

*Cover from THE THREE PIGS by David Wiesner. Jacket illustrations copyright © 1987 by David Wiesner. Reprinted by permission of Clarion Books/Houghton Mifflin Company. All rights reserved.*

- THE TRUE STORY OF THE 3 LITTLE PIGS!, written by Jon Scieszka and illustrated by Lane Smith (Viking); hilarious; popular title in this subgenre.

- THE THREE PIGS, by David Wiesner (Clarion). This creatively illustrated retelling won the Caldecott Award.

- THE THREE LITTLE WOLVES AND THE BIG BAD PIG, written by Eugene Trivizas and illustrated by Helen Oxenbury (Macmillan). The pig's the bad guy here.

- GOLDILOCKS AND THE THREE BEARS, retold and illustrated by James Marshall (Dial); Caldecott Honor.

- GOLDILOCKS RETURNS, by Lisa Campbell Ernst (Simon & Schuster). She's back! A grown-up Goldilocks, armed with a tool belt, opinions, and unlimited energy, returns to the scene of the crime to make things right.

- THE THREE SPINNING FAIRIES A TALE FROM THE BROTHERS GRIMM, retold by Lisa Campbell Ernst (Dutton). Lazy, selfish Zelda cooks up a scheme and gets her just desserts.

- THE STINKY CHEESE MAN AND OTHER FAIRLY STUPID TALES, written by Jon Scieszka and illustrated by Lane Smith (Penguin); zany fun that made a name for this team.

- MISS SMITH'S INCREDIBLE STORYBOOK, by Michael Garland (Dutton); see the read-aloud plan for this book in *Children's Book Corner, Grades 1–2.*

- THE THREE SILLIES, retold and illustrated by Kathryn Hewitt (Harcourt). Lush watercolor and gouache illustrations accompany this silly, silly, silly story.

- CLEVER BEATRICE, written by Margaret Willey and illustrated by Heather Solomon (Atheneum); see the read-aloud plan for this book in *Children's Book Corner, Grades 1–2.*

- PECOS BILL, retold and illustrated by Steven Kellogg (Morrow). This story of a Texan hero is appealing in every way.

- JOHNNY APPLESEED, retold and illustrated by Steven Kellogg (HarperCollins); delightful, action-packed spreads.

- MIKE FINK, retold and illustrated by Steven Kellogg (HarperCollins); a tall tale about "the most famous of the ring-tailed roarers and river wrestlers" in America's frontier history.

- PAUL BUNYAN, retold and illustrated by Steven Kellogg (HarperCollins); spunky illustrations of one of the most beloved of tall-tale heroes. See the read-aloud plan elsewhere in this resource.

- JIM AND THE BEANSTALK, by Raymond Briggs (Putnam). In a twist on the classic, Jim earns gold coins by helping the old giant feel young again.

- THE FAIRY TALE LIFE OF HANS CHRISTIAN ANDERSEN, written by Eva Moore and illustrated by Trina Schart Hyman (Scholastic).

## SEASONS, HOLIDAYS, AND SPECIAL DAYS

- FESTIVALS, poems by Myra Cohn Livingston and illustrated by Leonard Everett Fisher (Holiday House); a collection of poems on an array of festivals celebrated by people of different faiths and cultures.

### Winter

- WINTER POEMS, selected by Barbara Rogasky and illustrated by Trina Schart Hyman (Scholastic). Twenty-five poems from Shakespeare to Sandburg to Japanese haiku celebrate the season.

- GOODBYE GEESE, written by Nancy White Carlstrom and illustrated by Ed Young (Philomel); migration south; lyrical and lovely.

- OWL MOON, written by Jane Yolen and illustrated by John Schoenherr (Philomel); timeless classic about a winter evening's outing; see the read-aloud plan for this book in *Children's Book Corner, Pre-K–K.*

## Groundhog Day

- THE GROUNDHOG DAY BOOK OF FACTS AND FUN, written by Wendie Old and illustrated by Paige Billin-Frye (Whitman). With this book you'll never run out of facts about this animal and his day in the sun (or not); also discusses the "reason for the seasons," hibernation, and Punxsutawney Phil's reliability; includes riddles and Groundhog Day party suggestions.

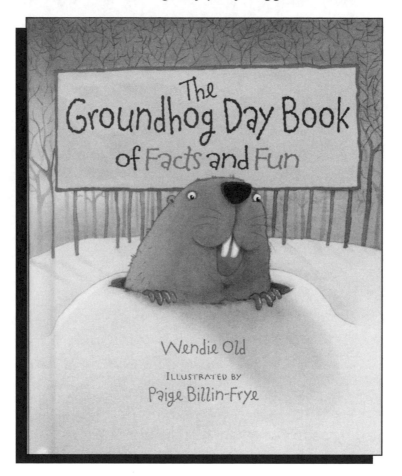

*Cover from THE GROUNDHOG DAY BOOK OF FACTS AND FUN by Wendie Old, illustrated by Paige Billin-Frye. Copyright © 2004. Reprinted with permission from A. Whitman & Co.*

## Valentine's Day

- THE STORY OF VALENTINE'S DAY, written by Clyde Robert Bulla and illustrated by Susan Estelle Kwas (HarperCollins); straightforward history of one of our oldest holidays; includes craft ideas and a recipe at the back of the book.

- FOUR VALENTINES IN A RAINSTORM, by Felicia Bond (HarperCollins); making the perfect card for special friends; a perfect picture book.

- IT'S VALENTINE'S DAY, poems by Jack Prelutsky and illustrated by Yossi Abolafia (HarperCollins); a nonfattening treat.

### St. Patrick's Day

- THE ST. PATRICK'S DAY SHILLELAGH, written by Janet Nolan and illustrated by Ben F. Stahl (Whitman). A shillelagh and its history are handed down through the generations.

- CLEVER TOM AND THE LEPRECHAUN, retold and illustrated by Linda Shute (HarperCollins); folk tale.

*Cover from THE ST. PATRICK'S DAY SHILLELAGH by Janet Nolan, illustrated by Ben F. Stahl. Copyright © 2002. Reprinted with permission from A. Whitman & Co.*

### Spring

- NAOMI KNOWS IT'S SPRINGTIME, written by Virginia L. Kroll and illustrated by Jill Kastner (Boyds Mills Press). Although she is blind, Naomi knows spring has arrived.

### Easter

- CHICKEN SUNDAY, by Patricia Polacco (Philomel); Children's Choice and ALA Notable Book about differences, friendship, and character.

- EASTER BUDS ARE SPRINGING POEMS FOR EASTER, selected by Lee Bennett Hopkins and illustrated by Tomie dePaola (Boyds Mills Press).

## Mother's Day

- HAPPY MOTHER'S DAY, written by Steven Kroll and illustrated by Marylin Hafner (Holiday House). A big family with a collective big heart plans a wonderful day for Mom.

- A HIGH-FIVING GIFT FOR MOM!, written by Judy Bradbury and illustrated by Cathy Trachok (McGraw-Hill). Christopher and his brothers visit a teachers' craft fair to buy a gift for Mother's Day.

## Summer

- SHOOTING STAR SUMMER, written by Candice F. Ransom and illustrated by Karen Milone (Boyds Mills Press). A dreaded visit from a cousin proves memorable.

- ANNA'S GARDEN SONGS, poems by Mary Q. Steele and illustrated by Lena Anderson (HarperCollins).

- ANNA'S SUMMER SONGS, poems by Mary Q. Steele and illustrated by Lena Anderson (HarperCollins).

- DOGGONE LEMONADE STAND!, written by Judy Bradbury and illustrated by Cathy Trachok (McGraw-Hill). Christopher sets up a lemonade stand on the hottest day of the year; simple fractions.

## Halloween

- BEAST AND THE HALLOWEEN HORROR, written by Patricia Reilly Giff and illustrated by Blanche Sims (Dell); a chapter book focusing on one of the characters of the Polk Street School, a series by the Newbery Honor Award-winning author, teacher, and reading consultant. Beast, for whom school is a bit of a challenge, writes a letter to an author about how much he loved the dog in his book. Only there was no dog in the book and now the author is coming to Beast's school for Halloween!

- TOM LITTLE'S GREAT HALLOWEEN SCARE, written by John Peterson and illustrated by Roberta Carter Clark (Scholastic). Lucy saves the day when Tom's idea for a Halloween prank goes awry; from the classic best-selling series of tales about this miniature family with tails.

- IT'S HALLOWEEN, poems by Jack Prelutsky and illustrated by Marylin Hafner (HarperCollins); no horror, just humor.

- HIST WHIST, written by e. e. cummings and illustrated by Deborah Kogan Ray (Crown); exquisitely illustrated.

- THE GHOST-EYE TREE, written by Bill Martin Jr. and John Archambault and illustrated by Ted Rand (Holt); a rhythmical wonder with just enough chill; the light-filled nighttime illustrations are perfect.

- FIVE FUNNY FRIGHTS, written by Judith Bauer Stamper and illustrated by Tim Raglin (Scholastic); a Hello Reader title of five funny, short Halloween tales.

## Thanksgiving

- THANK YOU, SARAH! THE WOMAN WHO SAVED THANKSGIVING, written by Laurie Halse Anderson and illustrated by Matt Faulkner (Simon & Schuster); a most incredible picture book by an inspired award-winning author, with art by an illustrator who knows what makes a picture book stand out; biography, history, power-of-the-pen message.

- THANKSGIVING AT THE TAPPLETONS', written by Eileen Spinelli and illustrated by Maryann Cocca-Leffler (HarperCollins); see the read-aloud plan for this book in *Children's Book Corner, Grades 1–2.*

- SARAH MORTON'S DAY: A DAY IN THE LIFE OF A PILGRIM GIRL, written by Kate Winters with photographs by Russ Kendall (Scholastic); photographed at Plimoth Plantation, Cape Cod, Massachusetts; see the read-aloud plan for this book in *Children's Book Corner, Grades 1–2.*

- SAMUEL EATON'S DAY: A DAY IN THE LIFE OF A PILGRIM BOY, written by Kate Winters with photographs by Russ Kendall (Scholastic); companion to the book listed above.

- ON THE MAYFLOWER: VOYAGE OF THE SHIP'S APPRENTICE & A PASSENGER GIRL, written by Kate Winters with photographs by Russ Kendall (Scholastic); companion to the books listed above.

- THE MEMORY CUPBOARD: A THANKSGIVING STORY, written by Charlotte Herman and illustrated by Ben F. Stahl (Whitman). Katie learns that it is people, not things, that make memories.

- TURKEY TROUBLE, written by Patricia Reilly Giff and illustrated by Blanche Sims (Dell); a Polk Street series special featuring Emily Arrow, a student in Mrs. Rooney's class; includes yummy recipes and fun, age-appropriate crafts.

## Christmas

- THE BEST CHRISTMAS PAGEANT EVER, written by Barbara Robinson and illustrated by Judith Gwyn Brown (HarperCollins); the best Christmas novel ever for middle grades.

- THE CHRISTMAS MIRACLE OF JONATHAN TOOMEY, written by Susan Wojciechowski and illustrated by P. J. Lynch (Candlewick). A widow, her son, and a sad woodcarver make for joy and a miracle.

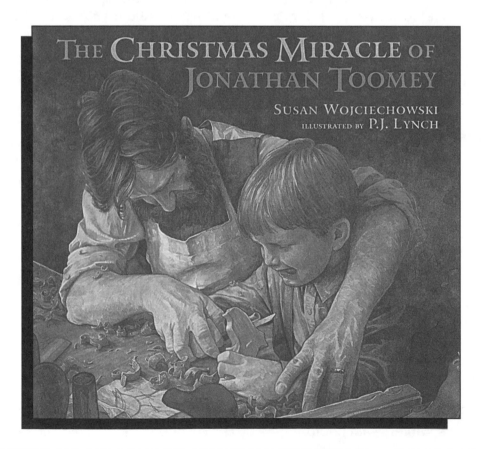

*THE CHRISTMAS MIRACLE OF JONATHAN TOOMEY. Text Copyright © 1995 Susan Wojciechowski. Illustrations Copyright © 1995 P.J. Lynch. Reproduced by permission of the publisher Candlewick Press, Inc., Cambridge, MA.*

- SANTA CALLS, by William Joyce (HarperCollins); a Christmas fantasy unlike any other.

- MIRACLE ON 34TH STREET, written by Valentine Davies and illustrated by Tomie dePaola (Harcourt); an illustrated chapter book of the classic Christmas story.

- THE CHRISTMAS MENORAHS: HOW A TOWN FOUGHT HATE, written by Janice Cohn and illustrated by Bill Farnsworth (Whitman); about a town that united against hatred; based on a true story.

- THE TWENTY-FOUR DAYS BEFORE CHRISTMAS, written by acclaimed author Madeleine L'Engle and illustrated by Carl Cassler (Dell). This is the story of a young girl waiting for the arrival of her new sibling with anxiety and eagerness.

- A CHRISTMAS LIKE HELEN'S, written by Natalie Kinsey-Wamock and illustrated by Mary Azarian (Houghton Mifflin); nostalgic tale of yesteryear Christmases in snowy, rural Vermont; beautiful art; a Parents' Choice Silver Honor Award.

- THE JOLLY CHRISTMAS POSTMAN, by Janet Ahlberg and Allan Ahlberg (Little, Brown); letters and cards lift from envelope pages.

- LITTLE TREE, written by e. e. cummings and illustrated by Deborah Kogan Ray (Crown); a Christmas poem illustrated with dreamy paintings.

- THE POLAR EXPRESS, by Chris Van Allsburg (Houghton Mifflin); see read-aloud plan for this book in *Children's Book Corner, Grades 1–2*.

- IT'S CHRISTMAS, poems by Jack Prelutsky and illustrated by Marylin Hafner (Greenwillow); silly, fun, re-readable.

## Hanukkah

- THE STONE LAMP: EIGHT STORIES OF HANUKKAH THROUGH HISTORY, written by Karen Hesse and illustrated by Brian Pinkney (Hyperion); free verse, first person accounts of key events in Jewish history as seen through the eyes of a child; written by a Newbery Award winner and illustrated by a Caldecott Honor Award winner.

- THE EIGHT NIGHTS OF HANUKKAH, written by Judy Nayer and illustrated by Yuri Salzman (Creative Media Applications; Troll); history, activities, story, and song.

- THE CHRISTMAS MENORAHS: HOW A TOWN FOUGHT HATE, written by Janice Cohn and illustrated by Bill Farnsworth (Whitman); about a town that united against hatred; based on a true story.

- THE STORY OF HANUKKAH, written by Amy Ehrlich and illustrated by Ori Sherman (Dial); story of the Jewish Festival of Lights; beautifully illustrated.

- HANUKKAH: FESTIVALS AND HOLIDAYS, by June Behrens (Children's Press). Follow along as a family celebrates the eight days of Hanukkah.

*Cover from THE STONE LAMP: EIGHT STORIES OF HANUKKAH THROUGH HISTORY written by Karen Hesse and illustrated by Brian Pinkey. © 2003 Reprinted with permission of Hyperion Books for Children.*

- THE JAR OF FOOLS: EIGHT HANUKKAH STORIES FROM CHELM, written by Eric A. Kimmel and illustrated by Mordicai Gerstein (Holiday House). "Chelm is the traditional town of fools . . . [who] are not stupid . . . unfortunately they are nearly always wrong," according to notes by the author.

- JEREMY'S DREIDEL, written by Ellie Gellman and illustrated by Judith Friedman (Kar-Ben Copies). Jeremy makes a Braille dreidel for his father, who is blind.

- THE MAGIC MENORAH: A MODERN CHANUKAH TALE, written by Jane Breskin Zalben and illustrated by Donna Diamond (Simon & Schuster); an early chapter book. Stanley shines the shammash and poof! just like a genie, an old man appears.

- CHANUKAH LIGHTS EVERYWHERE, written by Michael J. Rosen and illustrated by Melissa Iwai (Harcourt). A young boy contemplates the lights on his menorah and in the world around him.

- HANUKKAH HA-HAS: KNOCK-KNOCK JOKES THAT ARE A LATKE FUN, written by Katy Hall and Lisa Eisenberg and illustrated by Stephen Carpenter (HarperCollins); lift-the-flap knock knock jokes.

### Kwanzaa

- SEVEN SPOOLS OF THREAD: A KWANZAA STORY, written by Angela Shelf Medearis and illustrated by Daniel Minter (Whitman); about teamwork, family, and the principles of Kwanzaa; see the read-aloud plan elsewhere in this resource.

## POETRY

See the "Tips and Techniques for Teachers and Librarians" section of this book for an extensive list of recommended poetry anthologies and collections.

For additional recommended book titles listed by genre, refer to the "Parent Pull-Out Pages."

# Subject Index

# Title Index

# Author Index

Aaseng, Nathan, 279
Ackerman, Karen, 258
Adler, David A., 193
Ahlberg, Allan, 248, 307
Ahlberg, Janet, 248, 307
Alexander, Lloyd, 225
Alexander, Sue, 249
Amato, Mary, 185, 220
Ancona, George, 271
Anderson, Jon, 285
Anderson, Laurie Halse, 188, 226, 257, 263, 305
Anderson, M. T., 269
Andrews-Goebel, Nancy, 268
Archambault, John, 290, 305
Arnold, Tedd, 228

Bahr, Mary, 292
Banks, Lynne Reid, 186, 220
Bartoletti, Susan Campbell, 190, 229
Bartone, Elisa, 261
Bates, Katharine Lee, 251, 257
Bauer, Marion Dane, 172, 287
Behrens, June, 307
Bennett, Nadine, 285
Berger, Melvin, 195, 278
Bernstein, Daryl, 285
Bickel, Cindy, 95, 96, 126, 275, 276, 281
Birch, David, 31, 297
Black, Holly, 190, 225
Blumberg, Rhoda, 230, 257
Blume, Judy, 168, 199, 221, 224, 248, 268
Bobrick, Benson, 256
Bolin, Frances Schoonmaker, 154
Bond, Felicia, 302
Bond, Michael, 194
Borden, Louise, 264, 286
Bourke, Linda, 289
Bradbury, Judy, 284, 304
Branley, Franklyn M., 195
Briggs, Raymond, 135, 300
Brink, Carol Ryrie, 232
Brooks, Bruce, 295

Brooks, Walter R., 190
Brown, Don, 269
Bruchac, Joseph, 298
Buehner, Caralyn, 288
Bulla, Clyde Robert, 171, 179, 254, 261, 288, 292, 302
Bunting, Eve, 291,
Burleigh, Robert, 117, 121, 248, 252, 254, 262, 269
Busch, Lou, 246, 252
Buzzeo, Toni, 296
Byrd, Robert, 17, 22, 208, 262, 267, 279

Caffey, Donna, 273
Calkins, Lucy McCormick, 202
Cameron, Ann, 195
Carle, Eric, 157
Carlson, Nancy, 287
Carlstrom, Nancy White, 301
Carr, Jane, 153
Carroll, Lewis, 154
Caseley, Judith, 179, 248
Christopher, Matt, 193
Ciardi, John, 157, 233
Cleary, Beverly, 166, 182, 188, 199, 221, 222, 223, 225, 232, 247, 292
Clements, Andrew, 73, 79, 80, 81, 99, 101, 103, 195, 222, 275, 286
Codell, Esmé Raji, 202, 236
Cohn, Amy L., 262
Cohn, Janice, 101, 288, 307
Cole, Joanna, 185, 273, 287, 298
Connor, Leslie, 27, 30, 258
Conrad, Pam, 172
Cooney, Barbara, 268, 271, 292
Corey, Shana, 266
Corvino, Lucy, 208
Coville, Bruce, 186, 199, 225
Creech, Sharon, 182, 295
Cressy, Judith, 252
Cullinan, Bernice, 202, 236
cummings, e. e., 159, 305, 307
Cummings, Pat, 268

# Illustrator Index

# Index of Resource
# Books and Authors

# About the Author

JUDY BRADBURY is an author and teacher. She is the author of the Christopher Counts! children's picture book math series published by McGraw-Hill/Learning Triangle Press. She is also a frequent workshop presenter.

Judy has over 20 years of experience teaching in the public school system and providing private tutoring. A lifelong advocate of promoting reading, Judy pioneered a New York State-funded summer community reading program and has developed remedial/enrichment reading and writing programs for high school students. She is an active member in organizations such as the International Reading Association and the Society of Children's Writers and Illustrators. She lives in western New York with her husband, daughter, one big dog, and two cats that came for Christmas and stayed.